Food in Cuba

Food in Cuba

The Pursuit of a Decent Meal

Hanna Garth

Stanford University Press

Stanford, California

Stanford University Press
Stanford, California

© 2020 by the Board of Trustees of the Leland Stanford Junior University.
All rights reserved.

No part of this book may be reproduced or transmitted in any form or by any means, electronic or mechanical, including photocopying and recording, or in any information storage or retrieval system without the prior written permission of Stanford University Press.

Printed in the United States of America on acid-free, archival-quality paper

Library of Congress Cataloging-in-Publication Data

Names: Garth, Hanna, author.
Title: Food in Cuba : the pursuit of a decent meal / Hanna Garth.
Description: Stanford, California : Stanford University Press, 2020. | Includes
    bibliographical references and index.
Identifiers: LCCN 2019016001 (print) | LCCN 2019018052 (ebook) | ISBN
    9781503611108 (ebook) | ISBN 9781503604629 (cloth: alk. paper) | ISBN
    9781503611092 (pbk: alk. paper)
Subjects: LCSH: Food supply—Cuba. | Food consumption—Cuba. | Food
habits—Cuba. | Quality of life—Cuba. | Cuba—Social conditions—1990–
Classification: LCC HD9014.C92 (ebook) | LCC HD9014.C92 G37 2020
    (print) | DDC 338.1/97291—dc23
LC record available at https://lccn.loc.gov/2019016001

Cover design: Jason Alejandro
Cover image: Neighborhood market in Santiago de Cuba. Photo by the author.

For my grandmothers,
Irene Royal Garth
and
Carol Dean Fitzmaurice

Contents

Acknowledgments

First and foremost, I thank all of the people in Cuba who shared their lives and their stories with me. Without their willingness to tell me their stories, this book would not be possible. I am particularly grateful to Maria Isabel "Maruchi" Berbes Ribeaux, my official "tutora" while in the field. From my first trip to Santiago, Maruchi has provided a home away from home for me in Cuba; in that safe space we shared many meals and conversations that were integral to shaping this project. Her husband, Marcos Antonio Salomón Guerra, may he rest in peace, became one of my closest friends and fearlessly corrected any false assumptions I might have had about Cuban life.

Furthermore, I am immensely grateful to the Casa del Caribe for their institutional support and the sponsorship of my visa during fieldwork. At the Casa del Caribe, I am particularly appreciative of Julio Corbea Calzado who served as my unofficial mentor, guiding me through their archives and introducing me to people across the city of Santiago and El Cobre. I also thank Orlando Verges, Kenia Dorta at the Casa del Caribe, as well as Elba Iris and Marlene for their assistance with my visa process.

In the field I learned from and became friends with a small group of women, Grete Viddal, Kristina Wirtz, Jalane Schmidt, Sarah Hill, and A. Kilolo Harris Evans, who also carry out research in Santiago de Cuba. I am also grateful for the advice and camaraderie of fellow Cubanists P. Sean Brotherton, Hope Bastian, Paul Ryer, and Amalia Cabezas. My scholarly formation was deeply influenced by the intellectual community of the UC-Cuba academic initiative, which I have been a part of since 2008; in particular I thank Raul Fernandez, Nancy Burke, Anita Casavantes Bradford, Susanna Rodríguez Drissi, Ayesha Nibbe, Teishan Latner, Tom McEnaney, Maki Tanaka, and Alissa Bernstein.

At UCLA, I had the good fortune of working with Carole H. Browner, Robin Derby, Linda Garro, Akhil Gupta, and Jason Throop. I was a regular participant in the Mind, Medicine, & Culture group, and the Culture, Power, & Social Change group in Anthropology, as well as the Food Working Group in Geography. At UCLA my life and work were deeply influenced by the thinking, work, and lives of Mara Buchbinder, Jessica Cattelino, Hadi Deeb, Ellen Sharp, Amy Malek, Rachel George, Rebekah Park, Jenny Walton-Wetzel, Anna Corwin, Kristin Yarris, Oscar Gil-Garcia, Katja Antoine, Karen Ishizuka, Yanina Gori, Marisa Berwald, and Hannah Reiss.

Well before UCLA, the initial seeds for this book were sown during my undergraduate years in the Department of Anthropology at Rice University, where Eugenia Georges and James Faubion mentored me alongside Kate Goldfarb and Cynthia Browne. At Rice, Roland Smith and Gloria Bean also supported me in many ways through the Mellon Mays Undergraduate Fellowship program, where I first met Uri McMillan who continues to be a part of my life as a mentor and friend. After completing my BA, the Mellon program in partnership with the Social Science Research Council and the Woodrow Wilson Foundation have supported my work and provided an intellectual home. I am so grateful to be a part of this community; in particular I thank Cally Waite, O. Hugo Benavides, John Mckiernan-Gonzalez, Darren Ranco, Miguel de Baca, Fareeda Griffith, and Jacqueline Lazú for working with me at various SSRC workshops, as well as Vanessa Agard-Jones, Freda Fair, Kafui Attoh, Ren-yo Hwang, Sylvia Zamora, Teresa Gonzales, Katerina Gonzalez Sligmann, Priscilla Leiva, Dixa Ramirez, Jonathan Rosa, and Esme Murdock, who read and gave invaluable feedback on chapter 4.

A University of California President's Postdoctoral Fellowship (PPFP) in the Department of Anthropology at the University of California, Irvine from 2015 to 2016 was invaluable in bringing this project to completion. I want to thank my wonderful mentor, Leo Chavez, for offering feedback on my work-in-progress. Raul Fernandez, my honorary mentor, also offered critical feedback on several chapters. I am indebted to Keith Murphy, Mrinalini Tankha, Kris Peterson, Valerie Lewis, Damien Sojoyner, Sylvia Nam, and Belinda Campos for offering generous advice on various aspects of my work. My ongoing connections to PPFP have fed my scholarship and my soul; for the morsels they have fed me, I thank Tiffany Willoughby-Herard,

Tanya Golash Boza, Jerry Zee, Xóchitl Chávez, Anthony Jerry, Grace Hong, Kelly Lytle Hernandez, Maylei Blackwell, Rocio Rosales, Alicia Cox, Christina Schwenkle, Mark Lawson, and Kimberly Atkinson.

In July 2016 I joined the faculty of Anthropology at the University of California, San Diego. I have had the pleasure of working with excellent colleagues there who have supported this work in various ways. I have had the pleasure of participating in the Critical Anthropology Workshop and learned a great deal from the faculty and graduate students members. I am also grateful to those who gave feedback during a presentation of my work in the Psychological and Medical Anthropology seminar, where Steve Parish, Tom Csordas, and Janis Jenkins gave excellent suggestions for improving chapter 5. Many thanks to Dredge Kang, Isabel Rivera-Collazo, Amy Non, Jade d'Alpoim Guedes, Bonnie Kaiser, Aftab Jassal, Rihan Yeh, Pascal Gagneux, Nancy Postero, David Pederson, Suzanne Brenner, and John Haviland. Saiba Varma gave brilliant feedback on several chapters. I am especially grateful to my colleague Joe Hankins, who has shown unrelenting support of me as a scholar and human being, and helped me to organize a book conference in the Department of Anthropology at UCSD in Winter 2018. The book workshop, sponsored by the UCSD Division of Social Science, was immensely helpful in refining and clarifying my argument thanks to the expert feedback of James Ferguson and Nancy Burke and a small group of my department colleagues. I also thank Lilly Irani, Patty Ahn, Erica Cho, Hoang Nguyen, and Sal Nicolazzo.

I have benefited from the engagement with this book at various stages in department colloquia and invited talks. I thank audiences at Spelman College; the University of California, Irvine Program in Public Health; the University of California, Irvine Department of Anthropology; the University of California, Riverside Department of Gender and Feminist Studies; the University of California, Riverside Department of Anthropology; the University of California, Santa Cruz Department of Anthropology; the University of California, Santa Barbara Department of Anthropology; Scripps College Department of Anthropology; Scripps College Africana Studies; the University of Southern California Department of American Studies and Ethnicity; and the UCLA Mind Medicine and Culture group.

Since 2015 I have had the pleasure of exchanging writing with a group of scholars who all have had ties to UC Irvine Anthropology at some point. This group has given me invaluable feedback on my work, and I cherish our weekly virtual meetings. This group has included Angela Fillingim, Taylor

Nelms, Mrinalini Tankha, Saiba Varma, and Lee Cabatingan, who over the years have read and given invaluable feedback on every chapter of this book.

I thank Michelle Lipinski at Stanford University Press and the anonymous reviewers for their dedication to improving the work and their patience with me as I worked through the revisions.

Extending beyond my formal institutional affiliations, I have greatly benefited from my community of friends. I thank Michael Powell, Natilee Harren, Sarah Grant, Lisa Garibaldi, Sarah Raskin, Vanessa Díaz, Garrett Broad, Ashanté Reese, Jenn Wilson-Gonzalez, Katrina van Alkemade, Becky Levitt, Lucy Culwell-Kanarek, MW Wilson, and Vanya Hollis.

I thank my family for their support: my parents, Patricia Fitzmaurice and Byron Garth, my grandmother Carol Fitzmaurice, and my sister Sara Garth have all graciously witnessed the process of writing this book. Special thanks go to my mother-in-law, Phyllis Morrison, who has provided hundreds of hours of free childcare to allow me to complete this book. I also thank my aunt, Siobhan Fitzmaurice, for facilitating and subsidizing my first trip to Cuba in 2001. To my friends who are like family, Erin Schilling and Martina Hinojosa, I am so grateful that we have stayed so close over all of these years.

My greatest gratitude goes to my partner, Christel S. Miller, my rock, my home, through the difficulties of international fieldwork and the joys of our two kids. I also thank Jackson and Franklin for their patience and all of the ways in which they give me life.

Preface
Why Cuba?

My interest in Cuba was initially sparked by a *National Geographic* issue in June 1999 that featured Old Havana. On the cover a young boy with a red towel draped around his neck was hanging out of an old American car, his gaze fixed on the camera. I felt like I was looking into his eyes. At the time I was an avid photographer and taking a political philosophy class at the University of Minnesota, where I was enrolled in my last two years of high school as part of the Minnesota Postsecondary Enrollment Options Program. I was drawn into the political and economic conundrums of the island in John J. Putnam's *National Geographic* feature and equally taken by David Alan Harvey's photographs of Havana. As a young, rebellious thinker I was enticed by Che Guevara's story; I quickly read his books and thought through his theorizations alongside Marx and other political theorists I was reading in my political philosophy class. Shortly thereafter, my Canadian aunt offered to subsidize a trip anywhere I wanted to go as a high school graduation gift; I chose to travel to Cuba.

During my first trip to the island, my fascination only grew stronger. As a teenager I had idealized socialism and its revolutionary principles. On my first trip to Havana, I remember how perplexed I was when the Cubans that I met told me how difficult their lives were, how much they wished things were different and that they lived somewhere else. Through my young eyes Cuba was idyllic in so many ways. As a low-income family in a small town in Wisconsin, my family did not have full health insurance coverage when I was a child. Knowing this, I idealized a political system that offered free health care to all. As a high school student, knowing that I would have to pay for college myself limited where I applied and what I imagined was possible for my future. By comparison, Cuba's free education system seemed like a dream. Yet, the Cubans I met told me that everything was more complicated than it appeared through my eighteen-year-old eyes.

Aside from a curiosity about socialism, I was initially drawn to Cuba as a dreamlike escape from my own life. As a queer woman of color growing up in a predominantly white small town in Wisconsin, I was always the Other, the outlier, the outsider. Everywhere we went, people stared at my family and me. Racist microaggressions and more overt racial slurs were commonplace in my life. I never really saw people who looked like me in my hometown. When I traveled to Cuba, the difference was like night and day from where I grew up. I blended in, people didn't seem to pay much attention to me, they didn't yell out racial or homophobic slurs at me. I felt comfortable, so comfortable that being in Cuba made me realize how uncomfortable I had been my whole life. I began to see how much my own sense of self was distorted by the systems of social stratification and ethnoracial hierarchies that I grew up with.

This feeling was part of what kept me coming back to Cuba. Even after I traveled to dozens of countries in Asia, Africa, and Latin America, Cuba was where I felt most at home. But as I grew older and lived in different, more diverse places in the United States, and grew a family of my own, I began to make a home for myself in the US. Cuba is not my home, but it is a place that allowed me to grow into myself and I will always love it for that.

These were some of the things that motivated me to conduct research in Cuba. Based on the encouragement of a good friend, Grete Viddal, whom I met while taking a class on the Cuban Revolution at Harvard University, I decided to travel to Santiago de Cuba during the summer of 2008. Before that trip I was uncertain as to whether I would do research in Havana or somewhere else on the island, but after spending three months in Santiago that summer I decided that I preferred to conduct research there. Santiago reminded me of the good things about the town I grew up in, though my hometown is over ten times the size. Like my hometown, the pace of life felt slow in Santiago. People were friendly, and they did things like stop to say hello to one another. Compared to Havana, Santiago felt small enough that I could move across the city with a bit more ease. While I had experienced Cubans as generally very warm and inviting, in Santiago I felt even more welcome and was quickly able to make friends.

Around the same time, I began to realize that I had a long-standing personal interest in food. Between college and graduate school, I began reading chefs' biographies for pleasure, and Michael Pollan's *Omnivore's Dilemma* and Barbara Kingsolver's *Animal, Vegetable, Miracle* fully captivated me. Before beginning my PhD program, I completed a master's degree in public health, and my thesis project was based on food and nutrition research and the implementation of a feeding program in the Philippines. Realizing that my love of food could be part of my career, I decided to center my research on food in Cuba.

With my focus on food, in addition to my feeling most comfortable in Santiago de Cuba, the city and its people made problems of inequality, access, and adequacy even more salient for me. Santiago's majority Black population has faced ongoing forms of institutionalized discrimination; its distance from Havana and discrimination toward its population mean that fewer resources arrive to Santiago. Given this context I observed that *santiagueros* experience a palpable struggle to access foods and meet their basic needs. My initial observations of the intensity of the struggle to access basic needs in Santiago was what made me call into question what an adequate provisioning system entails, and drove me to unpack adequacy and the everyday struggle to get by in Santiago de Cuba.

Food in Cuba

Introduction
In Pursuit of Adequacy

Amalia needed to buy fresh corn on the cob.[1] It was late June, just when the very first sweet corn from the very first harvest began to hit the market. When accessed and processed at just the right time, this corn on the cob produced the juicy corn—locally referred to as *tierno* (tender)—perfect for making *hallacas*, a local Santiago de Cuba version of fresh-ground cornmeal rolled with meat and stuffed into cornhusks, similar to *tamales*.[2] The essential ingredient for good hallacas is fresh sweet corn: the juicier the kernels, the better the hallacas.[3] Braving the already sweltering heat of the summer, I joined Amalia in her search. Like most *santiagueros* (people from Santiago), she did not have a lot of extra money, so she could not afford to pay for transportation, and our shopping trip was to be on foot.

We began our search at the Plaza market, one of Santiago's oldest food markets located near the city center. The Plaza is a large, old, warehouse-like building that has been used as a market for over 150 years.[4] The interior was dark, with the only light coming in through open doors and windows located at the top of the 40-foot walls. The market had hundreds of feet of countertops for vendors to display and sell foods of all kinds. This was a bustling marketplace at various points during Cuba's past, from the 1860s to the 1930s, but on this day there were only about a dozen people selling food, most located in one small corner of the large open space.

Amalia greeted several marketeers from whom she regularly purchased food, but it quickly became clear that there was no corn there. She asked where we might find corn: we were directed to the Trocha y Cristina market in another part of town, which is where Amalia and I quickly proceeded to next. The hallacas were for a party to celebrate the birthday of her favorite niece, who had always admired her homemade hallacas; Amalia was determined to prepare them for the party.

Amalia led us for a walk along La Alameda, a main thoroughfare connecting the docks, warehouses, and markets of the entire city. This was a more scenic route, and it gave her a chance to stop and ask several people who work in food distribution if they knew of any corn in the city. After 45 minutes of inquiring with no leads, drenched in sweat and parched, we arrived at the Trocha y Cristina market. There was no corn there either. We walked the aisles of the open-air market, each stall selling more or less the same variety of items—tomatoes, squash, small peppers, small bunches of fresh herbs, and a few small cucumbers.

After asking all of the vendors about corn, it seemed that the search had been fruitless. However, Amalia found one of the market managers, and he told us that while there was none in the state-run markets, he knew of someone selling fresh corn from the countryside out of their home nearby. And with that, we had moved from the official spaces of food acquisition to the unofficial ones, shifting our approach to food acquisition. We walked uphill 15 minutes to the house, but the person had sold out of corn earlier that morning. She suggested another location, another 15 minutes away, but when we arrived there the vendor knew nothing about any corn and seemed doubtful that we would find it anywhere in the city. Exhausted after trekking across the city all day, Amalia buckled on her original decision not to spend money on transportation, and for the equivalent of less than five cents, we took a communal *camión* (truck) to another market near the city center on Calle Martí. After an hour of waiting for the camión we finally arrived at the market, our last-ditch effort, only to find that there was no corn there either.

We finally gave up for the day and sat on a bench in the park. Amalia was clearly distressed and needed this moment to calm down after such a difficult morning. We did not know why there was no corn yet that year. She wondered out loud: Was there a problem with the local crop? Was it diverted to Havana this year? Had the state shifted land use toward exports? Corn could have been scarce for any number of reasons or some combination of all of these. Amalia began to connect her situation with the broader context of global food production and distribution, contemplating the competing political and economic factors that might be behind the lack of corn. However, she could not let the corn go; she wanted so badly to make hallacas for this party that she was still racking her brain about how she could possibly find some in time. To help get her mind off the search and out of genuine curiosity, I asked her when she started making hallacas. She replied,

> I remember watching my mother make them every year during both seasons as a child. That was how I learned to make them. Over time one gets more experience and gets better. Everyone in my family made them, my mother, her mother, every generation.

Amalia spoke nostalgically about hallacas. She reminisced fondly about her childhood and other dishes made from corn that her mother often prepared. She remembered everything as delicious, as having a better flavor than foods today. She recalled her mother's hallacas as always requiring the juicier kernel of summer corn. Through her personal and family connections to the dish, she linked corn accessibility to her cultural and national identity; it was part of what it meant to be Cuban and part of a connection to her family. As we sat on the bench, her nostalgia dissipated, and she lamented our inability to acquire corn that day. "Now everything is *una lucha* (a struggle)," she sighed. We got up from the bench and started walking back to her house.

The Politics of Adequacy

Although making hallacas within the narrow window when fresh corn is available is a seasonal task, the taxing and relentless labor of searching for ingredients—the *lucha* (struggle)—to make a meal is an increasingly cumbersome undertaking that people in Santiago de Cuba tackle on a daily basis. This book weaves together the lives of Amalia and others like her who struggle to find food that meets their standards for a decent meal and a good life. As Amalia's search reveals, many Cubans invest a great deal of time and energy into food acquisition both for special occasions and for everyday consumption. This arduous search for food requires investments of substantial time and energy at the expense of other activities, including work and leisure. Despite what is lost in the search for particular foods, I observed many santiagueros bypass a variety of foods that might seem to an outsider like fine alternatives to scarce items. For example, Amalia could have foregone her search for corn and instead of hallacas made another dish with the squash, tomatoes, and cucumbers that were available at every market stall. Instead, she insisted on searching for the particular items that she nostalgically links to her memories of her mother and her own identity. I argue that this insistence on acquiring specific ingredients is part of a refusal to lower their standards for the foods they consume and part of their desire to consume what I call a decent meal, which is tightly bound to their sense of a right to a decent life.

This book is an ethnography of still socialist, post-Soviet Cuba, where "nadie se muere de hambre" (no one dies of hunger).[5] This is a saying echoed in daily conversations, sometimes as an honest reflection on the successes of the Cuban revolution, and other times in a tongue-in-cheek manner while complaining about the difficulties of food acquisition. After my initial trips to the island, it quickly became clear that for many Cubans, the process of acquiring food is not only laborious; it is also a major source of daily stress and anxiety. On street corners, in newspapers, on buses, and in living rooms across the island, families and friends are constantly engaged in dialogue about rising food prices, the shifting availability of food, and the decreasing quality of various food items. The ways in which food is consumed and shared are central to human social and cultural life. Amalia's quest for the perfect corn for hallacas is part of her nostalgic desire to connect her memories of her mother's kitchen with her niece's life, to pass on traditions, to share something that is dear to her, and to demonstrate her love and care for her family by way of food.

When access to food shifts and acquisition of the ingredients that people love to eat becomes more difficult, strained, or impossible, then acquisition comes to the forefront of their concerns. One of my central arguments in this book is that food acquisition is an important process along the chain of production-distribution-consumption. Increasingly, it is also essential to consider how we acquire our food, where our food comes from, and how the social, economic, and political aspects of obtaining food impact our lives. Just as food consumption itself was long ignored by anthropologists who saw it as innate, universal, and not particularly culturally interesting (Farquhar 2002), in many societies across the globe where household-level food acquisition is relatively straightforward, the process of acquiring food is not thought to be an important cultural activity; rather it is often seen as an economic issue that is more related to local channels of distribution (Mintz 1985).[6] In Cuba, as acquisition has become more difficult, the economic aspect of food acquisition is deeply connected to intimate forms of sociality and the ways in which people negotiate their social position.

A study of food acquisition in Cuba may seem puzzling given that the island has virtually no malnutrition or hunger. Indeed, the United Nations' Food and Agriculture Organization (FAO) honored Cuba for maintaining extremely low levels of hunger and malnutrition, citing particular praise for Cuba's national food ration, which still provides about half of an individual's monthly nutritional requirements at very low cost. The Cuban government also provides supplements and additional rationed items for children, the elderly, and those with certain chronic illnesses. But it is precisely this context that allows me to illuminate the ways in which food scarcity is experienced outside of conditions of famine and starvation, but still within a food system that is rapidly changing. Cuba's food system, like most across the globe, is entrenched within the web of distribution of the global industrial food system, and as the Cuban state struggles to buy food on the international market, food access shifts at the local level.

To understand this contemporary Cuban condition of food scarcity without hunger or malnutrition, I introduce "the politics of adequacy." I ask the simple question: what makes a provisioning system adequate? and adequate to what ends? When I ask Cubans about their food system, repeatedly I have heard the responses "no alcance" (it is not enough) and "no es suficiente" (it is not sufficient). What I have found, and what this book centers on, is that there are multiple dimensions of what is meant by *enough* and *sufficient* that matter deeply to people. If food security, subsistence, and sustenance are about access to sufficient nutrients and mere survival, then I propose that the framework of adequacy can account for what is necessary beyond basic nutrition, prompting us to ask not whether a food system sustains life, but whether it sustains a particular kind of living. That is, whether a food system adequately supplies what we need for the social, cultural, and personal dimensions of a good life. The politics of adequacy is about who determines what is necessary to live a good life, how it is determined, and must include both the political economy of food access and the social and affective experiences of eating (Farquhar 2002). Adequate conditions relate to multiple scales of social concerns: those of individuals (caring for oneself), those of family and community (caring for others), and collective forms of ethical commitments and senses of belonging. When there is a shift in access to foods that constituted long-term ways of eating, communities may rethink or reframe the basis of a good meal and a good life.[7] The boundaries of acceptable eating and a decent cuisine, as well as maintaining those boundaries, are important social acts. These social acts keep groups of people together, both symbolically and physically, around the table in times when consumption landscapes are changing. Food consumption is a profoundly relational process where care, social distinction, and dignity are enacted. Careful attention to and the extension of our understanding of adequacy, as it relates to food distribution systems, is therefore a necessary expansion of our understanding of basic needs. The focus here is on the adequacy of the system and whether the provisioning system yields the possibility for living a good life or not.

This book is an exploration of the blurred boundaries between mere survival or sustenance and a good life or a decent meal, a concept that I elaborate below and fully explicate in chapter 1. It explores how people *struggle* to close the gap between the two. Ultimately, I argue that the inability to access particular foods creates, for some santiagueros, a sense of crisis over individual subjectivity, family life, and what it means to be Cuban. By turning our attention to local understandings of adequacy, we illuminate aspects of lived experience that take us beyond a construction of people as "simply or only living in subjugation or as the subjected" (Sharpe 2016, 4), but as humans struggling for a respectable life. Within the politics of adequacy, the notion of politics functions with respect to the ways in which local Caribbean life articulates with systems of global power (Trouillot 1988, 1995; Agard-Jones 2013; Bonilla 2015) and how those "excluded from power can become legible political subjects" (Postero 2017, 17). This book analyzes the various dimensions that people struggling to become or remain legible political subjects must navigate to fulfill their desires to live a good life. They struggle to resolve problems amid the tensions between state socialism and individual and family needs. I examine the ways in which santiagueros grapple with the amount of time and energy they spend struggling to acquire food with the goal of assembling a decent meal and how often that ideal meal is met. I do not find that people's concerns are wrapped up in questions of health, nutrition, caloric sufficiency, or any number of things that food studies and nutrition commonly associate with food adequacy. Therefore, I call for an expansion of our understanding of adequacy to be more aligned with the United Nations' Committee on World Food Security's definition of food security: "the condition in which all people, at all times, have physical, social and economic access to sufficient safe and nutritious food that meets their dietary needs and food preferences for an active and healthy life" (UN CFS 2018).

To illuminate the ways in which Cubans experience their food system as adequate or not, I focus on the multiple dimensions of social stratification and ethics that are at stake here: individual social positions and care for the self; family and community and caring for others; as well as other forms of collective adequacy that shape ethical commitments and belonging at the levels of community and national identity. These commitments are shaped by gendered and racialized expectations of social interaction. I analyze the multiple levels that Cubans have to navigate through the local frames of *luchando* (struggling) and *resolviendo* (resolving), concepts which I explain later in this chapter, in order to fulfill their ideas about what is adequate and what makes a good life.

For many Cubans, the desire for an adequate provisioning system revolves around the yearning to consume "a decent meal." Cuban consumers use the category of the decent meal to maintain the boundaries of "real" food. Categorizing their meals in particular ways is deeply entangled with desires to live in idealized ways in the face of change. The concept of a decent meal involves a cuisine that not only provides nourishment, but also a meal that is perceived as categorically complete with starch, beans, meat, and vegetable components and the opportunity to serve an aesthetically plated meal. The decent meal contrasts with food that is somehow lacking in the previously stated dimensions and would not be deemed appropriate to serve to others as well as potentially being a source of shame for the individual who must eat it. Beyond economic and caloric measures, the aspiration to eat a decent meal is an intimate performance of social status at the level of the family and the self. As I elaborate later in the book, this intimate performance is also entangled with raced, gendered, and classed social expectations.

In Santiago de Cuba an adequate food system has come to represent not only the ability to eat, but also a cluster of promises around what it means to be civilized, live a good life, notions of *Cubanidad* (understood as "general condition of being Cuban"), family values, and countless other potential meanings.[8] For many santiagueros, mealtime represents a space of consistency, a space where care for the self and loved ones is cultivated. The decent meal is an intimate performance that is fundamentally about how social actors constitute their world, and the performative is woven into everyday life in myriad ways (Butler 1993, 1997). The focus on intimate domestic performance is ideal, as I have found that in the context of socialist Cuba the domestic sphere is highly valued. There is social value and meaning derived from state-based wage labor and work as a part of social identity. The decent meal is a type of private performance, which facilitates the social role of food as the locus of care. Therefore for meals to remain central to the maintenance of the self and the social, the particular foods that are nostalgically tied to identity must be at the table. The ways in which santiagueros continuously insist on decency and dignity in their cuisine implies an underlying belief that the ability to consume a decent meal should be a basic guarantee.

Acquisition and Adequacy in Food Studies

Food studies and the anthropology of food are increasingly vast fields of study encompassing consumption as a way to understand how people take up notions of tradition and authenticity (Coté 2017; Mannur 2007; Sutton 2001; Weiss 2016), as well as value (Oxfeld 2017) and connections to the gendered dimensions of our lives (Barndt 2008; Counihan 1999; Vester 2015) and the myriad ways in which food and political economy are entangled (Caldwell 2002; Farquhar 2002; Farquhar and Zhang 2005; Holmes 2013). As Counihan (1999), Van Esterik (1999), and Guthman (2008) among others have argued, food is more than mere calories; it is central to practices of self-care and caring for others. Sidney Mintz was one of the first anthropologists to insist on the importance of understanding both the cultural dimensions and the systems of distribution in food studies, and the need to understand this is increasingly recognized as central to food security (Mintz 2006; Oxfeld 2017; Pottier 1999). While the politics of adequacy framework can be applied in many arenas, this book focuses on adequacy in the context of food. It bridges at least two areas of food studies, those concerned with the social and cultural meanings of food, and those concerned with food access. Specifically, I focus on processes of acquisition, which both expands our understanding of the processes that enable food consumption and demonstrates why an adequacy approach can shed more light on barriers to food access. I argue that the politics of adequacy, a focus on local determinations of whether or not a food system is adequate, should be central to food studies. We must understand adequacy—the cross-cultural determinations of what quantity and quality of food is necessary and under what conditions it is accessible—before we can understand food security or sovereignty. Only through understanding adequacy can we determine if food security or sovereignty have been met.

Often studies of food security fall under one of two realms: those focused on food production and those focused on food distribution.[9] Given that the majority of Cuban food is imported, a focus on food distribution, rather than production, is more fitting for understanding household food access in Cuba.[10] As our food system becomes increasingly global and industrial in scale, and our food must travel thousands of miles before we access it, critical food scholars have noted the shifts in consumption and social change that come along with this (Wilk 2006; Mintz 2006). The global industrialization of foods has meant that while some foods in some forms have become ubiquitous, such as white rice or wheat flour, others, like the fresh sweet corn that Amalia searches for, have become scarce, niche, or available locally only seasonally (Goodman and Watts 1997; Friedmann 1993). In analyzing the tensions between fast and slow food, Mintz pointed out that one of the effects of the global industrial food system was what he called "settling for the mediocre" that comes from the uniformity of cheap foods distributed across the globe, "a flattening of variation, dissolving subtlety" (Mintz 2006, 7). However, as Amalia's search for corn demonstrates, and as I argue throughout the book, the Cubans in this study refuse to accept mediocrity—they will not settle for caloric intake—but insist on a particular cuisine. For them, an adequate food system gives them access to what they need to produce the rich, dynamic cuisine that they are historically and socially connected to.

The rapid circulation of cheap industrial foods across the globe has increased access to calories. At the same time, people are turning their attention to local and sustainable agricultures, to indigenous epistemologies of land and food, and to rethinking the effects of the global food industry on our health and subjectivity (Holtzman 2006; Mintz 2006; Nettles-Barcelon 2007; Paxson 2013; Weiss 2011, 2012). It appears that nostalgia for particular ways of eating is fueling the demand for access to specific foods. As communities yearn to eat in particular ways, we are increasingly aware that the social role of food matters deeply for who we are as people (Williams-Forson 2006; Reese 2018). These two positions around food access, the right to sufficient calories and the right to meaningful food, are increasingly held in tension. This tension is central to the politics of adequacy. How can people utilize an increasingly globalized food system to attend to their local needs?

Noting this tension between fast food and slow food, Sidney Mintz has called for "food at moderate speeds" (2006, 10). Building on this notion, I argue that an adequate food system allows people to access and maintain desired local foods, supports ethnically specific cuisine (Mintz 2006), and at the same time offers up the possibility that food consumption may remain or become a practice of self-cultivation that is part of the politics of the good life. In Cuba I have observed a widespread desire to maintain the connection between locality and food, reaching back to particular imagined historical and traditional culinary practices. This nostalgia is similar to the relationship between food and subjectivity in other socialist/postsocialist contexts. By centering my analysis on acquisition, I expand our understanding of the process of food distribution as more than just production and consumption. Turning our attention to processes of acquisition also troubles the food security versus sovereignty debates, as I reveal the difficulties people face in acquiring food even in environments considered to be food secure and thought to have food sovereignty, as in the case of contemporary Cuba.

Post-Soviet Food

The scholarship on post-Soviet/postsocialist food studies has aptly demonstrated the ways food retains and takes on new meanings as political and economic conditions shift. Although I argue that Cuba is still socialist, the body of work on food in postsocialist settings illuminates how the boundary between socialism and postsocialism is not straightforward (Buraway and Verdery 1999; Caldwell 2004; Dunn 2004; Palmié 2004; Verdery 1996). This body of work has shown that food is deeply connected to imagined community and remembered histories (nostalgia and identity). With a few notable exceptions, much of this work, however, has been concentrated on a particular historical moment (the 1990s) and the post-Soviet transition in Eastern Europe, where those countries were rather suddenly inundated with globalized food systems, cheap fast food, foreign food, and a sense of nostalgia for their "own" local food systems resurfaced. For instance, Nancy Ries has documented the centrality of everyday potato consumption for Russian physical survival during various periods of economic hardship, as well as what she calls a "cognitive resource," or "an object in the world 'coupled' to the social mind and thus an irreducible vehicle of thought about and action in the world" (Ries 2009, 182). Therefore, in the context of Russia's transition from socialism to capitalism, the potato serves as a symbol for Russians to reinterpret their changing world while it simultaneously gives structure and meaning to their daily lives, as it may seem that everything but the potato is changing.

Melissa Caldwell (2002) shows that in post-Soviet Moscow the distinction between "our food" and "not ours" aligns with the notion that locally grown foods are superior to "new" imports. This is one of the ways that Muscovites make meaning of their shifting nation-state's participation in the global food market. While Cuba had not yet faced the influx of consumer goods that many of these postsocialist republics did in the 1990s, the socialist rationing system itself as well as its slow reduction gave rise to many similar sentiments in Cuba as people defined and insisted upon eating in a particularly "Cuban" way.

The Cuban context, with a centralized socialist distribution system, has a very different postcolonial sociohistorical context. The Caribbean has always been modern (Thomas 2004) in the sense that the colonial plantation system based on the labor of chattel slavery produced agrifood products for export and imported consumer goods from around the world. It sits within a "centuries-long process of global interconnection" (Allen and Jobson 2016, 131). Like other places across the globe, this is a setting where tradition and modernity are not on opposite ends of a spectrum but collide and overlap in various ways such that it is possible to be "nostalgic for modernity" (Brenner 1998, 12). Cuba's "traditional" cuisine is made up of ingredients that originate in different corners of the globe (Palmié 2005); it is a modern cuisine based on the tradition of bringing together local and imported ingredients in particular ways (Garth 2013). Elizabeth Pérez (2016) has argued that working in the Cuban kitchen, particularly when preparing food for religious ritual, fosters particular affective states. In this context, Amalia's nostalgia for hallacas and intense desire to access the corn to make the dish can be a form of longing for modern tradition, one that is deeply impacted by local histories and global distributions as Cuba's socialist food system shifts in the post-Soviet era. However, this transition is not characterized by a sudden and dramatic inundation with consumer goods, but rather ongoing conditions of scarcity and uncertainty.

The State, Socialism, and the Politics of Distribution

In any society, the distribution of goods and services is determined by deeply political and social questions of who should receive what proportion of the goods produced in (or imported by) a given society (Ferguson 2015).[11] In Cuba, citizens (and some noncitizen residents) are guaranteed a set of basic entitlements regardless of their status as wage earners.[12] The

Cuban welfare state provides various forms of social protections, including retirement pensions, subsidies for childcare, free primary education, subsidized medical care, affordable public transportation, and basic food staples.

Cuba's dependence upon and interaction with the global industrial food system are defined by the centralized socialist state. For instance, all of Cuba's food imports are handled by the state agency Alimport (*Empresa Cubana Importada de Alimentos*) (Cuban Imported Foods Firm). The Cuban nation-state is still identifiable and a central part of everyday life in Cuba. The state is simultaneously an "imagined state" (Anderson 1983; Appadurai 1990) that people think of as an all-powerful personified actor, and an actual governing body still functioning at the level of the nation-state through centralized economic and political structures. While Cuban political economic relations are increasingly transnational (Trouillot 2003), in my analysis Cuba is not neoliberal, as some scholars have recently claimed (Perry 2016). Rather, I argue that Cuba is still socialist, largely because the centralized state still owns the means of production, the vast majority of Cuban property, and maintains a nationalized egalitarian redistribution system (see also Brotherton 2008). As a socialist welfare state, operating within a transnational network of capitalist societies, social entitlements are central to Cuban state sovereignty. Cuba's maintenance of stellar social indicators, even during an economic crisis, has certainly been a factor in preventing international interventions in Cuba. The distribution of social welfare is still managed by the Cuban nation-state and is not in the hands of transnational corporations or state-like entities (Sassen 1998; Gupta and Sharma 2006).

The Cuban food rationing system is one of the many state-based entitlement systems that are central to what makes Cuba still socialist. The desire to maintain culinary traditions and the anxiety about change in Cuba today should be understood against the backdrop of the food distribution system officially established over 50 years ago, on March 12, 1962. Every Cuban is eligible for a ration card, with which they can purchase basic food items. The ration is commonly referred to as *la libreta* (the notebook). Prices are very heavily subsidized, but households must still pay a small amount for the rationed foods, which are distributed at *bodegas* (ration stations), *placitas/puestos* (posts), and *carnicerías* (butcher

FIGURE 1. Typical Cuban Bodega. Source: Author

shops). However, the items included in the ration fluctuate with national scarcities and surpluses.

The food ration is absolutely essential for most families to survive. While the rations are the most common and important way that santiagueros acquire food, few people are able to survive on rations alone. Those who I spoke with stated that the food provided in the ration only lasted from one to two weeks rather than the full month. Nonetheless, the ration still provides every Cuban citizen, regardless of socioeconomic status, with many of the basic nutrients they need for part of the month and the ingredients to make culturally appropriate Cuban cuisine. Most Cubans, like Amalia, pick up and use all of the items on the ration card each month. The ration creates a baseline of equality with respect to food access, and, given that there is a bodega and carnicería every few blocks, it is relatively easy to access. The service hours are adequate and, although lines often form just before the workday begins and after it ends, waiting times are usually 30 minutes or less, which is reasonable for most Cubans who have begrudgingly grown accustomed to long wait times for all services.

TABLE 1. Items Available in the Ration in January 2012

Bodega Items	Monthly Quantity Per Person
Salt	1 kg (per three months)
Rice	5 lbs.
Beans	10 oz.
Raw sugar	3 lbs.
Refined sugar	1 lb.
Cooking oil	250 ml
Coffee	4 oz.

Carnicería items	Monthly Quantity Per Person
Chicken	6 oz.
Fish	6 oz.
Additional meat (ground meat with soy, bologna, or more chicken)	8 oz. (10 oz. if chicken)
Eggs	1st–15th of the month: 5 eggs @ 15 cents each
	16th–31st of the month: 5 eggs @ 90 cents each

Source: Author

TABLE 2. Additional Items in Elderly and Children's Ration

Item	Daily Quantity Per Person
Fortified fruit puree (compote)	12 oz. can (up to 4 years)
Powdered formula or milk	1 liter (age 0–7)
Soy yogurt	1 liter (age 7–14)
Additional rice	5 lbs. (age 0–14)
Supplemental rice	5 lbs. (over age 60)

Source: Author.

Unfortunately, the extremely subsidized food ration does not include many highly sought-after food items, like corn to make hallacas. As an example, the items detailed in Table 1 were available on the ration (per adult per month).[13] Table 2 includes the additional items rationed to children and the elderly. All of these items together cost the consumer about 25 national pesos (CUP) per month, the equivalent of 1 convertible peso (CUC) or a little more than $1 USD.

Over the past few decades there have been significant changes to Cuba's food and agriculture systems. Beginning in the early 1990s, after the collapse of the Soviet Union, then its major trade partner, Cuba entered into a period of extreme economic difficulty known as the Special Period in Time of Peace.[14] From 1989 to 1992, imports were cut by 73%, from $8.1 billion to $2.2 billion (Preeg and Levine 1993). In the 1990s many food products became scarce, and those that were available had prohibitively high prices. With the drastic reduction of oil, fertilizer, and pesticide imports from the Soviet Union, the agricultural crisis gave rise to food emergency: the bread ration was cut by 20% in Havana to three ounces daily and the bread price was raised by 30% outside of Havana (Chaplowe 1996). In the mid-1990s, caloric intake fell drastically, particularly among the lowest-income Cubans who could not access dollars, grow their own food, or access networks to acquire food.[15] According to the USDA, in 1993 daily caloric intake in the eastern provinces of the island was only 65% of the 1989 levels (USDA 2008). There was also rarely any food available for purchase and a significant reduction in the quality and quantity of food available in state day-care centers, workplace cantinas, school cafeterias, and other long-standing state-operated food centers (Jiménez Acosta, Porrata, and Pérez 1998).

In order to grapple with the food shortages, the state attempted to introduce new foods into the Cuban diet. Soy and other vegetable proteins were substituted for meat, soy products were substituted for dairy, and people were encouraged to eat more vegetables, tubers, and legumes. Meat products in Cuba increasingly include nonmeat fillers. The ground beef included in the ration is a 50-50 blend of meat and textured soy product. The Cuban state refers to these products as nonidentified edible objects or *objeto comestible no identificado* (OCNI) (Nova González 2000, 51). During this period a typical household spent 15 hours per week waiting in line for food, a task that was usually shouldered by women (Eckstein and Wickham-Crowley 2003). This dire situation led to a rise in black-market activity in the early 1990s.[16]

Today Cuba has recovered significantly from the worst of the Special Period. However, for many the quality of daily life has not returned to the era of Soviet mutual aid. The Cubans I spoke with who lived through the period expressed that they still felt uncertain about where their next meal would come from. In recent years the ration has been cut back even further, and more products have been made available at unsubsidized markets, which the Cuban state calls "liberated" foods. As items are liberated from the rations, consumers must acquire food through an elaborate system of state-run subsidized and unsubsidized markets in two different currencies, the national peso and the convertible peso. I elaborate on the ways in which households navigate this food system in chapter 1.

I consistently found that one of the foremost concerns of many santiagueros is the supplementation of their monthly food ration with food items that they view as essential to maintain their ideal of Cuban cuisine. Off the ration, santiagueros access food at subsidized national peso markets, unsubsidized national peso markets, national hard currency markets, the black market, and through informal gifts and trades (Garth 2009). Deciphering the ration system alone is complicated, and, in addition, santiagueros must acquire food through other avenues that are also complex and difficult to use, as illustrated by Amalia's quest for corn. The different ways of acquiring nonration foods have benefits and drawbacks with respect to quality, quantity, variety, and affordability (Garth 2009). The food system as a whole, like the ration, is changing rapidly. This context is one where an "anthropology of decline" (Ferguson 1999) can be applied to understand how a society that once had an abundance of material goods deals with a sudden and sustained decline in access to material goods (see also Pertierra 2011).

Cuba's contemporary food provisioning system must be understood in the context of other aspects of the socialist entitlement system, which together compose the foundation for the possibility of living a good life. In addition to their food rations, Cubans are entitled to virtually free education, although the quality of the education system appears to be on the decline (Blum 2011; Casavantes Bradford 2014). The free universal health-care system established under socialism has also begun to show signs of wear and tear in the past few decades (Andaya 2014; Brotherton 2012; Burke 2013). Although these state welfare programs have faltered in the post-Soviet era, it is important to remember that, like the ration, these programs have also provided a much-needed cushion of the basic need for education and health care. Nevertheless, families are increasingly forced to turn to "private" and black-market resources for care, thus creating a *doble moral* (dual morality) of having to undermine the egalitarian system in order to access health care (Allen 2011; Andaya 2014; Brotherton 2012; Cabezas 2009; Rosendahl 1997; Wirtz 2004). The notion of the doble moral, which I further elaborate in chapter 4, applies to circumstances where someone faces conflicting ethical stances in a situation and must undermine part of their ethics to uphold another aspect.

These reductions in entitlements give rise to ongoing conditions of uncertainty. Manduhai Buyandelger has characterized "the unpredictable as the hallmark of postsocialism" (2008, 236), and building upon her argument, I argue that the state of uncertainty also characterizes ongoing forms of socialism. Cubans, though still living in socialism, share with others in postsocialist post-Soviet states the experience of living through and responding to ongoing sociopolitical change. The changes in the socialist provisioning system that impact fundamental aspects of everyday life, like food access, leave citizens in a constant state of flux, always uncertain about whether or not they will be able to obtain the items they have grown accustomed to having. In myriad contexts, in the midst of mounting uncertainty and precarious existence, individuals and communities grapple with how they will maintain the freedom necessary to build meaningful lives.[17] This feeling of uncertainty is increasingly experienced in capitalist and neoliberal contexts as well, but as this book illuminates, uncertainty and precariousness are not only conditions of neoliberal capitalism nor only of postsocialism, but conditions shared across settings. Many Cubans have experienced the past 60 years, and more intensively the past 30 years, as a condition of constant change and ongoing uncertainty.[18] While some experiences of uncertainty manifest in relatively tangible emotional states, more often my interlocutors experience daily life as a constant tension between situations that they can grasp and easily make sense of, and those that slip through their usual sense of what is going on. This is akin to what Daniel White has referred to as the "gap between how bodies feel and how subjects make sense of how they feel" (White 2017, 177). This existential uncertainty is folded into the other forms of uncertainty that permeate daily life. Cubans try to mitigate the experience of uncertainly through their desires to consume particular foods in particular ways.

This uncertainty can be understood within what P. Sean Brotherton (2012) has characterized as Cuba's own form of socialist governmentality. Most often used in neoliberal contexts, governmentality is generally understood as the ways in which techniques of governing through discipline and technologies of self-government direct people to act in particular ways (Foucault 1991). It is a way of understanding how "power is exercised in society through social relations, institutions, and bodies" (Gupta and Sharma 2006, 277). In Cuba, socialist governmentality is a constant mode of tacking back and forth between the state sector and social networks, enacted through carefully calculated tactics and strategies (Certeau 1984). The tactics and strategies of food acquisition in conditions of scarcity are critical "ways of operating" that come to "constitute the innumerable practices by means of which users re-appropriate the space organized by techniques of sociocultural production" (Certeau 1984, xiv). Rather than moving power from the state to private entities and institutions, socialist governmentality functions in the realm *lo informal* (the informal) (Fernandez 2000), where state institutions are subverted, undermined, or directly pilfered from to take care of the needs of individuals and their families (see also Brotherton 2012). In this context, the notions of *luchando la vida* (struggling for life) and *la lucha* (the struggle) describe both ongoing daily efforts to achieve the goals of revolutionary society, and obstacles that individuals face to get beyond the controls and barriers that have been in place since the revolution (Garth 2013), that is, to *resolver* (resolve) their everyday problems. In reference to the tactics of luchando la vida, this common Cuban refrain is often repeated: "no se puede hacer nada, pero se puede resolver todo" (you can't do anything, but you can resolve everything). To *resolver* often means navigating around the barriers of the official state system by turning to networks of friends, kin, and acquaintances.[19] The tactics and strategies for luchando la vida are akin to what James Ferguson calls "improvisation under conditions of adversity" (2015, 94). Under socialist governmentality, Cubans are simultaneously made increasingly responsible for taking care of their own basic needs while remaining deeply entrenched within the "centralized state apparatus" (Gupta and Sharma 2006, 277). This particular context, which links struggle to the revolution and socialist values, is part of what makes la lucha in Cuba distinct from struggling to acquire food in other contexts (Carney 2015; Page-Reeves 2014).

With growing interdependence, the boundaries between the role of the state as provider and the role of civil society in maintaining social welfare have blurred in recent years (Gupta 1995, 2012b). Since at least the 1990s, Cuba's egalitarian health-care and social welfare programs have been slowly decentralizing (Brotherton 2012; Hearn 2008), and the responsibility for social welfare has shifted away from the national government to individuals, families, and the community. However, although civil society increasingly functions with heavy "individual investments of time, energy, and trust in broad networks of community support" (Hearn 2008, 2), the role of the centralized socialist state in the distribution of basic needs is indispensable in Cuba today. Cuban individuals, families, and communities struggle to work with what the state provides; the state and civil society function together to make the system work (Hernández 2003). That said, in the tension between the expectation that a state will provide basic needs for its citizens and the amount of effort the people must undertake to actually get food on the table, there are multiple dimensions of ethical dilemmas. State provisioning systems are part of a sociopolitical structure of the ethics of food distribution, and individual and community social practices around food sharing also have deeply ethical implications (Sen 1987, 1998).

Within the system of luchando la vida in lo informal there are locally agreed upon ethics for action. As I elaborate in chapter 4, there are certain ways of operating that teeter between licit and illicit, but regardless of their legality these tactics are locally understood as ethical actions necessary for survival. However, as food becomes more scarce families may engage in tactics of acquisition that are not considered ethical (again regardless of their legality). Indeed, "The compulsion to acquire enough food may force vulnerable people to do things, which they resent doing, and may make them accept lives with little freedom. The role of food in fostering freedom can be an extremely important one" (Sen 1987, 1). This ethical dimension matters; it demonstrates what Cubans perceive as a shift in the practice of socialist governmentality, and they experience it as a change in the accepted ways of operating within socialist governmentality. The Cuban state is embodied in this breakdown (Gupta 1995), and we can see the modality of socialist governmentality is not fixed but a mutable, ever-shifting process (Gupta 2012b). I argue that as the lived experience of the socialist state provisioning system changes and ways of operating transform, social positioning shifts and new subjectivities emerge.

Santiago de Cuba

This book centers on food in the everyday lives of Cubans living in the eastern city of Santiago de Cuba, the island's second largest city.[20] Santiagueros insist that Santiago seems to always be hotter than Havana, and they insist that there is more dust in Santiago than any other city on the island. Aside from the heat and dust, Santiago is the seat of many aspects of Cuban culture. Santiago is the birthplace of many genres of Cuban music, from son to conga. Cubans and foreigners alike argue that Santiago has a decidedly Caribbean feel due to its close proximity and histories of interaction with Haiti, the Dominican Republic, and Jamaica.[21] Descendants of these nearby places add homemade hot sauce to the normally heat-free Cuban cuisine, and in the mountains surrounding the city, families tune in to radio and television stations from Jamaica and Haiti.[22] The local research institution, Casa del Caribe, hosts delegates from a neighboring Caribbean country each year at the annual Festival del Caribe. The region was the locus of the inception of the Cuban Revolution, where Fidel Castro created his 26th of July Movement.

Despite a relatively large population of nearly 500,000 people, santiagueros often self-identify as *guajiros* or peasants.[23] If Havana is symbolic of the official narrative of the Cuban nation-state, then for many Cubans across the island Santiago represents the subaltern.[24] Under Cuba's largely centralized economic system, Santiago's location—nearly 500 miles or a ten-hour drive on a good day from Havana—is a major structural barrier to resources. Foods and other products are transported to Santiago by truck, train, or boat. Due to problems with infrastructure, from roads in disrepair to the poor functioning of refrigerated trucks, many foods sensitive to spoilage do not arrive in Santiago in edible condition.

In many Havana-centered ethnographies of Cuba, the rest of the island is portrayed as a vast field of *marabú* (weeds) or *solo paisaje* (just scenery).[25] Depictions of anywhere in Cuba that is not Havana as a veritable wasteland contribute to the ways in which eastern Cuba is further marginalized. In addition to the practical barriers to resources, there are also social barriers to resources within the context of systematic institutional prejudice against santiagueros and people from the eastern provinces of Cuba, a region also known as Oriente.[26] For instance, Cubans living in Havana often refer to santiagueros who move to the capital as *palestinos*, likening them to Palestinians living in Israel, and some *habaneros* (people from Havana) see santiagueros as an unwanted population that strains the already-stretched resources of the capital (Bodenheimer 2015; Stout 2014). For santiagueros, this is the ultimate insult to those who are only hoping to better their life possibilities in the heart of Cuba's centralized economy.

Despite this widespread prejudice, Santiago is also celebrated for its vibrant Black culture.[27] Many santiagueros are proud to continue what they perceive to be African traditions not only through music, dance, and ritual forms, but also culinary practices. Santiago's Carnaval celebrations are Cuba's most famous, and people from all over the world make the trek to Santiago to participate (Wirtz 2014).[28] Many santiagueros, regardless of their skin color or individual identity, explicitly link their *comida criolla* (creole food) to their collective African ancestry. Within the largely Havana-based anthropology of Cuba, this book offers an ethnography of daily life in Santiago that is grounded in the tension between the celebration of Black cultural forms and the prejudices that santiagueros face in the daily struggles of their lives.

In Cuba, race alone is not viewed as a salient category for identity. Instead of race, skin color becomes one way in which Cubans label and distinguish themselves. There are three official skin colors by which Cubans are categorized by the government: *blanco* (white), *negro* (black), and *mulato/mestizo* (mixed). Yet while these are the officially recognized skin colors throughout the country, there are myriad other ways that people identify and are identified.[29] As various santiagueros explained to me, rather than race, a person's way of conducting themselves and outward appearance, including skin color and *nivel de cultura* (level of culture), a local social category akin to social status, play a larger role than biological descent in defining a person's identity. As I further describe in chapter 1, the nivel de cultura identifier is an important form of social stratification that is implicated in the ways in which people define their social position and quality of life. Level of culture is distinct from socioeconomic class and more closely related to social status and education level. It is strongly linked to skin color, formal education, and generations of class-based social training. Without ever explicitly mentioning race or skin color, level of culture functions as a white supremacist ideology that uses the logics of "uplifting" the race through respectability politics, a way of delineating appropriate forms of Cubanidad as linked to whiteness, and policing Black bodies and the behaviors of low-income Cubans (see also Carby 1992; Davis 1998; Willoughby-Herard 2010). In this setting, color, class, and social stratifications like nivel de cultura are considered simultaneously when determining social positions. Rather than race itself being conceptualized as biological, the whole color-class hierarchy is thought to be biological, or at least naturalized. This essentialization of class-color hierarchy is a form of "cultural racism" where older conceptualizations of biologized race have been replaced with new forms of discrimiation based on "culture" (Wade 1993; Stolcke 1995). Many Cubans argue that understanding skin color, class, and level of culture instead of race is a more useful way to understand discrimination and social stratification. This is a social practice deeply embedded in histories of racialization and racism on the island.

Given the historical and socioeconomic conditions of Santiago, the city provides an urban setting to view food acquisition and symbolism in a very distinct cultural and social context as compared with Havana, which allows us to see how the politics of adequacy play out in the everyday lives of some of the most marginalized and disenfranchised people in Cuba. This helps to illuminate the relationship between adequacy and inequality.

Studying Food in Santiago de Cuba

Building on preliminary fieldwork from the summer of 2008, which fell during a global economic crisis, and summer of 2009, I conducted long-term ethnographic fieldwork in households in Santiago de Cuba in 2010 and 2011, and I have continued to visit the island throughout the writing of this book.[30] To understand the myriad ways in which santiagueros grapple with the changing availability of food in Cuba today, I studied 22 households across the city, intentionally selected for diversity in terms of household characteristics, including skin color, neighborhood, and socioeconomic status. Some of the participating households were introduced to me through my sponsoring institution, the Casa del Caribe, who also hosted me and facilitated my educational visa in 2010 and 2011.[31] After a few initial invitations, I began to find households on my own, through introductions by friends or the households that had participated earlier. I tried to include households where at least two members were of working age (18–60) and that included at least one other household member.[32]

I chose to use more in-depth, intensive methods with 22 families in

FIGURE 2. Preparing Corn for Hallacas. Source: Author

order to gain an understanding of the complexities and paradoxes of daily life from research participants' perspectives. My fieldwork involved "deep hanging out," a person-centered approach that focused on lived experience (Levy and Hollan 1998). I spent 12 to 18 hours per day for three weeks to one month with each of the households in the study.[33] I tried to observe all of what I call their "ingestive practices" and all household food acquisition, activities which take place at any moment, some rather quickly, others very slowly. I developed observation protocols, collected time allocation data, photographed household kitchens and meals, asked household members to keep food diaries, conducted a series of interviews with all of the consenting adults, and I tried to ingest all of the food and drinks that they did and nothing more. Although I was sure to just sit back and observe at first, toward the end of the time in each household my deep hanging out often became a form of observant participation as I would be enlisted to do things like hold a baby, cut tomatoes, wash dishes, feed pigs, or any number of household tasks. I was careful to oblige requests to help out around the house without stepping too far into someone else's social role and without shifting household food practices too much. Indeed, the main reason I decided to spend three weeks to one month in each household was that I found that it took a week or two for people to stop performing for the researcher and slip back into their normal habits. This ethnographic depth provided critical insight into everyday life in Cuba.

Although I privileged depth of information, by virtue of the fact that Cuban households tend to be quite large I was still able to study over 100 individuals during the course of this research. I also conducted interviews with some individuals whose households did not fully participate in the study. I interviewed several people who work in food distribution in some way and found a few nonagenarians (people in their 90s) for life history interviews. While most of my invitations to participate in the study were accepted, a few households declined to participate. I cannot be certain why they did not participate. However, a few households told me that the fact that I am American and do not have family ties to Cuba made them nervous about surveillance from either government. Nevertheless the households that were included in the study offer the depth and breadth necessary to understand the lived experience of food acquisition and consumption in contemporary Santiago de Cuba.

Chapter Overview

Each chapter of the book analyzes the politics of adequacy at multiple levels. Chapter 1 focuses on the lived experience of the politics of adequacy and the ways in which skin color and class impact the process of food acquisition. What would the search for corn look like for someone with more or less income than Amalia's or for someone who faced different forms of discrimination because of their skin color? I delve into the ethnographic data to explore relationships between the stressful experiences of food acquisition and participants' notions of an ideal or decent cuisine, ideals that derive from memories of previous eras and remembered pasts told by those who lived through earlier food systems. Although most households struggle to access food regardless of their class or racial status, it is also clear that low-income and darker-skinned individuals face more barriers to accessing food and therefore must invest more time and energy in what often results in less quantity and lower quality meals. I argue that a deeper understanding of processes of food acquisition across race and class augments our understanding of food distribution and its role in food security.

Chapter 2 attends to the ways in which remembered histories, nostalgia, and orientations to the past come to bear meaning on contemporary Cuban life. Drawing on ethnographic data in which santiagueros reference historical periods they recall as important in shaping their notions of a decent meal, a good life, and an adequate provisioning system, I detail three historical periods that they commonly invoke. The first is the period of Cuban independence when the rise of Cuban identity and the notion of Cuban cuisine came about. The second is the period just before and after the 1959 socialist revolution when food distribution and everyday life radically shifted as Cuba became a socialist republic. The third period is during and after the Special Period of the 1990s, a time of economic crisis after the collapse of the Soviet Union. I weave together ethnographic data referencing these periods with historical information to illuminate the ways in which nostalgia for the past influences how people experience the present.

In chapter 3, I analyze household-level dynamics and the gendered dimensions of food adequacy, elaborating on the ways gender inequalities are exacerbated by the changing food system. Despite women's much improved ability to access education, work, and health care, as the Cuban food system shifts away from state provisioning, women take on disproportionate amounts of increasingly difficult, time-consuming, and unpaid household labor. I demonstrate the ways in which deeply entrenched patriarchal ideologies and locally conceived ideals of "virtuous" womanhood drive this gendered division of labor. I argue that when the gendered forms of care for the self and care for the family that are enacted through food preparation and provisioning are undermined by an inadequate food system we begin to see the foundations of household and social relations begin to unravel. Attention to the tremendous burdens of work that have shifted from the state onto individuals, and the ways in which these tasks are often shouldered by women, reveals the depths of the impact of the faltering welfare state. In turn, giving detailed attention to food and the politics of adequacy reveals not only that women take on much of the work to hold the food system together, but as this work becomes increasingly difficult, the stress, anxiety, and other burdens on women have significant impacts on the family and household dynamics more generally.

Broadening beyond the household, chapter 4 focuses on the dynamics of food adequacy and social relations in *la comunidad* (the community) as santiagueros conceive of it. I argue that the collapse of the Cuban food system has profoundly shifted participants' ethical orientations to resource sharing with their communities. As state provisioning contracts, this chapter reveals the ways in which Cubans turn to different tactics and strategies for acquiring food. These tactics and strategies are understood within a locally conceived ethics of exchange, a system built around reliance on a network of *socios* (acquaintances) and the *palanca* (leverage) to acquire goods and access services though informal channels, lo informal. While there are many aspects of these practices that are technically illegal, such as buying and selling food on the black market, these are commonly accepted as licit practices. On the other hand, as it becomes increasingly difficult to access goods and services, Cubans turn to tactics that may not fall within commonly understood ethical practices. Yet, they turn to such tactics as the only way to access food, which is necessary to survive. This conundrum leaves many Cubans questioning whether there is a shifting ethics of acquisition under way in Cuba that may undermine the ethics of the New Man, which involved the curtailing of individual desires for the needs of the collective. I show that as the state provisioning system wanes, santiagueros must increasingly rely on social networks to access foods, and yet scarcity within those networks can lead people to turn to practices of food acquisition that undermine the very social connections that they rely upon to survive. This difficulty becomes a personal and social bind that demonstrates the ramifications of an inadequate food system.

Building on the arguments about the connections between food acquisition, the community, and local understandings of ethical practices, in chapter 5 I turn to the ways in which the changing food system can become extremely difficult and result in an emotional or social breakdown. Here I turn to the more person-centered, experience-near aspects of my research, giving attention to the lived experience of struggle. The narratives detailed here illuminate the ways in which struggling is an ethical orientation and moral process in and of itself. I turn to moments with palpable and visceral emotion to understand the affective states in which santiagueros find themselves during this time of transition in Cuba. Through my analysis of these moments and their own reflections, I outline the ways in which the changing food system leads people to breakdown. These breakdowns, which are often experienced as unwelcome and lamentable, become evidence of the inadequacies of the state provisioning system. Through these affective states, Cubans grapple with the politics of adequacy and reflect on what basic needs are necessary for a good life.

Finally, in the conclusions I draw together themes highlighted throughout to argue that the waning of Cuba's socialist food provisioning system has had a profound influence on associated social interactions, placing strain on family and community relationships. This is interpreted locally as a "change in character," which I demonstrate is connected to shifts in subjectivity. I detail how shifts in subjectivity impact how my research participants imagine community and imagine themselves within a nexus of national and transnational relationships. Building on my development of the politics of adequacy, I show how this analysis of post-Soviet Cuban subjectivity contributes to our broader understanding of issues of adequacy and the politics of distribution.

1

La Lucha

In late May 2009, I joined Monika, a *mulata*-identified low-income women who was 25 years old at the time, on a morning trip to the market to buy her household's food for the day.[1] We traversed Santiago from her city center home to the Trocha y Cristina market toward the bay, passing by many small food stands and ambulant vendors along the way. Monika was committed to shopping at Trocha y Cristina, where she had spent many years building relationships with the vendors, and felt she could find the best quality food as well as the widest variety of options in one location. As we walked, Monika spoke about planning the day's meals. She had pork cutlets, black beans, and rice at home to use for lunch; she would need onions, garlic, peppers, and some spices to cook the meat. She would need plantains for the *tostones* (twice-fried plantains) to serve alongside the meal. Tomatoes or avocado would do for the salad. For dinner, she would serve a soup—*caldosa*[2]—for which she would use some of the pork she already had at home. In addition, she would need squash, *yuca, boniato*, and chard.[3] She wanted to make sure to buy enough onions, garlic, and peppers for the soup as well. She had dried cumin at home, but she also wanted to use fresh *culantro* and *oregano cubano*.[4] Finally, she would pick up some fruit, maybe mango or *mamey colorado* to mix with her children's yogurt ration in a refreshing smoothie as their afternoon snack.[5]

Just as she had finished telling me her shopping plan, we rounded the corner and arrived at the market. Then suddenly Monika let out a scream: "¡Ay! ¿que pasó?" (Oh, what happened!?). We stood in shock before a completely leveled, empty lot of dirt. Bulldozers and dump trucks still on site, it

FIGURE 3. Bulldozed Market Space. Source: Author

appeared that the market had just recently been torn down. A man sitting on the curb nearby offered the comment, "The state tore down the market last night. Something about trying to curb the rising prices of food here."

Monika started to panic. She paced back and forth, inhaling and exhaling rapidly, her eyes darting back and forth. She finally sat down on the curb with her head in her hands. I tried to console her, linking my arm around hers. Eventually I asked, "Why don't we just go to another market?" She threw her hands down and yelled, "You don't understand anything! It is not that easy!" She moved a few feet away with her back to me. Eventually taking a deep breath, she turned back to me and said, "Ya, vámonos" (Enough, let's go).

We walked back to her house, uphill, in silence. When we arrived she threw her purse on the table and said, "I am going to take a shower and I am not leaving the house for the rest of the day. I need to rest my mind (*descansar la mente*).[6]" For lunch that day she served white rice with fried eggs, a dish called *plato de puta* (slut's dish) in local parlance, not considered a decent meal by any account. She sent her husband and two children to her mother-in-law's house for dinner, explaining that the market closure meant that she did not buy enough food for dinner.[7] The weight of the market closure set in, the precariousness of her household food acquisition came to light, and her ability to cope gave way. Monika did not join her family for dinner; instead she explained to me that she needed to stay home to "rest her mind," due to both an honest need to rest from her stressful day and a sense of shame over not being able to provide a decent meal for her family.

Like Monika, many household cooks in Santiago have the goal of creating a decent meal for their loved ones. They spend a great deal of time and energy each day in search of ingredients to make that idealized, decent meal. The goal is to not have to serve plain white rice and a fried egg, or a similar "crappy" meal, which they might consider to be sufficient for some people but not for "decent folk" such as themselves. The process of putting together a decent meal is a time-consuming pilgrimage as they seek to compensate for inadequacies in the state food rationing program. As I moved through the city with Santiago families in search of food, they orally expressed concern, and I could sense their anxiety as they sought out vendors, some in the black market, where desired foods might be found. Often their search was unsuccessful, leaving them frustrated and feeling that their meals, while keeping them alive, were not satisfying in other ways. As their searches for the ingredients that make a decent Cuban meal were stymied by a lack of money or because the foods were just not available, santiagueros become frustrated with the Cuban food system. This search for food is stressful and anxiety-ridden, filled with worry over whether they would be able to procure enough of the right kinds of food to feed their families. They express the tension between the inability to acquire the food they desire and the reality of their everyday meals as a sense that "they are going crazy." These Santiago families implicitly reflect on the politics of (in)adequacy and the ways in which shifts in the food provisioning system significantly impact their lives. In contemporary Cuba families across socioeconomic statuses experience the politics of inadequacy as they attempt to create meals that inevitably pale in comparison with memories of the "golden age" of food consumption, which I detail in chapter 2. Food is not simply food, but a reflection of identity, filled with emotions that color experiences of the changes in the food system, which families in Santiago, and all of Cuba, must endure.

This chapter introduces the everyday lived experience of food acquisition in post-Soviet Cuba. I argue that with careful attention to people's practices of acquisition we can see the inadequacies of the food system as evidenced by the overwhelming effort invested in acquiring food and the forms of stress and anxiety that derive from the uncertainties of food access. Monika's story, like many others in this chapter, introduces the foundation for some of the arguments made throughout this book, from the gendered division of labor and expectations of women (chapter 3), to the provisioning of food as an ethical act (chapter 4), to stress and affective responses (chapter 5). These dimensions of food acquisition refract in different ways for different households.

Class, skin color, and other local forms of social distinction are among the major fault lines that impact the differences in the ways santiagueros experience and reflect upon food acquisition and consumption in the context of the waning socialist welfare state.[8] As I will show, skin color and particular forms of racialization, as well as the ways in which santiagueros categorize themselves and others as part of lower, middle, or upper social classes, matter for the experience of food acquisition. Also, the local social category of "level of culture" as a form of social distinction is connected to but differentiated from skin color and class. I have found that class, skin color, and level of culture are social categories that can either broaden or contract a household's ability to access food in contemporary Santiago. These categorizations have a strong bearing on how food acquisition is experienced and the possibilities that are imagined by different santiagueros as they traverse the city in search of food.

After documenting the ways in which social categorizations can impact the experience of food acquisition, I explain the concept of the decent meal. The ability to put together a decent meal for family and friends is the goal that many santiagueros have when they set out to acquire food. However, due to the shifting availability of the foods that are necessary to create that decent meal, assembling a decent meal is often a difficult task, a process that santiagueros sometimes categorize as a struggle. In spite of all of these obstacles, families devise solutions to overcome the difficulties of the food system. Overall this chapter details the day-to-day tactics and strategies that households employ to overcome the inadequacies of the food system, which are exacerbated by or alleviated by their relative social positions vis-à-vis class, skin color, and level of culture.

Class, Color, and Culture

To understand the desire to eat a decent meal and live a decent life, we must understand where indecencies might lie, in particular those that fall along lines of class-status, race or skin color, and "level of culture." Class and socioeconomic status are extremely difficult to measure in Cuba. According to official Cuban state discourse, class struggles should theoretically dissipate under a socialist society. However, in practice, class divisions have remained throughout Cuba's socialist period, and with ongoing economic difficulties at the state level and increased levels of inequality, socioeconomic classes remain a part of society. My research participants self-identified and categorized others as *clase baja/gente humilde* (lower class), middle class *clase media/gente normal* (middle class), and *clase alta/gente con posibilidades* (upper class). Giving close attention to the lived experience of food acquisition illuminates the ways in which class differences persist in Cuba today. While the end result may be low levels of malnutrition across class divides, a close analysis reveals the unequal distribution of labor necessary to maintain those low levels of malnutrition. Those from lower socioeconomic status backgrounds invest large amounts of time and energy into food access, losing the ability to spend their time on other activities such as work or leisure.

In Cuba, as in many locations, class and race are deeply interconnected.[9] After the 1959 socialist revolution, Fidel Castro announced the state's commitment to eliminating racial discrimination. Similar to class differences, the general assumption was that once the socialist revolution had succeeded there would be no issues of racism because under the Marxist view when class was eliminated issues of race would not be a problem. Yet, like class, race and prejudice persist in socialist Cuba, though often in different forms that are increasingly hard to identify. As I mentioned in the introduction, Cubans often opt to discuss difference in terms of skin color, rejecting race as a Western construct that does not apply well in post-revolutionary Cuba. The correlation between class and skin color continues to mean that Black Cubans are often low-income and considered lower class (clase baja/humilde), while those with higher incomes characterized as upper-class (clase alta/gente con posibilidades) Cubans are often white. While these correlations are tied to colonial and early postcolonial concentrations of wealth, a high concentration of capital still remains among white families. This is particularly true as many of the emerging economic activities and the investment of foreign capital are concentrated among white Cubans, who are more likely to have connections in the diaspora or greater ability to access work in the tourist sector.

Although Cuba is deeply Black, steeped in remembered histories of ancestral ties to Africa and its diasporic reverberations through the island (James Figarola 1974; Wirtz 2014 2017), race relations have never honored that Blackness with equal treatment for dark-skinned Cubans. Cuba has been characterized as a white-aspiring society, where people have accepted the myth that *mestizaje*—the biological and social mixing of races and cultures—will ultimately promote racial unification under whiteness (Spence Benson 2016). Scholars have argued that this valorization of mestizaje erases and marginalizes Blackness (Harrison 1995; Wade 2001); others note the slow process of revalorizing Blackness (Simmons 2009) and the multiplicity of race in Cuba. Cuba's specific history of race relations is based in histories of Spanish colonial rule and chattel slavery. Before the 1959 revolution, race relations on the island were characterized by inequality, segregation, prejudice, and varying degrees of racial discrimination, in part a product of Cuba's history as a slave society. With limited job and educational opportunities, dark-skinned Cubans were more likely to be poor than those with lighter skin and also suffered disproportionately from infant mortality and shorter life expectancy. Inequality and discrimination were largely to blame for these discrepancies in morbidity and mortality.

The 1959 socialist revolution got off to a rocky start with respect to race relations. Early on Castro all but ignored Black Cubans, yet later he shifted to paternalistic propaganda about the ways in which the revolution could help Black Cubans become better educated and improve health indicators in the Black community, as a way of improving well-being overall in Cuba. Early on the revolution set up a "misleading dichotomy between Blackness and Cubanness" in the slogan "!Negros No . . . . Ciudadanos" (Not Blacks, Citizens)(Spence Benson 2016, 2), which the government used in campaigns and political speeches as if to say that to be Cuban one must not be Black. Cubans were increasingly convinced to shed their racial identities in favor of a unified Cuban identity tied to socialist nationalism. And yet this deep-seated anti-Blackness sits alongside an awareness and celebration of the cultural, religious, and culinary dimensions of Blackness in Cuba (Beliso-De Jesús 2015).

From the Marxist perspective adopted by Castro and the socialist Cuban state, racism is rooted in the capitalist economic base. By this logic once socialism replaced capitalism as the economic base, racism and other social ills in the superstructure would simply disappear since a capitalist base no longer sustained them. After the revolution, race became a taboo subject for public discussion: the state successfully convinced many Cubans that under socialism all problems of inequality including racial and gender-based discrimination would simply disappear (Fernandez 2010). Individuals feared that talking about racism would be interpreted as saying antigovernment, antisocialist, or anti-Castro things, which was strictly prohibited.[10] Furthermore, many Black-identified Cubans continue to be deeply grateful for the antiracist reforms of the revolution, what some have called the "Gracias Fidel Syndrome" (Moore 1988, 44; see also Allen 2011); they thank the revolution for making Black Cubans equal and have difficulty seeing the persistence of racist forms. Although food access was cumbersome among most of the households in this study regardless of class or skin color, those households with darker skin color faced greater barriers to food access both due to direct experiences of discrimination, fear of discrimination, and institutionalized forms of prejudice that render these households with less income and fewer options for making money in Cuba's post-Soviet economy.

In Santiago de Cuba, race and class should be understood alongside *nivel de cultura* (level of culture). In Cuba the nivel de cultura identifier is an important form of social stratification that is implicated in the ways people define their social position and quality of life. In Cuba level of culture is distinct from socioeconomic status and more closely related to social class and education level. It is strongly linked to skin color, formal education, and generations of class-based social training. For instance, those with a higher nivel de cultura are more likely to have read classic novels, be familiar with theater, ballet, and opera, and appreciate the fine arts. A person with a high nivel de cultura also has a sophisticated palate and appreciates some of the foods considered to be rare and associated with high culture in Cuba, such as wine, champagne, capers, and olives. Nivel de cultura has historically been linked to race. Those with lighter skin were thought to have an inherently higher nivel de cultura. Today the category of nivel de cultura is still used, though most Cubans claim that it is no longer tied to race in such a biologized fashion. When I spoke with scholars in Santiago about how to gauge nivel de cultura they usually referred first to education level. A colleague at the Casa del Caribe explained the concept in this way:

> A person with a high level of culture likes the fine things in life. They read the classical literature, listen to the symphony, know all of the famous Cuban theater, they like to talk about these things with their friends who also know about these things. So it used to be that drinking fine wines and eating things like champagne, caviar, olives, and capers was tied to nivel de cultura, but we don't have those things anymore.

Building on this understanding of level of culture, it is clear that despite revolutionary reforms, prejudice and discrimination persist by way of a class-color–based discrimination linked to social categories such as nivel de cultura. This can take the form of cultural racism, which my interlocutors do not identify as racism per se but rather as a more generalized form of prejudice that is linked to color and class. In this context Black Cubans simultaneously experience prejudice and defend the socialist revolution as fundamentally antiracist, pointing to forms of prejudice and discrimination linked to color, class, and level of culture rather than labeling their experiences as part of racism. Level of culture therefore becomes color-blind, race-coded language that links appropriate forms of Cubanidad to whiteness while devaluing Black people and Black cultural forms.

Within the class-color-culture stratification, one's social position matters for food access and influences the difficulties one might face in acquiring food. These social positions also matter for how people reflect upon and understand the decency and dignity of their household food consumption practices relative to other households. As I elaborate below, local notions of the decent meal and alimentary dignity have been shaped over time and in conjunction with the shifting political economic conditions in Cuba.

What Is a Decent Meal?

Cuban household cooks search the city for particular ingredients, insisting on acquiring only those ingredients, when there are a variety of other foods available. For instance in the case from the introduction, during her search for corn, Amalia encountered squash, tomatoes, onions, green peppers, plantains, all ingredients sufficient for making a variety of things. And Monika could have gone to a different market, slightly shifting her plans for the day's meal. Yet in the search for ingredients, both Amalia and Monika, and many others like them, refused to adjust their plans and insisted on searching for particular items to create a specific vision of the meal that they would produce. There appeared to be a shared notion of what a "real" or decent meal should constitute, which in practice was rarely achieved due to the scarcity of necessary ingredients or the money with which to purchase them (Garth 2013). While both searches, and many like them, failed, and in the end an alternative dish had to be made, the insistence on producing a particular type of food is a social phenomenon central to the politics of adequacy. Drawing on my research participants own categorizations of their foods as "real," "decent," "good," and "dignified," I call this particular type of food a "decent meal," a conceptual category that can be used in a variety of contexts to denote the ideal meal of a particular group of people (Garth 2019). A decent meal involves a cuisine that not only provides adequate nourishment, but also implies the ability to assemble a meal that is perceived as categorically complete (Douglas 1966, 1972). In the case of Cuba, the decent meal is one that includes a starch, beans, meat, and vegetable components and the opportunity to serve an aesthetically plated meal (Garth 2019). Portion size matters; sufficient amounts of meat and vegetables are often taken into consideration when assessing a meal. The decent meal contrasts with food that is somehow lacking in the previously stated dimensions, and would not be deemed appropriate to serve to others as well as potentially being a source of shame for the individual who must eat it. The decent meal was often an ideal that was not met.

As 58-year-old Omaro described the decent Cuban meal:

> Well if you are studying food in Cuba—Cuban food that is [. . .] all you need to know about is rice and beans—what we call here *congris*—and then pork and *viandas,* that's all we eat because that is *our* food. What the Cuban people live, our way of living is *congris*, pork, and *viandas*.[11]

The notion of a specifically Cuban diet, which consisted of a particular balance of different types of foods—meats, starches, and vegetables—was continually reified by many of my research participants in comments similar to those made by Omaro. The foods he mentions are commonly viewed as authentic Cuban foods, which, when consumed together, comprise a decent meal and a dignified cuisine. Omaro's inclusion of three starches—rice, beans, and tubers (viandas)—was an ideal shared across Santiago families. These views establish a romanticized ideal of "real" Cuban food, one that is enveloped in remembered traditions, local understandings of place and local histories of place (Garth 2009). Omaro also underscores that this notion of a Cuban way of eating is also a way of living, a way of life—rendering it a broader category of social meaning that moves beyond the realm of just eating, merely satisfying hunger, to an important part of what it means to be Cuban.

FIGURE 4. A Decent Meal. Source: Author

Assembling a Decent Meal

Regina's Search for Lunch

Leaving the city center, where many middle-class Santiagueros live, I walked through Santiago's commercial district, made up of just a few streets lined on either side with state-owned food stores with shelves filled with virtually all the same items, like rows upon rows of mayonnaise, mostly made in Cuba with some imported exceptions. Turning out of the commercial district, I walked down a long street of mobile food vendors, again mostly selling the same things—during these winter months it was lettuce, tomato, papaya, and other fruits and vegetables. At the end of this street I crossed from the city center neighborhood into what those living there called El Hoyo (The Hole), somewhere between Santa Rita, Santa Úrsula, and Chicharrones, which marks the beginning of a large poor and marginalized Santiago neighborhood. Most of the people who live here are Black or *mulato*. From the neighborhood's edge I walked downhill (as most of the area is low-lying and thus subject to flooding and the runoff of all of the city's water). At the top of the hill one can see that during some past era this was a relatively nice neighborhood—some colonial-era houses remain, though crumbling. For the most part the houses have been sectioned off into smaller dwellings, or have collapsed, and new structures have been built with a hodgepodge of tin, wood, and repurposed brick. Downhill from this main street there is a stark change in the landscape. The sidewalk ends. A perpetual puddle of watery sludge lines the side of the partially paved, partially dirt road. There are no trees, no greenery at all along the street, though a few trees that pop up from behind and between dwellings are guarded by those who value the coolness that their shade provides in the summer.

Walking down this hill to the bottom of the first of many Santiago-area valleys, I arrived at a narrow door with a *mal de ojo* symbol painted on it—to keep away bad spirits and evil people. This was the door to Regina's house. Regina is a 46-year-old, low-income, Black-identified santiaguera.[12] As I arrived at her house around 8:30 a.m., Regina was still lying in bed. Of all of the heads of household in my study, Regina woke up and started her day the latest. Regina's three-year-old grandson, Chichi, had opened the front door and was sitting just outside it, next to a gutter with a constant flow of wet trash and sludge that gathers just to the south side of their house in big puddle around a clogged drain. Chichi was sitting in his underwear, singing a popular reggaeton song while stirring around the slimy mix with a piece of wire. He looked up quickly at me, and then returned to his focus on the sludge, yelling "¡Mamá! ¡La Americana está!" (Mom! The American is here!), as he slightly inclined his head toward the door signaling me to go inside.

As I walked in, I could not see, and I had to stop in the living room to let my eyes adjust to the dark; the house has no windows, and no light comes in from the outside. As I stood waiting for my eyes to adjust, Regina got out of her bed—which is in the kitchen. She yelled for me to head on back to the kitchen, as she looked around to assess what there was to eat. I sat on her bed, which was along one of the kitchen walls, and we made small talk, while she gathered three cloves of garlic, half an onion, and a pack of red food coloring powder. She held it all in the palm of one hand and said, "This won't get us very far." Since she was not planning to leave the neighborhood, she decided to stay in her "house clothes." She slipped on her worn flip-flops, stating, "You can come or you can stay."

Like many lower socioeconomic status families (gente humilde), this is how almost all of Regina's mornings begin. She wakes up late, and the first thing she does when she gets out of bed is see what there is to eat. It is almost always virtually nothing. She does not bathe, change her clothes, or do anything other than put her shoes on and go out to *buscar algo pa' comer* (look for something to eat). Her first stop is her neighbor's house, where she pokes her head in and asks, "¿que hay?" (What is there?). Her neighbor, who is like a sister to her, gives her the daily update on how the bread is that day—too airy, too hard, stale, or, on rare occasions, good— what is available in the ration station that day, what's at the corner market, and what the regular morning street vendors have. She tells Regina about any food "deals" and "rip-offs" that may be overpriced or lower in quality than one should expect.

On most mornings, within 30 minutes Regina has returned to the house from small vendors in her immediate area with enough ingredients to create a decent breakfast for at least a third of the people who live in her house; in order of priority, they are the children (youngest to oldest), pregnant women, sick women, other women, sick men, young men, working men, and then finally, older, out of work men.[13] There are 24 people who officially live in Regina's house, which she inherited when her mother passed away. Four of her siblings had nowhere else to live, so they and their spouses remained in the house. Over the years these nine adults and most of their children all have Regina's house listed as their official dwelling, which is where they receive their food ration. Assessing how many of them actually live there at any particular time is quite complicated because they tended to come and go, staying with lovers and friends more often than at Regina's house. I decided to focus my study on the eight people that I observed as almost always eating at least two meals a day there.

Twice divorced, Regina has two children, one from each marriage.[14] When her mother was alive, she was the primary caregiver for both children, and Regina worked as a professional dancer. She danced with one of the top-rated dance troupes in Cuba, traveling to over 15 countries across the world. After her mother passed away, Regina stopped working and became the primary caregiver for her disabled daughter, who was 26 years old at the time of my study. Regina receives a small amount of money from the state as compensation for her care work. That is the only money Regina has, and it is scarcely enough to feed her daughter, let alone herself and the others that linger at mealtime.

While breakfast ingredients are often acquired relatively quickly, putting lunch together is generally much more of an ordeal. Each day, shortly after she finishes preparing, serving, and eating breakfast, she must begin her search for lunch ingredients.[15] Most fundamental to the decent meal, Regina must acquire rice, which requires that she leave her immediate area. Aware of the many ways in which she is discriminated against because of her dark skin and low socioeconomic status, she makes sure to bathe and dress in "respectable" clothing whenever she leaves her neighborhood. She carefully ties her hair back with a bow and wears the second nicest outfit she has—the nicest one is reserved for parties, weddings, and funerals. Her clothing is like a thin layer of armor she must put on to face the prejudice that lurks in various nooks and crannies of the city center.

On this particular day, as on many others, Regina dutifully walked the 14 uphill blocks to the large unsubsidized state market, La Plaza; as she entered she slowed down to let her eyes adjust to the dark windowless warehouse, having just come in from the Santiago summer sun. She blinked and slowly scanned the countertops to survey what was available. She held in her hand just a few coins, not enough to get much at her neighborhood food stand. She had made her way to the city's central market hoping to find lower prices to stretch what little she had into a meal for at least the women and children in her household. The others would have to fend for themselves.

She clutched her canvas bag to her chest as she walked past counter after counter of underripe tomatoes, and she rattled off her thoughts out loud to me as we walked through the market. She was not interested in tomatoes—it would take far too many to make enough sauce. She stopped in front of one stall that had plantains—she didn't have any oil for tostones, but she could boil them to make *fufú de plátano,* a traditional dish made by mashing boiled plantains with pork fat, garnished with fried pork skin. Noting to me that she was keeping the plantains in mind, she moved into the next room where there were more stalls. She paused to examine the *quimbombó* (okra), noting the price at the first stall—was it cheaper than in her neighborhood? She remembered it being the same price there, but she knew that she could get the man working at her neighborhood market to throw in a few pieces for free. She explained to me that they would not do this for her here—they did not know her and would not favor her because of her dark skin. She decided to just pick up a few onions and cooking peppers at the Plaza, and she would walk back to her neighborhood to get okra and hoped she would get a few extras thrown in for free.

Now, she turned to her most important task: rice. It would not be a

FIGURE 5. Mercado La Plaza, Santiago de Cuba. Source: Author

meal without rice. She told me that she knew that her neighbors and tight-knit social network, who were always willing to help out, did not have any to lend, so she decided to drop in on Asulema, a lighter-skinned, *mulata*-identified cousin who was a bit better off than Regina and lived in the city center. The door was open, so she called out her cousin's name as she walked into the fully furnished living room. Asulema was in the kitchen, well into the day's lunch preparations, and delighted to see her cousin. She wiped off her hands and met Regina with a kiss on the cheek. She dispensed a little cup of coffee for each of us from her thermos—always full of coffee, just in case a guest drops by, she explained. Asulema, who meets the standards of a virtuous woman (a concept elaborated in chapter 3), was in the midst of preparing a decent meal for her family. She served the coffee to Regina and me along with a glass of water, asking how things were down in "The Hole." Regina later told me she felt a sense of shame in having to ask her more well-off cousin for food; in an effort to save face she tried to make conversation, but it was clear that she wanted something from Asulema. Asulema finally asked Regina if she needed anything and after she said no, and Asulema asked again, Regina finally asked if she could borrow a few

FIGURE 6. Food Stalls in La Plaza. Source: Author

cups of rice. Asulema scooped about five cups out of her full bin of rice directly into Regina's canvas bag with the other vegetables. Regina thanked her and got up to leave, explaining her quick departure as necessary so they could both get lunch on the table at a decent hour. The tensions of class, color, and level of culture difference were brought into stark relief in this interaction as I watched Regina completely shift her behavior and disposition from how she acted at home, cultivating an air of properness as she sat in her cousin's home making small talk, all the while intently focused on her need to acquire rice and the ticking clock creating mounting pressure to return home to start the process of cooking lunch.

On her way back home she stopped by her butcher friend's house to see if he had any scraps he could give her. Indeed, he gave her the leftover pieces of meat that were still on his cutting block, giving her just enough for flavoring and fat in her quimbombó.

Understanding Regina's Daily Struggle

Regina's tactics of food acquisition on that particular day are typical of the low-income households in my study. The daily quest for food and complexities of navigating the changing food system routinely provoke high levels of anxiety and stress. The deep-seated forms of racism and prejudice that Regina constantly fears exacerbate the difficulties of food acquisition. As the monthly rations run low, Regina and other heads of

FIGURE 7. Small Neighborhood Butcher. Source: Author

household of lower socioeconomic status often start each day with no food in the house and spend their mornings trying to piece together enough for a meal with what little they have. For Regina, the intensity of waking up to a bare cupboard heightens the pressure on the daily search for affordable food. Budgeting and meal planning are difficult given that she has so little. She often resorts to borrowing food or money to feed her family. Furthermore, when Regina moves beyond her neighborhood she worries that she is judged by a strict standard of "right behavior," which is a largely based on white, middle-class, socialist ideals. While budgeting and planning are not upheld as the ultimate virtues of women in her close social circle, her inability to plan and properly control her home environment reflects poorly on her within this larger social realm. As Regina's quest illustrates, the difficulties of food acquisition lead many santiagueros to characterize the process as a *lucha* or part of *la lucha*—a daily struggle to acquire food.

Despite these struggles and although she had one of the most dire food-access situations of my study, Regina was among the happiest and least overtly stressed participants. It could be that she expressed stress in a different way that I did not observe, or it could be that she has grown so accustomed to living in these conditions that she no longer gets angry and stressed about it, or it could be that she and the women of her social circle have a different set of values for what constitutes a "good life." Indeed, in one of our interviews Regina told me that she remembered extreme hardship as a child and that her parents' and grandparents' generations were plagued by the cycles of Black urban poverty that were so common before the revolution. She said, "Gracias a Fidel" (Thanks to Fidel) her life was better than those who had come before her.[16] This way of framing her life is part of what makes Regina less stressed about her daily situation than others of higher socioeconomic status, who remember when their lives and their kin's lives were much better. As Regina strives for a decent life, she makes comparisons to those whose lives appeared to be much more difficult, measuring against those forms of indecency; she does not reflect upon her situation as among the worst she can imagine and for that she thanks Fidel Castro and the 1959 revolution.

Although the stresses cut across class lines, the daily practices of food acquisition vary across neighborhood, skin color, and social class in Santiago de Cuba. Like other low-income households, Regina's social networks are limited mainly to friends and family who live in the same neighborhood, many of whom are also struggling to make ends meet. Borrowing and lending food is a common daily practice in this neighborhood, but given that most people living there are resource-poor, borrowing from within this network as an approach to food acquisition does not generally yield good results. Regina must also rely on kin networks outside her neighborhood and social class, and she explained to me that this situation made her feel uncomfortable, because she feels more indebted or more obligated to repay her lender than if it were someone in her own neighborhood who might have a better understanding of her situation. This is one specific element of inequality between low-income and middle- and upper-income households in Santiago: the latter are more likely to be able to borrow significant quantities of food items from one another during times of scarcity or financial trouble.

Food Shortages and Inaccessibility

Like Regina and her rice, one of the central reasons santiagueros feel that the Cuban food system is inadequate is the underavailability of foods that they are accustomed to eating. Although food availability in general has increased significantly since the worst days of the Special Period in the mid-1990s, there are often shortages of specific food items (Garth 2009). It may be the case that a particular item is not available in any market across the city, or it may be that the item is only available at a higher price in pesos, or in hard currency, thus rendering the item inaccessible to many

Santiago families. When a food that is seen as a central part of a Cuban meal is unavailable or inaccessible, even if there are other foods available, many of my study participants reported that they did not feel satisfied. Thus, they experience the food system as scarce and think of themselves as living within a food shortage. This form of food scarcity has received little attention from scholars of food security.

The lived experience of food acquisition described in these cases of searching for particular ingredients that are strongly linked to cultural and national identity is a dimension central to the politics of adequacy. As Cubans and others in similar international contexts live through large sociopolitical shifts at local, national, and international levels, their food access also shifts. But this does not necessarily mean that their understandings of how food and identity are connected also adjust. Melissa Caldwell (2002) has observed similar phenomena in postsocialist Russia, where the distinction between "our food" and "not ours" aligns with the notion that locally grown foods are superior to "new" imports. In Vietnam, Elizabeth Vann (2005) has documented desires to consume local products and the forms of anxiety people feel as once empty store shelves now fill with new products. While some communities try to maintain the ways of eating that they view as "traditional," in other cases new products are easily taken up and integrated into daily life, as in Coca-Cola in rural Guatemala (Yates-Doerr 2015). New foods may be taken up in a manner specific to the local setting, such as women using the McDonald's dining room as a space to comfortably socialize (Yan 2000) or giving the McDonald's french fry local meaning (Caldwell 2004). The social meaning of foods, new and old, are constantly renegotiated, and keeping up with these shifting meanings is a key component of understanding what makes a food system adequate.

Elvira's Dilemma

Elvira is a 38-year-old middle-class santiaguera who self-identifies as *mulata* but is often characterized by others as white because of her socioeconomic status. Elvira comes from a middle-class family in the city center. Although her family was historically low-income, because of her father's participation in the 1959 revolution and his role in the Cuban military, for which he has been granted certain privileges, her family has become middle- to upper-class. Elvira's brother lives in Havana, another marker of higher social status for the family, and her ex-husband lives in Tampa. Her ex-husband sends the family money each month, a large portion of which goes to keeping Elvira and her son Esteban well-groomed with the latest hair styles, acrylic nails, and donning the latest fashions from head to toe, yet another maker of higher social status. Esteban, like his mother, self-identifies as *mulato* but is almost always characterized by others as white.

Although they possess many different forms of monetary and social capital, Elvira and her family still struggle to acquire all of the types of food they desire. Elvira works out of her home as a self-employed seamstress. Although she does not have a business license, she sells hand-sewn purses out of her front door. She hangs the purses on the bars on the windows as an indication that she is home and ready to sell. She also repairs clothing, bags, and shoes. While she tries to be home as much as possible for her business, she leaves the house each morning to search for any materials she might need for her business and to acquire the household food for the day. She generally does not plan meals in advance but bases the day's meal on the most affordable foods that she can find in a relatively easy manner. She feels that she cannot spend all day searching for food, as she needs to get back to her business. Her mother, who lives next door, often helps her to acquire difficult-to-find food and will always offer to feed Elvira and her family if they cannot acquire enough ingredients for the day.

Representing the middle-class experience of food scarcity, Elvira talked about how difficult it is for her to go without rice toward the end of the month when the rationed rice runs low. Even though there might be pasta and other starches available, she is used to and expects to have rice with every meal:

> One day you tell yourself, just today because I don't have [anything] but then it's not just one day . . . one meal or two without rice in a row! That is what María Julia does, she doesn't eat rice, but me . . . I would die. To not eat rice . . . she can . . . but she must have a stomach like this [indicates small size with her hands] . . . the problem is that I have a very large stomach![17]

Rice is an essential part of the decent meal in Cuba; for many Cubans, rice is a key part of a daily feeling of satiation, the physical and psychosocial feeling of fullness, commonly a point when one feels they have had enough to eat.[18] Although Elvira cites María Julia as an example of the possibility of going without certain foods that are scarce, she personally feels that this is not a possibility for her. She invokes an embodied difference between herself and María Julia, and feels that she would "die" (suffer greatly) if she went a whole day without having any rice.

While on the surface this may not appear to be an urgent situation of food scarcity, for Elvira and many others, reduced access to foods such as rice that are central to their everyday diet causes a great deal of stress and anxiety.[19] As Elvira says, it may be somewhat acceptable to have one meal without rice, but when she has to go multiple meals or even days without rice she begins to panic. The way that she relates rice consumption to her stomach size indicates the ways in which she ties rice to a particular form of satiation that cannot be achieved by eating other foods. For Elvira, even with other foods available as substitutes, she does not feel that she can satisfy her hunger without rice. While her hypothetical death without rice is certainly hyperbolic, it is important to note that although she certainly would not die from starvation or malnutrition, a part of her may *symbolically* die if she is unable to access rice or other ingredients that she views as quintessential for satiation.

This type of panic and sense of crisis over access to particular foods was very common among my research participants and clearly indicated a sense of urgency around food access that goes beyond the state's goal of merely meeting nutritional needs. The realities of food accessibility reveal the ways in which santiagueros are entangled in a situation they see as a political subjection to the state's unpredictable and unclear food provisioning practices. However, at the same time, there is a deeply emotional side of food access that affectively links food with people's sense of subjectivity. Families of middle- and upper-class status, who also often come from many generations of families with that same class status, have come to expect a particular quality of life, and as they feel the effects of the declining entitlement system in Cuba, they retain the sense that they deserve access to a decent meal, to particular kinds of foods, because they are, and have long been, "decent" people. Without explicitly stating it, these families make claims of deserving a particular lifestyle because of their race, class, and level of culture.

Lack of Culturally Appropriate Foods

The ideals of Cuban cuisine were developed over a long history of *mestizaje* and the incorporation of myriad ingredients coming from different cultural origins into contemporary Cuban cuisine. Although Cuban cuisine is dynamic and adaptive, most of my research participants do have sets of basic parameters for what constitutes an ideal Cuban cuisine and the minimum or basic foods necessary to constitute a decent meal. Somewhat similar to her sense of urgency around the ability to maintain her ideals of adequate rice consumption, in the following interview excerpt from 2011, Elvira reflects on what she thinks of as the basic ingredients necessary to satisfy the minimum standards for her diet.

> Hanna: OK then, tell me about the situation right now in your house, the food situation?
>
> Elvira: The food is like the majority of Cubans . . . I have always said that I need to at least have one egg per day in the house. The only time that I didn't even have an egg, I said that although I could go 15 days without eating meat, I need to have my protein each night, an egg, at least an egg.
>
> Hanna: You prefer to have protein at night?
>
> Elvira: No, whatever time of day, when I have it, I eat it. I like to eat meat every day, one day one kind another day another kind, even though they say it's bad for you, but it's impossible, at least in my house, I earn [money] but how long does my salary last?[20]

While I found that most santiagueros generally share the view that rice is part of what constitutes a "real" meal, I found that there is more variability in opinion regarding how important it is to include meat with each meal. Most of my research participants preferred to eat meat with at least two meals per day, but few were able to achieve this standard. In the exchange above Elvira discussed how she would prefer to eat meat every day, to have a variety of different kinds of meat in her diet, but that she settles for her minimum standard of at least one egg per day. Her reflections on protein also underscore the desire for dietary variety in food consumption that was expressed by most of my research participants. Most people do not want to eat the exact same thing every day and prefer to be able to select among various types of protein. For instance, ideally a family would eat chicken one day, then pork the next, fish on the third day, and ground meat on the fourth. However, it is often the case that only one type of protein is available at a low cost (because the market was flooded with it), so people will go nearly the whole month eating only one type of protein.

In the case of Elvira's concerns about consuming rice with every meal, her anxiety stems from her feeling of dissatisfaction with substituted starches as unable to satisfy her hunger. In contrast, with respect to protein intake, Elvira and many of my research participants made more explicit links to their nutritional needs. When these basic standards for variety in food consumption were not met, many santiagueros became concerned that their basic nutritional needs were not being met. Especially when considering protein intake, research participants often felt like they didn't get enough red meat, or meat in general, and that too large a proportion of their protein intake was egg- and legume-based.

When participants felt concerned about whether their diets were meeting nutritional needs, their stress and anxiety around food access and acquisition became heightened and more urgent. Fear of nutritional deficiencies often invoked memories of the worst of the Special Period, when micronutrient deficiencies became so severe that there was an outbreak of neuropathy that included symptoms of vision loss. Present-day difficulties in food acquisition often caused my research participants to recall times during the 1990s when they spent hours and hours searching for particular kinds of foods to no avail. This invocation of memories of food scarcity clearly illustrates the trauma experienced by many santiagueros during the Special Period, and explains in part why seemingly banal concerns over variety in their diets is experienced by so many as an egregiously bad situation worthy of panic, fear, stress, and anxiety. This heightened stress and an added concern over food safety, particularly the safety of meat products, further exacerbates anxiety around food acquisition.

Food Safety and Poor Quality Foods

Due to decades of experience with faltering infrastructure, concerns regarding food quality and inconsistent availability are common issues for most santiagueros. Consumers in Santiago have no way of knowing whether food safety standards have been met for the foods that they consume. They often wonder: would food that was brought into the city on a refrigerated truck be guaranteed to have been kept at the right temperature when so often those trucks broke down or their systems failed? Would the blackouts throughout the city affect the refrigeration of meat and dairy inside the city ration stations and warehouses? Would delays due to paperwork and bureaucracy prevent foods from getting to the public before they went bad? People often do not trust that the state has their health and best interests in mind; they fear that the state would rather dump spoiled food on them then have to pay to replace it or face the repercussions of not providing the rationed quotas. Many families in my study have their own system and standards for evaluating the safety of their foods: they observe smell, taste, and texture before they consume foods, and they may adjust food preparation techniques if they are wary of the safety of a particular food item. Elvira and her best friend, María Julia, a 45-year-old white middle-class santiaguera, had a conversation regarding the lack of availability of meat and the poor quality of the "meat" products that are available.

> Elvira: Ah! So, because my husband doesn't eat chicken, for him to eat chicken it's just once in a while, so he eats [red] meat, of course! "The prohibited meat" but it's so hard to acquire! So, it's pork that he likes and so I always try to make sure I have it for him. I dunno, like a little pack of hot dogs or some croquette meat, that kind of thing, and maybe one day a little piece of ham . . . that ham, ummm.
>
> Hanna: Mortadella?
>
> María Julia: Yeah, that one ham . . .Vicky.
>
> Elvira: Yeah Vicky ham, which is sometimes vile, the last one that I bought . . . the same as a mortadella that was really good that they said was pure pork and that I had already bought before that was really tasty . . . but I guess it was poorly made or I don't know, it tasted like blood . . . horrible! Think about it, I was so traumatized that I haven't gone back to buy any more.
>
> María Julia: That's how it is . . .
>
> Elvira: [My husband] bought a small piece of mortadella, the ones that are made by the government. It smelled so bad, it was so bad that we went to return it, but they wouldn't give us our money back. They said it was from the last cycle so they couldn't return our money because they didn't have any money.
>
> Hanna: No? They took [the mortadella] back but didn't give you your money back?
>
> Elvira: We went back home with it. I was so traumatized by this, and note that he had bought the ones that they call *fiambre* that they say is made of pork, it should be normal, a sausage, but *everything was blood*. I had to make it into paste and not even as a paste would it work because it went bad. And then I added onion, and onion covers up everything, you know how strong onion is. I served it to my husband and he refused it and said "Don't serve me this anymore!" (She laughed) "It makes me

want to throw up. You eat it!" So I ate it that time, but now I have gotten to the point where I can't eat it anymore. Sometimes we go 15 days without seeing any meat. It's that bad, it's like everything here. Yes, in my house we always try to make sure we have vegetables. I try to get it however I can (*lucharla como pueda*), because if you make white rice with a fried egg and some salad that will get you by.

In this exchange Elvira begins by expressing her concern over what to feed her husband who strongly dislikes chicken and prefers to eat red meat. Her focus on feeding her husband the appropriate food rather than focusing on her own needs is typical of many Cuban women in my study. Both Elvira and María Julia recall their experiences buying state-produced ham, Jamón Vicky, that seemed to them to have gone rancid, and when they tried to return it they were not given their money back so they kept the meat and tried to find ways to make it tolerable. For Elvira this was the last straw with respect to eating these low-quality processed meats produced by the state; she has reached a point where she would rather use eggs for protein intake than go through the trouble of trying to make these poor-quality meats edible for herself and her husband. As she puts it, she "was traumatized by" this instance of meat consumption, and her husband reacted viscerally to the meat, feeling as if he were going to vomit when he tried to eat it.

While this meat traumatized Elvira, another family that I studied regularly ate this type of meat. Carla, a Black lower-class santiaguera, and her granddaughter Yaicel made fun of me one summer when I reacted to the smell of a similar type of meat. One day early in my research I was suddenly overtaken by what I perceived to be a strong smell of rancid food—in the middle of a conversation I had to get up and go outside. Carla yelled to Yaicel to come see what was the matter with me. Yaicel ran outside—I said, "There is some smell that is making me feel sick." She laughed and called to Carla who started roaring with laughter too. Although they also perceived the smell and were aware of why I was having that reaction to the meat, they regularly made croquettes with that meat when it was available in the rations. Later that day when Carla and her family sat down to eat the croquettes for lunch and I couldn't bring myself to eat the finished croquettes, the family again roared with laughter—"Even Hanna, who eats everything, won't eat these!" Yaicel said. "That means it's true that this isn't real food, it's true, thanks for confirming that for us!" And laughter continued, and they finished the croquettes.

Carla and Yaicel's dark-humor-infused response to the rancid smelling meat is a stark contrast to Elvira's disposition that the meat was traumatizing, an extreme offense to her sense of decency. Elvira's emotional responses to the changes in the food system, juxtaposed with her conceptualization of what an ideal Cuban cuisine should be, are integrally tied to her social position as a 38-year-old middle-class santiaguera who self-identifies as *mulata* but is often characterized by others as white because of her socioeconomic status. Elvira's assertion that without rice she "would die" is certainly an exaggeration, but it is true that she feels a sense of crisis and panic when she is unable to access rice because it is so symbolically tied to her sense of who she is as a decent middle class santiaguera. While Carla and Yaicel and many families like them may go days without real meat and several meals without rice, these families are less likely to go into a panic over what they are eating because there is less at stake in the lowering of their already low social position. Elvira's deeply emotional response to inconsistencies in rice and meat provisioning reveals the ways in which the experience of food acquisition can become a moment in which santiagueros are awakened to their shifting social positions in contemporary Cuba. This realization of the loss of middle-class lifestyles, coupled with memories of extreme food scarcity, is part of the intense emotional response to seemingly simple practices of food acquisition. This loss of a decent way of living is integral to why santiagueros often conclude that "there is no food" despite the fact that there appears to be plenty of food around. In contrast to the low-income experience of food acquisition, represented by Regina's story, the middle-class experience can be characterized by higher levels of stress over acquiring particular kinds of food when basic needs have already been met. There is relatively little fear of not having enough to eat. However, there is a deep-seated sense of entitlement to certain types of food, and when that desire is not met, middle-class families often have a great deal of anxiety about the possibility that they might not be eating a decent, dignified cuisine, as elaborated in the introduction. For these families, an adequate food system would entail access to all of the ingredients necessary to create a decent meal.

Food Acquisition: Making It Work with Money

Both Regina and Elvira must draw on family and community members in their process of acquiring food. As the state provisioning system wanes, and more food is only accessible through hard currency or the black market, people must rely on their communities both for information about where to acquire certain types of foods and to access black-market foods. Through the community, people learn about food availability and receive warnings about low-quality foods they might fall prey to. Everyone, regardless of social status, benefits from the information that circulates through social networks. This increased reliance on social networks for food access can be problematic for groups of Cubans who are marginalized and discriminated against. This is true of Black Cubans, as we saw in the case of Regina's fear of prejudice from market vendors, and it is true of some LGBTQ Cubans.

Building Community with Wealth: Carlos's Kitchen

Armando, who is a white-identified 68-year-old upper-class santiaguero, and Rodulfo, a Black-identified upper-class santiaguero who is 45 years old, are two gay men who cohabitate but are not in a relationship. Both of them were rejected by their families once people found out they were gay, and they have since formed a very close bond over the ten years that they have lived together. Armando works as an engineer and Rodulfo as a doctor, and they also have the good fortune of sharing about $300 CUC (about 8,000 Cuban pesos) a month in remittances from Armando's sister, who lives in Miami. Because they both work outside of the home, it is very difficult for them to complete the domestic work of cooking, cleaning, and taking care of the home. Additionally, their lack of social connection to family and the ways in which homophobia limits their social network mean that they cannot rely on others to assist in food acquisition in the ways that people like Regina and Elvira can.

With some of the money from Armando's sister, they were able to hire Carlos as a live-in domestic worker. To some extent, Rodulfo and Armando are able to use their financial resources to shift some of the stresses of food acquisition onto someone else; however, they are aware of their precarious situation and often reflect on how hard their lives would be without the extra money to hire Carlos. Carlos, a 35-year-old white santiaguero, is also a gay man who was left with nowhere to go after he came out. Carlos comes from a low socioeconomic class background but has access to money and other resources because he lives with Armando and Rodulfo. Carlos quickly became accepted as a part of the family after he started working in their home. Because homophobia is still prevalent in Santiago de Cuba, the fact that they are out gay men impacts their ability to access resources and thus impacts their food acquisition practices. Similar to Regina, they face inequality and discrimination, as they do not have the same ability to rely on family and friends for borrowing food, nor do they have the social connections in the community to acquire food as others might have. They are careful to hide their sexual orientation around new acquaintances and people who might be potential connections for acquiring goods, as they fear that being gay will lead people to discriminate against them.

Typical of upper-class households, Carlos has developed an elaborate system for planning meals, shopping, and food budgeting. The house contains a large freestanding freezer, so he is able to buy some items in bulk when they are available and freeze them for later use. They also have two refrigerators to hold large quantities of food that they plan to use relatively quickly. Carlos spends most of his mornings running around Santiago looking for deals on the black market. He tries to buy food in bulk and stock up on things that might become scarce. Carlos appears to enjoy his job and his role in the household. Rodulfo and Armando are shielded from the stresses of food acquisition and are able to enjoy the elaborate, well-prepared, decent meals that Carlos puts together for them.[21]

After preparing everyone's breakfast of toast with scrambled eggs and coffee, Carlos headed out to the street with several canvas bags. He did not usually bother stopping at the ration station or carnicería on his block; instead he headed straight to the *panadería* (bakery) to see if they would illegally sell him any flour, sugar, yeast, or other ingredients. He was able to buy some yeast because it was the only ingredient that they had enough excess of to sell him under the table without causing noticeable changes in the quantity or quality of ration bread that they produced. He then started toward the bay where the port and warehouses are and spoke with various contacts to see what was available on the black market. On a given day he might acquire some of the rationed items in bulk, such as 10-pound sacks of beans, rice, sugar, salt, or other goods. He might stumble upon some industrial-sized cans of fruits or vegetables that were destined for hotels or other tourist industry destinations. He would also be sure to acquire some sort of protein, either from the fishermen who sell down there, or the illegal lobster and shrimp dealers. Often he will acquire so much that he has to take a motorcycle home. On this particular day, he walked home with two heavy sacks filled with an industrial-sized can of tomato sauce, the yeast he bought from the baker, and a large bag of frozen shrimp.

Once he arrived home, he took everything out in order to assess which items he needed to use right away, which could be stored or frozen, and how to combine them with other ingredients he has. He decided to keep the shrimp frozen, but felt that he should use the yeast because he did not know how old it was or how it had been stored. After a brief rest, he headed back out to the local market, ration stations, and carnicería to pick up whatever was available. He was back home to start lunch around 11 a.m.; he usually serves by 1:30 p.m. when Armando and Rodulfo come home for their breaks. Once he got home he decided he was going to make pizzas to use the yeast and tomato sauce. With the meat that he picked up at the carnicería, he had all of the ingredients that he needed except cheese; while the dough was rising, he got out some of the CUCs (hard currency) that Armando and Rodulfo had left for him and went to the CUC store to buy a small amount of cheese. He did not want to use their small electric oven because this would mean being charged in the more expensive tier on their electricity bill, so he cooked the pizzas with gas, a much cheaper option, using a small stovetop contraption that he made out of old cans.

The Privilege of Household Help

Representing the upper-class families in Santiago, Armando and Rodulfo can afford to pay someone else to do most of their household labor; they are also able to give Carlos ample funds in advance so that he can buy in bulk and plan the household meals. This gives them access to a wider variety of food and makes the problem of food acquisition considerably less stressful. However, their food access is also disadvantaged because of their limited familial and social networks due to discrimination against gay people. In fact, their higher socioeconomic status is relatively rare for LGBTQ Cubans who still face discrimination in the workplace and in everyday life in Cuba. Still, their ability to pay Carlos to take care of the household food preparation and acquisition allows them to shift some of the day-to-day stress of Cuban life off of their shoulders. Although Carlos now takes on these burdens, this is a form of waged labor for him that in turn alleviates some of his financial stresses.

The arrangements described in Armando and Carlos's household are typical of high socioeconomic status households. The ability to hire help alleviates household members' stress, although there may be an added burden if paying for these services is somewhat difficult. Access to expensive or difficult-to-find household appliances, such as freestanding freezers, microwaves, or other kitchen tools, can also aid household help and the family members if they need to cook their own meals. For most middle- and low-socioeconomic status households, long-term food storage is not an option, so frequent food acquisition is required. Low- and middle-income families often have to make every meal from scratch: there are no premade sauces, no microwaved meals, no powders to mix into drinks; everything is peeled, ground, marinated, and produced out of the cook's labor. A higher socioeconomic household is more likely to buy items in the hard currency stores that facilitate kitchen work; they may choose to buy soda instead of freshly squeezing juice, or they might buy mayonnaise in a jar rather than whipping it up themselves. These conveniences are always out of reach for low-income households and a rare treat for the Cuban middle class.

Conclusions: Practices of Acquisition and the Politics of Adequacy

While all of the households in my study experienced some forms of difficulty in accessing food, social status and the nexus of skin color, class, and level of culture matter deeply for the experience of food acquisition. However, the difficulties of food acquisition are complex and do not just fall neatly in the ways that might be most apparent. Social positions relate to the ways in which people are able to access and acquire food, and also have a central role in determining what families define as adequate and their reactions when they are unable to meet their high standards for a decent meal. Those with more means are able to shift the burdens of food acquisition onto others; they are much more likely to be able to enjoy a decent meal through the struggles of their paid help. The households of the lowest socioeconomic status struggle to acquire enough to eat each day, gathering just enough food meal by meal. Their food acquisition strategies often feel loosely pieced together, as if each meal is whisked into the hands of family members with no time or energy to spare. It feels precarious, as if one small failure could bring the whole system down—and there is no resorting to buying a pizza or borrowing from equally precarious family and friends. People like Regina face an immediate and all-encompassing task of acquiring food in time for the next meal. This urgency leaves little time for bitter reflection. In some ways, these forms of struggling to acquire food are similar to the ways in which low-income families struggle to access sufficient food in other contexts, such as recent migrants to Southern California in Megan Carney's work (2015) or Salvadoran migrants in Sharon Stowers's work (2014). However, the struggle I describe here also contrasts to those found in these other works because struggling extends beyond low-income families to middle- and upper-class households in my research. And as I elaborate in chapter 2, the ideology of struggle takes on a specific meaning in the context of Cuban history.

By comparison, the middle class—those with enough to get by but not enough for extra conveniences—appears to feel the most anger, resentment, and sense of urgency over the inadequacy of their food system. As they struggle to piece together meals that do not even meet their standards of decency, they lament the loss of previous eras when food was cheaper and easier to access. They have the loudest demands for an adequate food system. Elvira and other middle-class heads of households feel comfortable airing their grievances with the current food system; they feel entitled to something better, for the middle-class inability to consume a decent meal may index for them that they are slipping from a decent standard of living to one that is indecent.

Layered on top of class and level of culture, prejudice and discrimination experienced by darker-skinned Cubans complicate the already tenuous experience of food acquisition. As basic entitlements are withdrawn, this changing food system exacerbates existing forms of racism and inequality, which may spiral into a cycle of impoverishment for low-income Cubans who are so often dark skinned. When food access is, in part, determined by social connections and channels of trust, those who are deemed less trustworthy because of racist ideas about skin color are unable to rely on essential social systems of access. Overt discrimination against darker-skinned Cubans is a real daily barrier to food access, and the psychological burden of fearing discrimination is an equally real obstacle that further complicates food access for Black Cubans. Still, due to the hard work and perseverance of Cuban families, meals are served despite these barriers.

The extremely complex food system entailing various types of markets with different goods at different prices, coupled with the dual currency system and rising food prices at a time of high unemployment, lay the groundwork for an overwhelming and stressful food acquisition process. However, it is a necessary chore, and, for most Cubans, there are no alternatives but to use this complex system. The accounts of household food acquisition detailed here demonstrate the ways in which Cuban families adjust to their changing food system by developing their own sets of strategies and tactics to acquire food beyond the ration and to maximize the use of all the foods they acquire (Certeau 1984; Certeau, Giard, and Mayol 1998).[22] Most Cubans reflect upon the increase in work necessary to acquire food as an undue burden, a form of unpaid labor that they undertake to make up for the decline in state provisioning in recent years. Nonetheless, it is part of what is necessary to survive in Cuba today, as it is in many diverse places across the globe.[23]

This daily labor to acquire food often goes unaddressed in studies of food security. By most measures of food security, Cuban households may not be considered insecure because in the end people usually get enough to eat. However, when we see the process behind food acquisition and understand the centrality of the link between particular foods and identity, we can see that food security is not black and white. Food acquisition, easily taken for granted in places with full-service grocery stores, is an extremely complex social and cultural process in Cuba today. Waiting in lines at ration stations, chatting with friends and family members about what is available where and at what price is woven into the fabric of daily life in Cuba. Furthermore, turning our attention to the process of food acquisition, rather than food security, highlights the hours of labor and stress that are behind the heaping plates of rice and beans on the Cuban table. Although many Cubans eat well, there are costs. The stress and time costs also articulate with the Cuban notion of struggle. Drawing on community and family, struggling to acquire a decent meal is an important social process that articulates with ideologies of Cubanidad, or a sense of Cuban nationalism, *but* it can also fosters feelings of bitterness and a desire for life to be easier.

Through their experiences of food acquisition and insistence on a food system that serves all of their needs, santiagueros express a particular politics of adequacy. This chapter has illuminated some of the reasons why Cubans' understandings of adequacy also include a concern for equality with respect to access to basic needs. These concerns for equality are part of the tenets of egalitarianism established through the logics of the New Man under Cuban socialism. However, as the entitlement system falters and families with the privilege of access to hard currency are better equipped to navigate the food system, inequality in food access is intensified. While lower-income people struggle just to get food on the table, they still idealize similar types of decent meals as those with more means. Nevertheless those people who are better positioned to access certain foods are both more likely to achieve the decent meal, and more likely to refuse to eat other kinds of foods, and resist the replacement of the decent meal with other forms of food—mere caloric intake. To further demonstrate Cubans' understandings of the politics of adequacy, in the next chapter I draw upon remembered histories, nostalgia, and orientations to the past that were important in shaping local understandings of a decent meal, a good life, and an adequate provisioning system. I show how the logics of adequacy developed over a long historical time frame and the ways in which people's memories and comparisons to past periods influence the ways that they envision an ideal present and future.

2

Antes

As we sat drinking beer at an outdoor table during Santiago's summer Carnaval celebrations, Mickey and I both took a moment to sit back and actually look at the labels on our bottles of Cuban beer. Mickey was a 41-year-old middle-class santiaguero who identified as Black and also as *moro* (Moorish) and *sirio* (Syrian). We were drinking the local brand called Hatuey, a beer honorifically named after a man of Taíno decent, thought to be Cuba's first national hero. He became legendary for his efforts to organize an indigenous uprising against the Spaniards in the early colonial period and is still a symbol of anti-colonialism and anti-imperialism. I asked Mickey if he felt that it could be at all offensive to use Hatuey's image as a marketing strategy for beer.[1] Mickey was confused by my question at first but eventually explained:

> Here in Cuba the martyrs who came before us are always honored. We are well educated about everything they have done for us. From when you start school you know about Hatuey and so now as I drink this I think of him and his courage in fighting against Spain. We also understand that our food and the whole agriculture system is connected to our fight for independence and ongoing fight to remain a nation of Cuban people. So, no it is not bad to use Hatuey like this, it is a central part of what we Cubans do.

In recalling the past to remark upon the present, Mickey is not alone. A strong historical consciousness among many Cubans has influenced the ways in which they reflect upon the contemporary moment. Remembered

FIGURE 8. Hatuey Beer Bottle. Source: Author

pasts are always part of creating and interpreting the present. Across individuals, neighborhoods, and households there are myriad ways of longing for different pasts. Visions of what constitutes a decent meal and an adequate provisioning system range from romanticized views merging history and ecology, to imagined traditions, to childhood memories. Food remains central to understandings of Cubanidad and what it means to be Cuban on the island today. Some people long for the periods they lived through with abundant imports from the Soviet Union, while others long for prerevolutionary access to US-produced brands. Cuba's independence came hand in hand with increased commercial influence from the United States, and this is reflected in my research participants' notions of an ideal cuisine. Some have actual memories of consuming these foods. Many desire imagined pasts they did not live through, gleaned through idealized notions of the ways their ancestors ate or family lore of periods of abundance. Although the details of nostalgia and longing for "authentic" consumption may be enacted in different ways, I found that the practice of defining "real" food and a decent meal were common social practices across skin color, age, and class (Garth 2019).

This chapter illuminates the ways in which Cubans invoke the past and their understandings of how the past comes to matter in the present. It is not a comprehensive history but instead turns to the ways in which histories are produced and reproduced in everyday life (Mintz 1985; Trouillot 1995; Palmié 2013). Parin Dossa (2014) has called this "social memory" and written about how violence and social suffering are remembered in everyday life. Drawing on Das (2003, 2007) and Waterson (2007), Dossa connects memory to food and argues that memory work can shift "our interpretation of history" (2014, 16). Along these lines, Cubanists have debated the evidence of various "truths" of Cuban nationalism and the histories of Cuba (Ferrer 1999; Finch 2015; Guerra 2005; Pérez 1995). These debates have made it clear that the "historical reality" of Cuba, the various projects of Cuban nationalism, and state socialism over time are not mutually exclusive but intertwined in the experience of everyday life in contemporary Cuba. The foundations of Cuban identity lie within a history of "racial capitalism, imperialism, and colonialism—the processes that created the current African diaspora" (Patterson and Kelley 2000, 13). In her analysis of race and performance in Cuba, Kristina Wirtz reminds us that "the past moves in and through the present, like a ghost, or a memory, or a sense of tradition, and it does so because living people selectively animate particular paths, choosing what will be remembered as history, what kinds of things will serve as signs of that history, what will be forgotten, and what relationship those signs defined as past will have to the present moment" (2014, 4). In such contexts, interpretations of how the present aligns with the past can be a symbol of value for those who aspire "to live an authentic life" (Weiss 2012, 624; Weiss 2011), where authenticity is grounded in "an imagined historical connection with recuperated cuisines and tastes" (Weiss 2012, 624). Indeed, the santiagueros that I worked with continually experience the present period in relation to their memories and idealizations of the past. It is through this infusion of the past into the present that santiagueros bring history to life and find value or a lack of value in the food that they put on their tables.

My research participants invoke, as central to their understandings of the social importance of food consumption in their lives today, past periods of transition that gave rise to the conditions of food access in Cuba today. The first period was Cuba's struggle for independence from Spain, which was inextricably linked to agricultural production and food consumption. Contemporary ideologies of what constitutes an adequate life can be traced to the island's fight for independence and sovereignty. Building on my research participants' narratives, I argue that this fight for independence and the rise of a Cuban identity, Cubanidad, coincided with the development of a particularly "Cuban" cuisine that is seen as a unique type of food which derives from the mixture of roots that make up Cubanidad. This is one past period, an *antes,* which Cubans idealize as better than the present.

The second historical period is the change in the food system after the 1959 socialist revolution. During this time there were radical shifts in food distribution, which necessarily shifted consumption patterns. At the same time that material conditions were changing, socialist ideologies of the New Man and notions of self-sacrifice for the greater good of the socialist project were inculcated into people's thinking. This period also includes the height of Soviet material aid, a time santiagueros now reflect on as the good old days of socialism, when "everything was available and at good prices." This period is also marked as an ideal past, *antes,* which santiagueros long for in the present, even if it would never be possible to actually achieve this idealization of the past.

The third period, which marks the end of an idealized *antes* and the beginning of ongoing struggles in the present, is the Special Period in Time of Peace and its aftermath. This period was the most commonly referenced past period in my research and likely most important historical period for many santiagueros. The Special Period was originally thought of as temporary; the government repeatedly characterized the scarcity and subsequent emergency measures as temporarily necessary to ensure that socialism would live on. However, as many of my interlocutors reflect, the scarcities and "emergency" measures of the Special Period seem to still be in place, or to be shifting into new but ongoing struggles that Cuban individuals must face on a daily basis.

I ground these historical periods in people's memories or remembered histories of the past, as a way of illuminating how past periods have come to bear meaning on the present. These memories of the past give the present its textured and layered temporality. This is a way of centering my interlocutors' experiences of remembering the past to understand forms of longing, tensions, and anxieties over the present and unknown future. These remembered pasts provide the groundwork for understanding the ways in which santiagueros conceptualize adequacy in the contemporary. Remembered pasts are often the basis for which santiagueros are able to assert that things should be better, because they recall periods when they perceived their food system as adequate. Orientations to the past are central to the ways in which santiagueros interpret their contemporary subjectivity as shaped by ideologies of Cubanidad, anti-imperialism, and struggle. These historical interpretations of subjectivity and remembered periods of adequacy are central to the ways in which Cubans understand what it means to live a good life and what it means to have a dignified cuisine.

Sugar and the Rise of Cubanidad

As I sat down with Geo, a 55-year-old, mestizo-identified, financially well-off musician for one of our first interviews in 2008, he asked if I needed additional sugar for the small cups of Cuban coffee that he had prepared for us.[2] He said, "We never have any food, but we always have sugar, always." He gestured toward two large sacks, which held approximately ten pounds of sugar total. This quantity of sugar was the standard ration at the time: five pounds of refined sugar, five pounds of unrefined sugar. Making all of their dishes and juices from scratch, most Cuban families quickly devour it all before the end of the month.

This moment sparked Geo to reflect on the importance of the sugar harvest in Cuba:

> Look, the sugar harvest, at the start of the revolution, the sugar harvest has great importance, obviously. The reason the harvest was so important was that cane sugar was the first exportable product from our country. The sugar production was central, and it was that way until the 1990s. In the 1990s or maybe a bit earlier, in the decentralization of sugar as the economic base, the country starts to open itself to tourism and other industry. This allows us to earn more hard currency for the country. This happens at the same time as the development of our nickel industry . . .

At this point in the interview I cut Geo off, thinking that he was straying too far afield of our interview about food. Geo quickly chastised me for this:

> Look if you want to know about Cuban food, or Cuba in general it is absolutely necessary to understand sugar and our sugar harvest. I am a musician; what should I care about farming? But nooooo, nooo. Sugar is Cuba. Sugar is our livelihood, our history. So I am telling you all of this context so you can have it there recorded and you can understand the basis of everything in Cuba. Sugar.

He continued:

> So it is of utmost importance that the sugar harvest has to be efficient. Historically it was different because we had slaves or people who worked for so little they were basically slaves, but now after the revolution we all have to work in the harvest. It has to be efficient enough that the production of sugar can be our economic basis. We plant the sugar, and we have to harvest it in three months. If we don't harvest it on time we lose the yield. So everything has to be optimum. Everything, even "cultural attention to the harvest," what the state says. From picking weeds, to not being lazy while working. We have to ensure that we get the most out of each crop. So even though this is changing because we are now more based on tourism, nickel, and biomedical technology, we still have a sugar export and we still produce for ourselves. Sugar now carries more symbolic weight, it is what made us.

As many Cubans are acutely aware, sugar has long been the center of the island's complex history with global and local power relationships, commodity flows, and notions of what it means to be an independent nation. The tensions between global and national power have been critical in the development of Cuban ideologies and identities. The simple act of adding sugar to one's coffee, an often thoughtless gesture conducted several times a day in Cuba, may become a trigger to remember the political and social meanings of production, consumption, and power. Indeed, for Geo the spoonful of sugar in my coffee made him recall the importance of the sugar harvest and the social meaning of transnational food distribution. It reminds Cubans like Geo of histories of land exploitation by colonial Spanish and US imperial forces (Funes Monzote 2008). A daily dose of sugar is quickly linked to anti-imperialism, the country's entire economic base, and the ways in which international relations are implicated in Cuban daily life.

Sugar is also key for understanding Cuban independence and the development of a Cuban cuisine, which developed alongside the rise of Cuban national identity. Concepts of struggle and nationalism are linked to concepts of Cubanidad (Cubanness) and *patria* (literally, fatherland). The logic of patria in Cuba today stems from a "19th-century conception of nationhood as a 'place-bound source of self-identification'" (Pérez 2009, 12). The notion of Cubanness, what it means to be Cuban, emerged out of the discussions and ideologies between Afro-Cuban small farmers and colonial administrators and plantation owners; "native Cuba" became linked to the dual emancipation from colonialism and slavery.[3] The defense of patria (and related anti-imperialist sentiment) became an undying Cuban devotion, exemplified through the ubiquitous saying: "To die for the patria is to live." The ethic of struggle within the logic of patria, for most Cubans, is a quintessential aspect of national identity. However, the meaning of struggle and what Cubans are struggling for has changed over time.

Ideologies of Cuban nationalism emerged at the same time that Cuban cuisine was forged. Struggle becomes connected to food as the island attempts to become more self-sufficient and adept at interacting with the international food market. Traditional Cuban dishes, derived from a mixture of new and old world ingredients, create *criollo* (creole) cuisine. Colonial-era Cuban cookbooks included many creole dishes, such as *ajiaco, olla cubana, arroz blanco criollo*, with ingredients such as *boniato, plátanos*, and *malanga*. Cuban political independence grew alongside the national narrative of mestizaje, which came to mean not only the mixing of races and cultures, but also of cuisines. Crucial to the ideology of Cuban independence, the desire for sovereignty was deeply instilled during this early independence period and has continued to reverberate through contemporary politics and national identity. These "traditional" dishes developed and cultivated during the period of independence are still symbols of Cubanidad, imbued with anti-imperialist and sovereign spirit. That is to say, for many Cubans the notion of what is "authentic" grew during this period, and understandings of authentic Cubanness of food, identity, and nationality all came together during this time. This decent meal signifies a certain sense of independent respectability and dignity that Cubans still long for today.

Fernando Ortiz, Cuba's most famous anthropologist, used a Cuban stew—the *ajiaco*[4]—as a metaphor to refer to Cuban culture as an ongoing identity process that is often "open to hybridity, heterogeneity and hyphenation" (Pérez Firmat 1987, 14). In his celebrated 1940 essay, *Contrapunteo cubano del tabaco y el azúcar*, Ortiz defined the ajiaco as a native dish, a Cuban stew consisting of different tubers that combined to symbolize the Cuban people.[5] A proper Cuban ajiaco is made by slowly boiling cuts of meat with these starchy root vegetables and seasoning them with a *sofrito*, a sauté of onion, garlic, peppers, cumin, oregano, and a bay leaf when available. According to Ortiz, Amerindians supplied the corn, potatoes, taro, sweet potatoes, yams, and peppers. Spaniards added squash and other tubers, while Chinese people added "Oriental" spices, and African people contributed *ñame*, a tuber similar to a yam, along with their culinary taste. The analogy represents the coming together of Natives, Africans, and Spaniards, among others, to create Cuban society. The key to the ajiaco metaphor is that as the ingredients are brought together to make the soup, they do not lose their original identity, but rather, mix together to create something with a new and different flavor; also, new ingredients can always be added. They do not "melt" together but comingle to create something unique while maintaining their individual constituency. Ortiz suggested that Cubans are "a mestizaje of kitchens, a mestizaje of races, a mestizaje of cultures, a dense broth of civilization that bubbles on the stove of the Caribbean" (1940, 165–169).[6]

The forms of mestizaje—the social and biological mixture of European colonizers, enslaved African people, and local native peoples that took place under the colonial plantation system—were crucial for establishing Cuban cuisine. The conditions of slavery, the diversity of the slave experience in Cuba, and the transition to freedom are essential for understanding the making of a national cuisine. As a part of the plan to gradually free the enslaved, a *patronato* (patronage) system was implemented as an intermediate stage between slavery and freedom. Previous slave masters were obliged to feed and clothe formerly enslaved people and educate their children; they could not separate families or send domestic servants to the countryside against their will, and they had to pay them a monthly wage. The idea behind gradually freeing the enslaved in Cuba was to slowly prepare them to become self-sufficient. Enslaved people had previously been given plots of land on which they were to grow their own food while enslaved, but as sugar became more profitable, plantation owners (then called *patronos* [patrons] rather than masters) seized that land to produce cane and imported food for the enslaved. During the gradual transition to freedom, the semi-free people, called *patrocinados* were once again given small plots known as *conucos* to start cultivating their own food. In addition to providing subsistence foods, the yields from the conucos could be sold at market.[7] Records of purchases show that animals, such as pigs, as well as maize, *yuca* (cassava), *malanga* (similar to taro), *boniato* (white sweet potato), and plantains were commonly purchased from *patrocinados* (Scott 1985).

These connections between struggle for independence and the slow breakdown of the plantation slave system with the development of a Cuban cuisine are reflected in my research participants' interpretations of the meaning of Cuban food in their everyday lives. For instance, in 2008, María Isabel reflected on making hallacas, a local version of tamales, stating that:

> What is most important is that our food is grown here on the *Oriente* soil—[that refers to the eastern part of the island], which is so fertile with a history—with our history—of the blood and the *lucha* of our African, French-Haitian and Cuban ancestors and years of *lucha* and victory that give the corn grown in the region a sweeter flavor and juicier kernels.

For María Isabel, part of the authenticity of the dish lies in her romanticized view of the relationship between ecology and history. She envisions herself, the corn, and the nation as growing out of the same soil, fertilized by the blood of her ancestors. However, as I illuminate in Amalia's search for corn in the introduction, due to changes in the Cuban food system many of the foods that are linked to Cuban identity in this way are increasingly difficult to acquire.

US Military Occupation

Cuba's postcolonial period was marked by the US military occupation of Cuba that began immediately upon independence from Spain. Cuba's fight for independence was slow, taking place over three wars between 1868 and 1898 (Pérez 1999). The final fight was part of the Spanish-American War, during which US troops were deployed to Cuba to assist in the fight for independence from Spain. In 1898 the US and Spain signed the Treaty of Paris, which granted Cuba independence from Spain. However, the US military remained in Cuba ostensibly to help transition Cuba to independence. In 1901 the US and Cuba signed the Platt Amendment, which called for the withdrawal of US troops but established a period of economic and political dominance of the US in Cuba, including the long-term lease of the military base at Guantanamo Bay. Through the early 1950s, about one quarter of the national income came from the sugar industry, which accounted for 80% of all of Cuban exports. Cuba was economically dependent on a single crop, sugar, and a single consumer, the United States. Sugar remains central to Cuba's story. During this time the United States had an overwhelming commercial influence on Cuba, and American products could be easily found at stores throughout the island (see Ryer 2015). This influence continued through the 1950s, when Cuba's most popular magazine, *Bohemia*, was filled with ads for Kellogg's Corn Flakes, Heinz Ketchup, Quaker Instant Oats, and other American products.

When I asked Juan, a santiaguero in his late 50s who grew up in an upper-class Cuban home prior to the 1959 revolution, to describe a typical meal from his childhood, he replied:

> People almost always ate rice and beans, in other words typical Cuban food: fried plantains, tostones, meat, salad, etc. Children always had a glass of milk. Now they say [milk] is not good for digestion. [Milk] has another way; the lactose takes a different amount of time to digest than other food. Before we always had a glass of milk . . . it was easy to get. The [milkman] brought it to your house, left it in front of your door, and there was never a problem with people taking it. The milkman came every day. Kids drank milk four times a day: breakfast, lunch, dinner, and before bed.

I commented that even by today's standards that is a lot of milk. Juan continued:

> Before kids were fat, if you see photos of kids in school *antes* [before the revolution] you will see fat kids—uh in private school. I'm referring to *private school*, because other kids didn't have these possibilities. Still, in general kids were well nourished. Before [the revolution] you could either go home to eat lunch or your parents gave you money to buy whatever was there—a sandwich, a soda—whatever there was that day.

I asked Juan to tell me about the changes that happened after the revolution and he lamented, "Things became scarce." When he elaborated on the scarcity he recounted that starting in 1959 or 1960, for example, "Corn flakes, a cereal just for kids, was not too expensive before, but suddenly it was off the shelves and has not come back since."

In addition to US-made cereals such as corn flakes, when asked about what changes occurred with respect to food after the revolution my interlocutors listed the following foods as essential to pre-revolutionary Cuban cuisine and now scarce: beef of any sort, "real" (not powdered or canned) dairy products, lettuce, capers, olives, chicken, turkey, duck, lobster, crab, calamari, and shrimp among others. However, those who longed for these food items tended to come from higher socioeconomic backgrounds prior to the 1959 revolution.

The fact that Cuba's independence dovetailed with an increased commercial influence from the United States is reflected in the present notions of an ideal cuisine: some Cubans have actual memories of consuming these foods, while they exist only in the imaginary for others. However, although some Cubans idealize the availability of consumer goods during this period, there were mounting tensions between the US and Cuba in the struggle for full Cuban independence and release from US domination. It was this circumstance that contributed to the eruption of the 1959 Cuban Revolution and shaped the agricultural and economic policies of post-revolutionary Cuba (Benjamin, Collins, and Scott 1984).

Revolution and the Height of Soviet Material Aid

The 1959 socialist revolution and the height of Soviet material aid in the 1970s and 1980s mark the second commonly referenced historical period that Cubans elicit when speaking about food in Cuba today. While the colonial period and pre-revolutionary period are commonly understood as clear antes references, the glory days of the revolution are often overlooked yet extremely commonly referenced as times when things were better (at least in hindsight).

María and Leo

Santiago's city center, *el casco histórico*, consists of narrow hilly streets. Sidewalks barely wide enough for one person are all that stand between the 16th-century homes and crumbling streets. Walking through the streets, I noticed how the lives of santiagueros poured out of their homes and into the lives of their neighbors and those passing by—through the open windows and doors the smells of coffee brewing, rice cooking, and meat stewing mingle with the sounds of pressure cookers hissing, Latin pop on the radio, and the bustle of people moving through the streets in and out of homes. María de la Gracia's home, painted bright pink, is a popular stop for her friends and family as they head to work or run errands on the city's principal commercial street, Calle Enramadas. In January 2011 I spent three weeks studying the daily food consumption habits of her household.

María de la Gracia is a white, middle-class santiaguera in her early 60s, who suffers from diabetes and hypertension.[8] Every morning I would join her for 6 a.m. walks through her Santiago de Cuba neighborhood. The morning walks were designed to help her lose weight and hopefully lower her sugar and blood pressure. When passing by places where significant moments took place in her life, María told me stories of her past. As we moved between dusty streets and crumbling sidewalks, around gutters filled with unknown liquid, we enjoyed the sounds of roosters crowing and birds chirping, before cars began moving along the streets and the noise of televisions and hissing pressure cookers began filling houses.[9] María always pointed out to me the beautiful things that my eyes were not trained to see—a tree in bloom above our heads, a newly painted colonial home, or sunlight reflecting off of a century-old tree.

One morning we wandered a bit further than usual so she could show me where she was born and raised, a "humble" neighborhood near Santiago's city center—Los Hoyos. Although María and her family consider themselves to be white Cubans, Los Hoyos is an "emblematically black neighborhood" (Wirtz 2014, 112). María felt a sense of shame being from Los Hoyos as a white person, as if a white Cuban *should* live in a better area. Yet, Los Hoyos is also a socially important neighborhood in that every year some of Los Hoyos' best carnaval performers win awards for the city's juried prize (Wirtz 2017). Los Hoyos was also home to General Antonio Maceo and General Guillermón Moncada, essential figures of Cuban independence. The neighborhood denotes pride in Cubanidad in many different registers (Schmidt 2015). María seemed to vacillate between pride in her humble beginnings in Los Hoyos and a sense of shame expressed in never wanting to return there, even just for a morning walk.

María was born in Los Hoyos in 1949. Some of her earliest memories were of her grandparents, who took care of her while her parents worked. Her father worked at the local rum distillery, and her mother worked cleaning the houses of well-off families in Vista Alegre, the historically aristocratic neighborhood in Santiago. She told me that although her family was poor, there was always enough to eat. She remembers her grandmother's Sunday dinners, a mid-afternoon meal that served as both lunch and dinner. Her grandmother always made soup—*una caldosa*—filled with vegetables, meat, and *viandas* that were perfectly seasoned.[10] Black beans with ham. White rice. Fried plantains. Pork steaks, so soft you did not even need a knife to eat them. Always with a salad and dessert.

María was nine when the socialist revolution happened. She remembers a period when neither of her parents had work—the distillery closed temporarily when it was taken over by the state, and the family that her mother worked for left the country. For María, those were the worst years she can remember. She remembers going to sleep without dinner and only drinking sugar water for breakfast. However, she also told me that this was a very short period and that her family quickly got back on their feet. Her father worked his way up to the managerial level at the rum distillery, and her mother worked in a state factory for many years, eventually quitting to take care of María's grandparents toward the end of their lives. During María's teenage years, she remembers that the economy had improved and access to food was relatively simple. Cuba's national food ration was established. Apart from the ration, food was available for purchase in different types of state markets. As she remembers it, siempre había de todo (everything was always available) y a buen precio (and at good prices).

As we walked away from her childhood home, she was reminded of meeting her current husband, Leonardo, for the first time. She told me that she met Leo when she was young, a child really. She was playing in front of her house and they exchanged a lingering glance. She knew of him from around the neighborhood, but this was the first time that she really noticed him. He must have noticed her too, because she remembers that he started to pass by the house every day at the same time. Though they eventually fell in love, their age difference was too great for them to get married when they first met, and Leo joined Fidel Castro's revolutionary movement, taking him away from the city. María admired Leo's devotion to Cuban socialism. She explained to me that though she supported his military service to Cuba and his decision to go to war to fight for socialism in Cuba and abroad, she could not wait for him to return before starting her life. When she was the right age, her parents felt it was best that she start her own family, so she married another man and had two children with him.

María established her first household during the height of Soviet material aid to Cuba. During this time, there was an abundance of cheap goods imported from the USSR and other socialist countries. María recalled that although she was poor when she married her first husband, they were able to get by because at the time, everything "was available and at good prices."

The Cuban government incentivized Cubans to work harder by paying extra for high productivity and created a "parallel market" where Cubans with extra money could buy any number of food items. María and others recalled that there were many types of canned products available—fruit, vegetables, and meat—as well as a variety of Russian cakes and sweets that disappeared during the Special Period. For María and many from her generation this was the height of Cuban socialism, the good old days that they reflect back on as their ideal.

Leo, a white, middle-class santiaguero, was 67 in 2011. One evening Leo and I sat at the dining room table throwing back shots of rum and he began to reminisce about his life. He took out a photo of himself with Fidel Castro in dark green uniforms in the late 1950s. Although he did not talk about those years much, on this particular night he was clearly proud of the years he spent fighting for Cuban socialism at home and abroad. Like María, he grew up in poor conditions in the neighboring province of Guantánamo. As he told it, they were "not living like humans." He grew up in a home with a dirt floor and walls made of used boards. His mother cooked meals behind the house over a fire on the ground. They never went hungry, but it was hard work to keep food on the table. He told me that he felt he had to join the fight for socialism because it was the only hope for families like his.

La Revolución

Fidel Castro and the 26th of July Movement, named for the group's first attempt to overthrow Batista on July 26, 1953, did not initially claim to be socialist; instead, after they overthrew the government of Fulgencio Batista and took power, they gradually adopted a socialist ideology. By 1962 Fidel Castro declared he was Marxist-Leninist. The socialist ideologies, largely Marxist-Leninist, of the early years of the revolution were intermingled with the writings of Cuba's national heroes and other symbols of nationalism. Fidel Castro himself characterized the flexibility of Cuban socialism as "a virtue, as evidence of the originality of Cuban revolutionary ideology, its autonomy from Soviet Communism and its link to the Cuban people" (Gordy 2015, 39). The movement leaders implemented various measures of wealth redistribution and significantly increased opportunities for employment and education. In the first few years after the revolution nearly 1,500 decrees were created in response to frustration about previous periods of corruption and eagerness for "socioeconomic change in a country with great disparities in wealth and access to basic services" (Gordy 2015, 63; see also Fagan 1969; Farber 2006; Pérez 1995; Pérez 1979; Pérez 1992; Pérez-Stable 2011[1993]).[11] Wages increased, social services increased, and living expenses were reduced. These political and economic changes have evolved over time into strong, often shared values among contemporary Cubans at the popular and political levels (Kapcia 2000).

Among these socialist entitlements, Cuba has had a food rationing system since 1962. The National Board for the Distribution of Foodstuffs, created in March 1962, established the rationing of rice, beans, cooking oil, and lard across Cuba. Soap, detergent, and toothpaste were rationed in 26 major cities and eventually across the entire island. Beef, chicken, fish, eggs, milk, and sweet potatoes were only rationed in Havana at first and eventually were included in the ration across the country (Benjamin et al. 1984). Initially the food ration was expected to be a temporary solution to the problems associated with transitioning to socialism, but the ration was not fully eliminated. The early ration booklet optimistically included ham, cheese, pepperoni, sausage, beef, pork, lamb, goat, fish, seafood, fruits, and vegetables; however, due to the lack of state resources, most of these items were never actually available.[12] Though not its original purpose, today, food rationing serves as the primary means to equitably distribute basic foods and avoid certain consequences of food scarcity.

As Cuban socialism matured, shifting ideologies and market mechanisms impacted the ways in which the government acquired food and other basic necessities. Some of the more idealistic economic objectives of the 1960s became unfeasible by the 1970s. There were too many material shortages for the state to deliver on its promises, and inefficiency plagued the system. As a result, the Cuban economy turned to market measures with the goal of increasing productivity and reducing waste (Mesa-Lago 1978). In 1972 Cuba joined the Soviet bloc's Council for Mutual Economic Assistance (COMECON or CMEA).[13] The introduction of market measures into Cuban socialism, particularly the use of material incentives for production, needed to be defended ideologically. The government embarked on a campaign asserting that it was possible to maintain socialism with some market measures and that this did not mean a return to capitalism. Over time, Cuba increasingly relied on the Soviet Union for trade. During this period the distinction between idealism and pragmatism was not always clear—leaders asserted that a pragmatic move could be made in service of the end goal of the ideal.

Cubans like María and Leo remember the difficulties of everyday life in Cuba before the 1959 socialist revolution. Coming from "humble" economic backgrounds, they both observed their parents and grandparents struggle to keep food on the table. While the initial years of the revolution were difficult, by the 1970s María remembers the height of Soviet material aid as ideal. During the 1970s the parallel market system was created alongside the ration, which still guaranteed everyone a baseline set of goods. Cuba was extremely dependent on the Soviet bloc for the vast majority of trade from 1972 until the collapse of the Soviet Union.[14] The Soviet Union paid much more than the average international price for Cuban sugar, subsidizing the price that Cuba paid for Soviet sales of petroleum, and supplying all weapons free of charge to the Cuban armed forces. The Soviet Union also provided very low interest loans in order to help Cuba pay off trade deficits from major economic development projects.[15] Habia de todo, de todo de todo, y a buen precio. (There was everything, everything, everything, and at a good price.)

Despite these ideological efforts, defenders of revolutionary ethics, like Che Guevara, advocated for the elimination of material incentives and a stronger reliance on moral incentives to increase production. For Che Guevara a shift in consciousness as a part of a new moral development was crucial to the political economic changes under way in Cuba. The Cuban *conciencia* (which can mean conscience or consciousness) was changed through explicitly political goals and revolutionary programs (Blum 2011); for Guevara (1965) it was part of a "commitment to action." Guevara maintained that a socialist revolution could only work if structural changes were coupled with changes in collective values. The socialist New Man would have to change his attitude about race, gender, labor, and individualism to become a cooperative, dedicated, hardworking laborer who was obedient and nonmaterialistic. This New Man would be colorblind and believe in and practice gender equity. Self-sacrifice for the good of the collective was central to the moral redrafting of the New Man: "Individualism, in the form of the individual action of a person alone in a social milieu, must disappear in Cuba" (Gerassi 1968, 115). For Fidel Castro this shift involved "an attitude of struggle, dignity, principles, and revolutionary morale" (1980, 59). Cubans were reeducated into this new morality via explicit programs in the educational system (Blum 2011). Transforming Cuban consciousness was the foundation for transforming to a communist economic system. The underlying goal was to shift Cubans away from material incentives and toward moral incentives.[16]

These two transitions—to socialism in 1959 and to Soviet partnership in the 1970s and 80s—mark periods of nostalgia for many Cubans. These are time periods that they remember as significant shifts in the availability of material goods, including food.

The End of *Antes*: The Special Period in Time of Peace

The fondly remembered period of Soviet material aid came crashing down during the Special Period in Time of Peace, which officially began on June 23, 1990. This period of economic breakdown was due in large part to economic reforms in the USSR, then Cuba's major trade partner, under perestroika, which began when Gorbachev took over in 1985 and continued to worsen until the disintegration of the USSR in 1991. As I mentioned in the introduction, the period was characterized by drastic reductions in food availability; estimates of caloric reduction range from 27% to 65% depending on the year and location. Cuba's mechanized industrial agriculture system was completely dependent on fossil fuels, and with no subsidized oil imports from the USSR to run machines or fertilizers for crops, domestic production halted. Food access was considerably worse in the eastern provinces, including Santiago de Cuba.

In my interviews, I found that when I would ask Cubans to reflect on the past—an open-ended time period—they would almost immediately begin speaking about the Special Period. This struck me as a sign of the period's significance and the period as a site of trauma for many Cubans. Indeed, the Special Period is often referred to as *lo peor* (the worst), *horrible* (horrible), *grave* (grave), and it is juxtaposed with periods that are reflected upon more positively like the height of Soviet material aid and the rise of Cuban independence. The Special Period for most santiagueros was the worst of times. María Isabel reflected on the transition to the Special Period:

> In the 1970s we more or less maintained our way of life, we had the same chemical and nutritional composition in our food, which was often imported from the Soviet Union, or China and other parts of Asia, Argentina. But nevertheless we maintained our way of eating with these imports. And then when the Soviet Union fell, that along with the embargo, we have suffered a situation so grave, so ugly, so terrible . . . we had to try to find solutions, we started raising pigs in our house. We couldn't buy fats, there was no oil in the stores, so we had to make fats with pork lard. We really suffered from the restriction [lack] of so

many foods. We lost so much weight, some people lost 40 to 50 pounds because we did not have enough to eat.

Many of the santiagueros I spoke with remembered the Special Period as dire, a time when people were going hungry, when nothing was available in the stores, and people were desperate. However, when I asked if they themselves experienced hunger or long periods without anything to eat, almost everyone I spoke with said that their family did not suffer as much because they were able to access some back channel to access food, such as a relative in the countryside, a friend who pilfered from the state, or some black-market activity they were involved in. A few people reflected on a period of a few days in which they went with very little food. For instance, when discussing changes in the Cuban food system, Julián, whose stories I detail further in chapter 5, recalled a day when he and his family could not find anything to eat. He remembered having just enough money to buy shaved ice with sugar water for his two children for dinner. As he recalled that evening to me, tears welled up in his eyes, and he became so emotional that we had to stop the interview. Like Julián, many santiagueros experience strong emotions in the present as they recall the emotional difficulties of dealing with food scarcity in the Special Period.

In response to this economic catastrophe the Cuban state introduced various measures to improve the economy. These measures were intentionally shortsighted to help the economy recover, even at the expense of longstanding socialist principles. The strategy was to open the Cuban market to attract foreign investment and long-term growth, and focus on the development of export industries, particularly biotechnology and electronics, while limiting imports and increasing agricultural self-sufficiency. In one such measure, beginning in 1993 the government allowed Cubans to hold and use hard currencies, including the US dollar.[17] Later, the convertible peso (CUC) was introduced and pegged to the US dollar. During this time the US dollar, the CUC, and the Cuban peso (CUP) were all in circulation.[18] In 2004 Cuba discontinued the use of the US dollar, but there continued to be a dual CUC and CUP economy, which came with its own set of problems and a dual market system for each currency (Tankha 2016, 2018). During the late 1990s the Cuban government also began allowing certain forms of self-employment (Domínguez 2005), as well as developing the tourism industry, which was thought to be a more economical venture despite "grave social repercussions" (Gordy 2015, 7). In 1995 private restaurants were legalized. The rise in small restaurants catering to both Cubans and international tourists shifted the food landscape by offering more options for those with some purchasing power. State farms were transformed into semi-private cooperatives called Unidades Básicas de Producción Cooperativa (UBPC), and from 1994 to 2000 the income of farmers in private cooperatives rose by 50% (Domínguez 2005, 19). The state and some local activists began developing urban gardens outside of Havana (Premat 2012).[19] In addition, the state reopened free agriculture markets that it had shut down in previous years, which allowed individual farmers to sell surplus above the state quota at unregulated prices (Gordy 2015). The economic measures of the 1990s were catalysts for rising rates of diverse forms of ongoing inequality in Cuba.

During the Special Period, the ethics of the New Man that were built up over the years of Soviet material aid began to dissolve. Socialist values were reformulated as new challenges of the Special Period arose. The economic crisis created financial and social conditions that forced Cubans to undermine some socialist principles in order to survive; participation in the black market rose, as did the phenomenon of pilfering from state jobs. One of the reasons that Cubans found the Special Period to be so difficult was that it forced them to undermine the principles of socialism and the New Man that they had bought in to. Many Cubans still experience a sense of double consciousness (*doble conciencia*) over the discrepancy between their actions and their beliefs. Doble conciencia is a dual morality central to the changing sociopolitical context of Cuba today, where Cubans simultaneously attempt to both uphold the traditional moral character of Cuban identity and undermine it through their changing actions (Blum 2011, 18).[20] After the Special Period, Cuba became a place where one is pressured to "think like capitalists but continue being socialist" (Brotherton 2008, 259). Everyday life is plagued by the stresses of la lucha, struggling to get by, which are exacerbated by the social and emotional difficulties of living in a dual morality (Weinreb 2009). Furthermore, as Holbraad has argued, "because people were committed to their Revolution . . . they were expressly dejected with its ailing state in the Special Period." (Holbraad 2014, 367). These disconnections between ideologies and everyday practices have caused several of my research participants to reflect deeply on the meaning of their lives and the meanings of Cuban subjectivity in the contemporary period, which I elaborate on in chapter 5.

Conclusion

This chapter detailed the three past periods that santiagueros tend to gravitate toward as they recall the role of food in Cuba's past. Their remembered histories and orientations to these past periods underlie the ways in which they understand the relationships between food, adequacy, subjectivity, and Cubanidad addressed in this book. These remembered pasts are central to contemporary understandings of adequacy, dignity, and subjectivity. The histories of global flows of capital and extraction, and the histories of resource distribution have strongly influenced contemporary Cuban ideologies of equality, counterhegemony, and anti-imperialism, which are central to understanding the politics of adequacy. The historical narrative of Cubanidad developed in the postcolonial era at the same time as the notion of an ideal Cuban cuisine. Cubanidad and Cuban cuisine are deeply entangled with ideologies of mestizaje, independence, and equality. These particular historical circumstances give rise to a contemporary sense of what an adequate life entails, and this account reveals the foundations of the political stakes of alimentary dignity, a decent meal, and the politics of adequacy.

Contemporary understandings of decency and dignity are linked to history and nostalgia for remembered pasts, as Cubans struggle to pragmatically and ideologically contend with their faltering welfare state. The historical roots of international trade and the development of Cuban identity, as well as the ideologies of redistributive justice, equality, and sovereignty, are deeply embedded in this struggle. With contemporary political economic shifts away from orthodox socialist doctrine, forms of socialist ideology are constantly negotiated and reinterpreted in the present. These factors also shape the ways Cubans reflect upon their changing food system in relation to their own subjectivity. Remembering the past can be one of the ways that people process the social and affective impacts of the present. Here a longing for the past, reminiscing about the past, and clinging to idealizations of the past can become a way of coping with difficulties in the present, a topic I elaborate on in chapter 5.

The provision of basic food needs under the socialist rationing system, although initially a practical solution, has become an important ideological and symbolic form of adequacy. As socialism has evolved, Cubans have come to see it as the state's duty to provide basic needs for all citizens. Basic food provisioning is thought of as something that the state owes Cubans in exchange for their labor and low wages, and it is seen as a right of all citizens regardless of their status as wage earners. For many Cubans, revolutionary principles, expectations, and moralities do not completely dissipate as the Cuban economy shifts. For many Cubans, an adequate food system is an indication of a strong socialist state that reflects their long-standing ideologies of justice, equality, and independence. Building upon these ideological foundations, in chapter 3 I turn to carefully woven ethnographic accounts of household food acquisition and the contemporary Cuban food system. Cubans face difficulties as they struggle to obtain the ingredients necessary to assemble a decent meal, to eat and live in a dignified way, and orient their lives out of historically situated ideologies.

3

Virtuous Womanhood

One cool spring afternoon, Elvira walked over to my house to tell me that the trip we were supposed to leave for the next day with her husband and son was cancelled. We had been planning to go to Guantánamo on a trip to visit their extended family, which would also be a chance for me to study the process of the rare trade of bacon-making with one of their cousins. Standing in the doorway of my Santiago house, Elvira—who had clearly done her hair and makeup and gotten dressed solely for the occasion of walking over to my house—simply said, "The trip is cancelled."

I invited her in, but she declined, so I asked what happened. Elvira explained that the trip was cancelled because her husband Joaquín could not get the weekend off work. I said that the three of us should just go without him. She gasped and said, "I can't go without him. Who will make his food and iron his clothes?" I replied, "He is a grown man. Even if he can't make his own food, he can just grab some street food; it is only two days." She looked at me like I was totally outrageous and said, "Well I can't go, so you and Esteban [her son] can go alone, but you will look like a slut if you go alone with him." She walked away and I called after her, "Will you please come with us?" She turned and said, "It's not the correct thing to do," as she walked back to her house. After she left I sat and reflected on what had just happened—the short interaction was rife with meaning. What had she meant by "the correct thing to do"? And really, why couldn't Joaquín feed himself for just two days? And why would it make me a slut if I traveled alone with Esteban?

This chapter foregrounds the ways the increased work involved in food acquisition and meal preparation is predominantly taken on by women as part of unpaid household-based labor. I analyze this as situated in the frictions between deeply entrenched colonial ideologies of gender and socialist reimaginings of gender and work. The daily practices of preparing breakfast, lunch, dinner, and snacks, punctuated by all of the other work it takes to get those meals into the mouths of husbands, children, and elderly parents, clearly illuminate the relationships of women not only to their families, but also to the broader political and social system. As the Cuban food system becomes increasingly cumbersome for its users, the responsibility of the state shifts onto the household, and women overwhelmingly shoulder the burdens of that system.

That said, I argue that women are not necessarily directly compelled to do this work as a duty to sustain Cuban socialism or as a duty to keep rates of hunger and malnutrition low. Instead, I find that women are influenced by local ideals of the "virtuous woman." A role that was most often held by those who identify as female, virtuous womanhood is central to local ways of understanding what it means to be a "good woman" in the household and in Cuban society more generally.[1] Despite Cuban state policy efforts to support women's presence in the socialist workforce (as detailed later in this chapter), women's social role as *dueña de la casa* (lady of the house) is upheld as the most virtuous responsibility of "a good Cuban woman."[2] That is to say, the idealized virtuous woman labors to care for and sustain the family. Santiagueros interpret the domestic work of women within a locally specific ethical frame, that of "the right thing to do." This framing is part of the local practice of cultivating virtuous personhood, a form of labor meant to cultivate the category of the "good person," as Elvira attempts to do in the beginning of this chapter. These sensibilities can be tied back to the tentacles of colonial governance in intimate spaces (Stoler 2002). Today, the gossip and jealousy that circulate by way of these interactions reinforce ideals of the "good Cuban woman."

The social phenomenon of virtuous womanhood, I argue, not only holds women to standards that are nearly impossible to attain, but it also problematically perpetuates the notion that only certain kinds of people who engage in these limited types of socially sanctioned behaviors are worthy of living a good life (Willoughby-Herard 2008, 2010). This problematic notion presents internal contradictions to Cuban notions of adequacy and the right to live a dignified and decent life, notions that have been historically tied to egalitarianism. These ideologies of egalitarianism, tied to the socialist revolution, are in direct tension with deeply entrenched colonial ideologies of proper womanhood. Furthermore, virtuous womanhood is a status that is often reserved only for white women in practice, and in some cases it can function to perpetuate anti-Black logics regarding what types of people are worthy of a good life (Mullings 1997; Mullings and Wali 2001).

Another overarching argument I make in this chapter is that the domestic sphere has become a highly valued locus of social life in socialist Cuba, which further solidifies the role of women's work as central to the functioning of Cuban socialism. In contrast to the household, state-based wage labor is important insofar as it guarantees a small steady flow of income and is crucial for facilitating the social connections necessary to access material goods, which in turn function to maintain the household. For many Cubans today, the value of laboring outside the home lies in one's ability to facilitate social reproduction within the home. Therefore in this setting, the household is not only the site of reproduction of a productive labor force (raising generations to be laborers, supporting laborers to be able to keep laboring), it is simultaneously the opposite: state-based jobs are the sphere used to support the domestic sphere. Wage labor at state-based jobs becomes the site of social reproduction in this context. The importance of virtuous womanhood and maintaining the domestic sphere is even more pressing when we see the domestic sphere is valued in this way.

As chapter 1 revealed, getting food on the table in Santiago de Cuba is often a daunting task, requiring hours of work. Santiagueras grapple with the seemingly insurmountable household tasks they must undertake, while some are simultaneously working outside the home in order to earn more money for the household as state subsidies diminish. Women also have to combine food acquisition, preparation, serving meals, and cleaning up after meals with housecleaning and caring for children, elderly relatives, and disabled relatives. Nonetheless, the difficulty of women's work has been overshadowed by the ultimate provider in Cuba: the socialist state. While at first glance Cuba appears to be food secure, by using an adequacy framework and turning our attention to the labors of women, we can see the struggles and difficulties that women face in ensuring that there is no hunger in Cuba. I argue that this household-based labor is the other side of *la lucha* (the struggle), and the home is the locus of *inventar* (innovating solutions) while the labor of "being in the street" is the central locus of *resolver* (resolving things). The tensions of the politics of adequacy are wrapped up in particular socialities of food provisioning and gendered subjectivities.

Negotiating Gender Roles and Food in the Household

Attention to women's household work illuminates elements of my larger research question—if everyone is talking about how "there is no food," how is it that santiagueros end up with meals on the table and little incidence of hunger or malnutrition? By and large the answer to this question can be found in observing the hard work of Cuban women. I understand the category of "women" and notions of "gender" as always negotiated and in flux (Behar and Gordon 1995; Boehm 2012; Rosaldo and Lamphere 1974). To understand how gender operates within contemporary Cuban society, it is necessary to situate Cuban gender ideologies within broader Latin American colonial histories and Cuban socialist ideologies. Building upon these foundations, in this chapter I illuminate the ways in which the idealization of virtuous womanhood becomes heightened in Cuba's post-Soviet socialist period.

Women in Santiago, whether they work outside the home or not, dedicate large amounts of their time to food shopping, cooking, cleaning, laundry, and child and elder care. This is part of the phenomenon others have called the *doble jornada/triple jornada* (the double or triple shift) (Freeman 1997), where women work outside the home, sometimes at two jobs (one state-sanctioned, the other not), and take on the majority of the domestic labor, including cooking, as well as the work necessary to maintain connections in the community, which are crucial for accessing food in Cuba (elaborated in chapter 4) (see also Lyon, Mutersbaugh, and Worthen 2017). At the same time, men, whether they work outside the home or not, tend to spend very little time on these tasks and instead focus on tasks such as fixing, constructing, and repairing machines, appliances, buildings, etc., and the elusive activity of being "in the street" (*en la calle*), which entails acquiring goods and making social connections to get goods and services, but can also include hanging out, drinking, and having sexual affairs.[3] Although difficult to pin down and sometimes frustrating for Cuban women, the unpaid activities of men also benefit the household in that the social connections they make are essential for acquiring scarce goods as the state provides less.[4] Much of this work "in the street" is in the service of the need to resolver, resolve problems with access to basic goods and services as we saw in chapter 1 and I will further illuminate in chapter 4. These morally valenced notions of "doing the right thing" or the action of being "in the street" are part of the assemblages of gendered subjectivities. Gendered subjectivities are often racialized ways that exclude nonwhite people from both the constraints of these categories of virtue and the potentialities that virtue may hold (Stoler 2002).

The category of the "good woman" is a social construction that is constantly in flux and remade, and also depends deeply upon other intersectional aspects of identity, such as skin color and socioeconomic status. In our discussions of food acquisition and preparation, several participants shared with me some of the characteristics of a "good woman," often as a way of telling me that if I wanted to be a "good woman" I should behave in particular ways. Some of these characteristics included going to bed early and waking up early; not drinking; not walking alone or with other women in the street too much, especially at night; not talking to men, or going places with men other than husbands, sons, or family members; planning meals and running an economically efficient household; serving (food to) husbands and children; cooking meals ahead of the hour of eating; keeping a clean house at all times; always being available in the home to serve husbands and children; and being always ready to receive visitors with coffee and conversation.[5] All things related to food are central to this local sense of the virtues of womanhood. These locally upheld virtues are thought to be characteristics that one can work toward as part of a practice to develop virtuous character (Mattingly 2010, 2013; Faubion 2001, 2011; Foucault 1988b, 1990; Aristotle 1976). Notions of ideal womanhood are reinforced through social practices of "visiting" and the interactions that take place at points of food acquisition, especially in borrowing and trading practices.

The ideals of virtuous womanhood in the contemporary landscape can be traced to a history of racialized, white European hegemony during the colonial period. While postcolonial Cuba attempted to shed Spanish colonialisms, some, like those related to the virtues and vices of gendered subjectivity, have been very difficult to eradicate even through the socialist period. These deeply ingrained "notions of respectability" (Thomas 2011) were part of the "intimate in colonial rule" (Stoler 2002) that remains central to Cuban understandings of what it means to be a good woman. In contrast, with varying degrees of success, the socialist revolution went to great lengths to inculcate the New Man with a particularly socialist ideology of self-sacrifice. However, notions of "honor" and "respect" from the colonial era still remain central to Cuban ideals of masculinity (Knight 1970; Lauria 1964). While these notions of virtue, honor, and respectability are deeply racialized and centered on notions of white supremacy, the ideologies have trickled into the lives of Cubans of all colors either in terms of an internalized desire to achieve these virtues, or as an external racist gaze judging them as never able to be virtuous.

My personal experience with negotiating the rules of gender roles for myself as I balanced the needs of my research with the confines of good womanhood were deeply influenced by my classed and racialized positionality in Santiago de Cuba. As I mentioned above, the women in my study constantly advised me to behave in ways that would fit the mold of a respectable woman. However, in order to conduct my research I had to break the rules. For instance, I was chastised repeatedly for walking in the streets alone at night, something that others thought was not safe for me, but more importantly implied that I might be engaging in nonvirtu-ous behaviors. To appease some of these concerns I asked male friends to walk with me, escorting me from the households that I was studying to the places I was sleeping. However, this also put me in violation, as walking in the streets at night with men is not appropriate for a virtuous woman. When I refused to stop this practice, rumors circulated about me, and the women in my study told me that I was developing a negative reputation. Some pleaded with me, with a sense of urgency, that I should scale back my research, finish things up before dusk, and get home at a decent hour, so that my reputation would be salvaged. These ways of disciplining me in the field were about teaching me the social norms of womanhood in San-tiago. However, they were also about disciplining me into a particular kind of racialized subject. As a light-skinned Black woman in the US, my class status and social behavior are critical components of the ways in which I am racialized in Cuba. Following the norms of virtuous womanhood in Cuba could be the social difference that tips me more toward a higher class status and whiteness rather than Blackness. The women who pleaded with me to behave in certain ways were not only trying to save my reputation; they were also trying to keep me from being categorized as Black, or lower class.

The rules governing gendered behavioral norms have been racialized since the colonial era. As throughout Latin America, in Cuba the *casa/calle* (house/street) divide is used to mark the distinction between white women's space and the spaces of men and Black women, with "men dominant in the public sphere and women in the private sphere of the household" (Safa 1995, 47–48) and Black women moving through public and private spaces as laborers. The notion of the casa/calle division of racialized, gendered spaces has persisted since Cuba's independence from Spain (Garth 2010; Smith and Padula 1996). For Black women, framings of matrifocality have

been used to characterize gendered norms. Matrifocality, or the centraliza-
tion and critical importance of the role of the mother in a household (Smith
1996; Smith 1962), is prevalent in the Caribbean, particularly among Black
women. Historically, marriage has been a sign of bourgeois respectability,
and the rejection of legal marriage among matrifocal households clearly did
not conform to colonial models of the nuclear family and male breadwinner. By contrast, while matrifocality is the rubric used to frame the lives
and labor of Black women, the notion of la dueña de la casa, the casa/calle
divide, and what I am calling "virtuous womanhood" have been used to
understand white women's lives in the Caribbean. This social world in which
a women's role is both upheld as virtuous and socially necessary is deeply
embedded in patriarchal relations. Traditionally the home is thought to be
a social and physical area over which white women have control and are
kept safe from the dangers of life in the streets, so that they may reproduce
and care for family (Andaya 2014; Stoler 2002).

While the categorization of women's place in the world is often linked
to Spanish bourgeois logics, it can be seen across racial lines throughout
various economic classes in Cuban society. However, as Helen Safa (2005)
has argued, the perception among Cuban people and within the Cuban
government that male-headed households are more desirable than female-
headed ones is not only an expression of racial hierarchies, but also of class
divisions. As many of these class divisions have blurred through the policies
of socialism, there has been a convergence of domestic practices between
white and Black, and between formerly middle-class and working-class sectors of the population, even while people retain distinctions about "respectable" household forms that maintain racialized and class-driven undertones.
Although household labor has been somewhat de-racialized, the politics of
respectability and the racial politics related to it remain in place.

This chapter builds upon feminist scholars of Latin America who have
demonstrated the ways reproductive and productive labor of women in the
household is undervalued and underappreciated (Allen and Sachs 2007;
Carney 2015; Counihan 2004; DeVault 1994; Mares 2017; Page-Reeves
2014; Texler Segal and Demos 2016). What I found in Cuba is similar to
what Mary Weismantel documented in Ecuador in the late 1980s, as political economic systems shifted there. While men were drawn away from the
household for different labor opportunities, the emergent economy there
drove "women's orientation increasingly inward" (Weismantel 1989, 5). As
women's care work has been shown to be crucial to the functioning of other

Latin American states, this chapter reveals how Cuba's ongoing socialist project depends heavily upon women's unpaid domestic labor. Furthermore, the data presented here also reveal how the intimate and quotidian gendered negotiations of food provisioning are deeply entangled with the structures of the global industrial food system (Alexander and Mohanty 1997; Grewal and Kaplan 1994; Boehm 2012; Tsing 1993; Wilson 2004).

Women and the Socialist Revolution

Just as Latin American neoliberalism is a gendered project (Schild 2007, 2013), Cuban socialism is also a gendered political project. Cuban household dynamics and gendered divisions of labor are heavily influenced by state-based ideologies (Andaya 2014). The Cuban interpretation of the Marxist position is that true gender equity can be established only through a socialist revolution, and that under socialism, gender equality becomes the standard. Several policies intended to "liberate" women have become institutionalized in Cuba, as in other socialist and communist countries, including encouraging women to work outside the home through the provision of equal work and educational opportunities, creating programs to help with domestic work and childcare, and mobilizing women into political and government positions within the Cuban Communist Party.[6] In Cuba, these efforts were established through the swift creation of laws and policies, but their implementation and uptake was relatively slow.

For Fidel Castro, the women's movement was meant to be a "revolution within the revolution" and not a separate struggle; thus, an autonomous feminist movement that empowered women to work toward equality was never established in Cuba. While women officially have equality in Cuba and many programs were established to ensure this equality, in practice there is still not substantive gender equality in the home or the workplace (Smith and Padula 1996). In addition, the underlying purpose of the programs established to improve women's equality after 1959 was to involve women in the revolutionary project of class equality rather than to establish a feminist movement.[7]

The Federation of Cuban Women (Federacíon de Mujeres Cubanas or FMC) was formed in 1960 to formalize women's participation in the revolution, specifically to organize Cuban women and encourage membership in the Communist Party.[8] The FMC created a number of programs that were instrumental in moving women into the workforce (FMC 1975).[9] They launched the women's literacy campaign in 1961 and developed a program to encourage rural parents to teach their daughters important skills for the labor force, such as sewing and clothes making. They were then encouraged to send their daughters to Havana through the Ana Betancourt program; these girls were known as Las Anitas. Through this program, young women learned what was considered to be proper grooming, proper ways of dressing and speaking, and domestic skills such as cooking and sewing. The Las Anitas program directly imbued revolutionary womanhood with forms of virtuous womanhood that were ideologically based in colonial-era gendered ideals. Nevertheless, these policies were very effective in increasing women's involvement in the formal labor economy. While the proportion of women in the state workforce has steadily risen, women are also juggling informal labor and black-market dealings to earn money in addition to taking on the vast majority of unpaid household labor.

The programs designed to encourage female participation in the workforce were coupled with attempts to change traditional ideologies concerning the family and gender roles. By the 1960s there was a national movement away from colonial definitions of a "proper" family. There was a move away from lifelong legal marriage as the ideal and increased acceptance of common-law marriage and visiting unions as typical Caribbean domestic arrangements, a move away from bourgeois traditions. More state programs were put in place to aid women in the household. An official program was implemented to cover salary during the three months prior to and three months after the birth of a child. An additional six months of unpaid leave may be taken, and mothers are guaranteed the right to return to their jobs.[10] The 1971 Plan Jaba was a program that allowed working women to drop grocery bags and shopping lists off at stores on their way to work, and store attendants would fill them with goods so that they could pick up and pay for the bags on the way home.

The Family Code of 1975 was another official position designed to promote equality and mutual respect between the sexes, establishing the equal right to work and obtain an education. In part, this was a way of encouraging men to share in household responsibilities. As a part of the Family Code couples agreed to share in household duties and childcare as a part of their marriage contract. The code also made it legal for spouses to divorce if one spouse was not sharing in household tasks. While the Family Code enabled women to move into the workforce by encouraging and mandating equal access to education and jobs, it did not directly propose specifics for how men should help with household duties and childcare. Cuban men were not interested in losing the household authority they traditionally held, and according to Fidel Castro, "a revolution was occurring among the women of our country, but no such revolution was followed by the men" (Garcia 2008, 99). Later, during the Special Period, a charter was added to the Cuban Constitution that officially granted men and women equal rights.[11] It placed particular emphasis on equality in the home.[12] Despite the equal-pay-for-equal work-mandates, women still earned less than men, making "80 to 85 percent of male salaries" (Safa 2005, 328).[13]

The Roles and Perspectives of Men

Although I did not find that most women are directly compelled by men to take on the labors of "virtuous womanhood," there are ways in which the roles, perspectives, and actions of the men in my study influenced how women understood their roles and guided their behavior. I found that for the most part the men in my study thought of themselves as financial providers for the household. Some men were indifferent to and ignorant of the forms of household labor that women in the household engaged in; others felt that they also "helped out" around the house in socially appropriate ways. For instance, with respect to the gendered division of labor in household food acquisition, Mickey, a 41-year-old middle-class santiaguero who identified as Black, explained his family's practices for acquiring food and other goods for the home, stating:

> It is really about muscles. I go to the market when we need a lot because I have more muscle to carry it up the hill. [My wife] goes when it is just a few things because she can carry it. She does most of the shopping for little things. I do the big trips. Things are changing now.

I pushed him further by inquiring about how things were changing, and he added:

> Sometimes it is the grandmothers that do all of the cooking in the house—this is not new, but other times children, both boys and girls, will make things and men as well. For example, sometimes I make the breakfast at home—it is something easy that I can do. Or my son will help prepare fruit or the salad for meals. Things didn't used to be this way.

A different perspective related to the gendered dynamics of family

FIGURE 9. Women Buying Meat. Source: Author

life in Cuba today was offered by Berto,[14] a 40-year-old Black man who works as a gardener. He reflected on the benefits of the revolution for his family:

> The childcare center is very cheap for us, because it is based on my wife's pay. She gets paid less. She takes our son at 7 a.m. and she goes to work. On her way home she stops to buy food for dinner. Usually either she cooks or my mother will cook something. My wife takes care of all of those kinds of things.

Berto failed to mention that in addition to dropping their son off at child-care in the morning, his wife also picks him up at the end of the day. They have access to low cost childcare only because his wife works in a state job that is eligible for day care. She does all of her household labor in addition to her job, as a nurse's aid, which, as he notes, pays less than his job. Berto quickly glossed over the labor that his wife and mother contribute to the household, indicating his indifference to how central these tasks are to making the household function.

In contrast to Berto's underestimation of the time women spend on

FIGURE 10. Men Watching a Cockfight in the Street. Source: Author

household labor, Mickey noted that in comparison to previous generations in Cuba, men are now willing to take on small amounts of household labor. Unlike Berto, who seems to be completely removed from household labor, Mickey is aware of which tasks might require his help, and he and his son attempt to contribute to household food preparation. In Mickey's view this has been a change over the generations; that is, Cuban households have progressed so that men and boys help with small tasks of food preparation. I found that in many households men have some food-related tasks that they take on, such as making one meal on a weekend, or a special dish that they know. However, while these tasks are nice gestures, they do very little in the way of alleviating the burden on women.

While it is true that some men appear to be taking on more household-based labor than previous generations, this is often a sensitive topic for men because it is still not socially accepted for men to take on domestic work. Engaging in household labor is often viewed as emasculating for some men. Some men and women feel that having men engage in household labor is too difficult for them emotionally and socially. For instance, Reina, a 54-year-old white female living in a middle-class Santiago neighborhood, told me that having her husband help out around the house was what led to her divorce.[15] As part of the 2010 countrywide layoffs from state jobs, her husband was out of work for the first time in his adult life, and rather than have him "in the street" she sought to put him to work on the house.

She had him repair a bathroom and refinish the wood furniture, as well as small everyday tasks like taking out the trash and going to the market. One day she asked him to clean the kitchen, a task that usually falls under "women's work," as she put it. She told me that the next day he packed up his stuff and told her that "he wanted a woman who would take care of him, not one that was his boss." She added that her efforts to keep him in the house, preventing him from cheating on her had been in vain, because he moved out of her house and right into his mistress's house. According to Reina, part of the role of being a good woman involves taking care of family, which includes not allowing family members to take on certain tasks that "should" be done by women.

Reina's story and those like it circulate quickly and widely among men and women who spend many hours a day visiting and gossiping with friends. During my study I overheard or was told stories like this—stories told by both men and women concerning relationship problems where the blame was placed on the woman's actions or way of treating her partner. These narratives reinforce local ideas of traditional gender roles, serving as a warning and fueling fear among those who deviate. While the traditional notion that men engaging in household labor is emasculating is still upheld in some households, Mickey's participation in food preparation and the active role of other Cuban men like Jorge Chino, detailed below, demonstrate that the gendered and generational dynamics of household labor are more nuanced than they might appear on the surface.

Portraits of Working Women: A Delicate and Draining Balancing Act

Ethnographic attention to the day-to-day lives of women in Santiago de Cuba reveals not only the quantity of work that it takes to get food on the table, but also the demands of doing it in a virtuous way and meeting all of the social expectations for a woman in Cuban society. This section details the everyday lives of three women in Santiago de Cuba whose households stand out as extremely well organized and who strive to uphold a high level of virtuous womanhood. These three cases are all of white-identified women, indeed the colonial vestiges of racialized social mores mean that few dark-skinned and few low-income Cuban women will ever be virtuous women (Stoler 2002; Willoughby-Herard 2010). While Black women may not strive toward virtuousness as often or intensely as white

FIGURE 11. Man Repairing Motorcycle. Source: Author

women, Black women are still judged by and held to many of the standards of virtuous womanhood. In turn, the standards of a "good woman" are also connected to how whiteness is constructed as normative and virtuous as part of colonial ideological legacies in Cuba.

María Julia

María Julia, briefly introduced in chapter 1, is a white-identified, middle- to high- socioeconomic status woman living in the city center. She is 45 years old, and has bachelor's and master's degrees in architecture and urban planning. She works for the city historian's office mostly focusing on heritage building repairs and laws intended to maintain the historical integrity of Santiago's historic city center. She works 40 hours a week but is able to do about a third of her work from home.[16] This works out well, allowing her to drop eight-year-old José at school, go to work, and then leave early to pick him up and finish her office work at home. She lives with and cares for her parents, who, although they are very independent, need her help with things, such as cleaning the house, doing their laundry, and any heavy lifting. As she explained it to me, her parents are now retired and need to rest, so she takes care of nearly all of the household labor, and they contribute their pensions to the household expenses.

María Julia consistently ensures that her family has a decent meal for breakfast and dinner each day; however, the result is that she is so exhausted she is rarely fully present for dinner with her family. Instead she is either too exhausted to be involved in conversation or has already eaten and fallen asleep. Food acquisition for her household is shared between María Julia and her mother. Her mother generally picks up the rations for the household, as the close proximity of the ration station and the relatively small quantities of food are manageable for her to carry back to the house. María Julia then does the extra shopping at markets to supplement the rations. She usually does this shopping on the two afternoons that she works from home. This family has enough income that they are able to buy some food items in greater quantity in order to avoid shopping daily. María Julia usually tries to buy 10 to 20 pounds of yuca, malanga, and other tubers at once. Her mother may also purchase the higher-priced produce from ambulant vendors that pass by each day to ensure that there is something for José to snack on or to have a fresh salad with lunch or dinner.

On my first day of working with her family I arrived at 6:45 a.m. because she told me that she "got up early," but it turned out that by early, she meant 4:45 a.m.! By the time I had arrived she had already made lunch and dinner for the day. She was also already halfway done cleaning the entire house when she stopped midway to prepare breakfast for herself, her son, her boyfriend, and her parents just as I arrived. She explained that she usually did things this way, so that she would dust, sweep, and mop the whole house except the kitchen before she finished her cooking. Then she would finish the cooking for the whole day, including breakfast, and finally, after serving and eating breakfast, clean the kitchen as her last task before showering and getting ready for work. She carried out these tasks every single day. María Julia is what I would call hypervigilant about cooking and cleaning. Because she does not go out to work every day I wondered why she did not just save the cleaning for her days off, or why she did not enlist some help from the three other adults who live in her household. When I tried to ask her this question she simply said "no es correcto" (it's not right [to ask for help]).

As I arrived that day she was already serving breakfast—one fried egg for each person, one roll of bread (*pan de bola*), coffee for everyone but her son, who had a yogurt and *zapote* smoothie. Her parents shared a banana as well. They ate quickly, clearly still sleepy and in a sort of automaton morning mode. As soon as they finished, María Julia cleared their plates and washed them. She swept and mopped the kitchen and wiped off all of the countertops. As she dumped the mop bucket in the plants, she kicked off her shoes and ran into the bathroom where she turned on the shower—cold water only in the mornings and not a full bath; she just quickly rinsed, making sure to not get her hair wet, as it was set in big rollers (another thing she did around 5 a.m. that morning). After she got out of the bathroom she threw on her robe, got her son dressed and his backpack ready, and plopped him down in front of the TV while she finished getting herself ready. She dressed and put on makeup in about 10 minutes and grabbed her son and flew out the door. Wearing high heels, she walked to the corner of the block where her son's school is and dropped him off. Then she walked back past her house to the bus stop. Some mornings she has to take a *moto* (motorcycle for hire) because she is running behind, but because I was with her on this particular morning, we would have to take the bus. Because she was worried about being late, I offered to pay for rides on a moto for both of us, which is something she is hesitant to do because it is expensive. She refused, stating, "50 cents when you only make 20 dollars a month is hard to justify when you could take the bus for a tenth of a cent."

A man on the bus gave her his seat and she was very grateful. I stood as she said to me, "It's so unfortunate that men and people in general in Cuba have lost the common courtesy to give up their seats for women and the elderly. Before a young lady would never have had to stand—some young man would have given up his seat for you, but Cubans have changed." I told her that I did not mind standing, and she replied, "Well you didn't do that much this morning so it's probably OK, but when I work like a bitch (*perra*) in the house all morning and then I have to stand on the bus on the way to work I get angry! (*me molesta*). It's the least they can do—[after] all that we do for them."

Before I left her at work, I asked about her plans for lunch. She said that she would not eat lunch, that she usually waits until she gets home because it's too much work to pack a lunch, too expensive to eat at a restaurant, and she is distrustful of the safety of street food; this means she doesn't eat until she gets home around 6 p.m. She must have seen my dismay because she was quick to add, "I've been doing it for ten years and I am fine, don't worry."

At 5 p.m. I waited for María Julia outside of her office. She came out around 5:15 p.m., and we headed toward the bus. I had eaten a pork sandwich for lunch so I was sated, but I could see that she was completely deflated—she was exhausted, weak, and it was hard for her to stand. She had to sit in the shade to wait for the bus because she thought she might pass out standing and that she couldn't even sit on a moto. We got on the bus, got a seat, and 20 minutes later we got off at our stop and she ran into the house, went straight to her room, and changed into her house clothes. Her mother had picked up her son already, and he was watching cartoons drinking a Kool-Aid-like drink. She kissed him on the forehead and went into the kitchen where she immediately served herself a heaping plate full of the rice with chicken (*arroz con pollo*) she had made in the morning for dinner that night. By 7 p.m. she was nodding off in the rocking chair in front of the television, and I headed home.

As I would find out over the course of a month studying her household, the day detailed here was quite typical for María Julia. To understand the logic behind her vigilance over her household, some background information is necessary. I first met María Julia during my first research trip to Santiago in 2008. I was introduced to her by her now ex-husband, who holds a high-level position in the local Santiago government. During my time there, María Julia discovered that her husband had been having an affair with his coworker, who was younger than her, and that the other woman was pregnant with his child. Although she wanted him to stay with her in addition to financially supporting the second child, instead he left her for the other woman. María Julia was devastated; she could not understand why her husband would choose to leave her when she did everything she should have done to "maintain the house" and bring in extra household income by taking a job in his office. She even would have "done the right thing" and stayed with him despite his (now) public infidelities. She felt that she was entitled to keep him: she had played by the rules and done what was expected. Instead, she ended up a single mother with an ex-husband that barely even speaks to her.

María Julia's job required that she continue to interact with her ex-husband. To recover after the breakup she took some time off and returned to her job about five months after he left her. A doctor's note indicating that she was too depressed to work allowed her to keep her job. She told me that as she began coming out of her initial depression, she was determined to prove to him that she was a perfect woman, a perfect mother, and that he had made the biggest mistake of his life. She went to work beautifully dressed and made up day in and day out, but he did not seem to notice. Eventually she started drinking. Reflecting on that period, she said she was so ashamed that she confessed her behavior to only one other person. At the same time, she was sure that others had noticed and judged her for it. She was both ashamed by the infidelity and her own behavior after he left her. However, by the time I began working with her household, things had turned around: she had stopped drinking, was dieting and trying to get in shape, and had a boyfriend who she thought was good for her and her young son.

María Julia is a highly educated woman with an excellent job by local standards. She is in a relatively comfortable socioeconomic position and able to provide a more-than-adequate lifestyle for herself and her son. But her dedication to the household contrasts with her own dietary practices; in general she neglects herself and does not practice self-care, instead putting all of her energy into caring for others. She has a clear set of ideas about what a good woman should do and feels that she failed to perform this role sufficiently in the past, so now she must work tirelessly to maintain a perfect household.

She told me her desire to keep up the appearance that everything in her household and relationships is perfect is a response to the stories that have circulated about her among the women in the neighborhood and in her social circle. Although I did not tell her, I had heard some of these rumors firsthand from her friends. They question María Julia: what did she do wrong? They feel that there must have been something that she did not achieve, some reason why her husband left her for a younger woman, a common action for a Cuban man that usually does not lead to any social shaming for them. She got wind of these rumors, and it further fueled her desire for perfectionism. She will not ask for help, because she wants to prove that she can do it all. She is completely exhausted but willing to push on so that her son can show up at school with "juice" from a powdered mix instead of just water, illustrating her achievements as a mother. At the same time she feels that this virtuous work should grant her certain rights and privileges, such as a seat on the bus. She told me that while her perfection did not make her husband come back, something she wanted for a long time, she does have a new man in her life, and so her perfection begets a reward valued by women in Santiago: the stable companionship of a man (cf. Browner 2000; Browner and Lewin 1982).

Except for the fact that she works outside the home, something the idealized traditional woman would never have done, but which a modern woman and ideal socialist would undertake, María Julia embodies a traditional, white Cuban ideal of womanhood. She measures her self-worth by the outside appearance of her family, her home, and herself, and she garners respect by maintaining a relationship with a male partner. This is a fundamental part of her subjectivity. In order for María Julia to uphold her own standards of her ideal self, she must work relentlessly in her paid and unpaid roles, constantly sacrificing herself to care for her family.

Caridad and Jorge Chino

Jorge Chino (JC), 45, and Caridad, 42, were one of the few couples in my study who both had formal employment outside the home. They are an upper-class family and both identify as white. Their two children live with them in their own modest home located on the same property as Caridad's parents' house, in one of Santiago's upper-middle-class neighborhoods where the pre-revolutionary wealthy class had lived. Many of the very rich left Cuba after the revolution and their homes were seized by the state. Now largely in disrepair, these homes were distributed to party members and those who fought for the revolution. Caridad's father acquired the property in this manner. Caridad and her family are proud to be devout socialists.

Caridad was very enthusiastic about participating in my study; she saw herself as a successful representation of women who work outside the home and still maintain what are viewed locally as good mothering practices. Caridad and JC are also exceptional in that they have been married for over 20 years, neither of them previously married nor having children outside of the marriage. Together they have raised their two children, Jorgito (17 years old) and Vira (8 years old), who are exceptionally far apart in age for most Santiago families. Caridad and JC waited many years to have a second child because their first was born with a disability. Both had worked tirelessly to navigate their way through the state bureaucracy and acquire the resources necessary to care for their disabled son. They had successfully gotten home health-care nurses, special transportation, and schooling for Jorgito, and they always secured for him the most modern wheelchairs available in Santiago.

To the surprise of many, Caridad has continued to work full-time outside of the home before and after both of her pregnancies. She works standard hours from around 9 a.m. to 5 p.m., Monday through Friday, at a state-sponsored art institute. She confided that she is very grateful to have been able to keep working, as it gives her a sense of self outside of her role as a wife and mother. She explained that she really enjoys her work and also feels that through her connections at her office she is able to bring extra resources beyond her salary back to the household. She has developed relationships that have helped her family acquire food, construction materials, entertainment such as movies and music, transportation, and even a family vacation at a local resort—all for free or at discounted rates.

Caridad and Jorge Chino are a rare couple who share household responsibilities. They equally share the tasks of food acquisition, each picking up specific things for the household on a daily basis. Jorge usually gets the rationed foods and stops at the cheaper markets on the outskirts of town when he works. He also acquires some food items directly from his employer. Caridad does some food shopping on her breaks from work. Since her office is located in the city center, it is convenient for her to pick up items as needed at the Plaza, one of the largest markets in the city. She also stops at small vegetable stands on her way home from work each day to purchase additional food items. Caridad is in charge of the laundry and the major household cleaning (sweeping, mopping, dusting, etc.), while Jorge Chino is largely in charge of getting the children ready for bed at night and for school in the morning. He also tidies up the house and makes sure that it is tidy enough so that Caridad can do her part of the cleaning.

Another exceptional characteristic of their relationship is that JC is one of the few men in my study who cooks for the household on a fairly regular basis. Because of the nature of JC's work as a taxi driver, there are days when he is off work and able to return home in the late afternoon before his wife gets home from work around 6 p.m. Without fail, if he gets home first, he makes dinner for the family.[17] One such afternoon I observed JC make a meal of Cuban-style *carne prensada* (meatloaf), tostones (fried green plantains), yellow rice, and salad. Through his job he sometimes is able to access beef cheaply on the black market.

On this particular day, he acquired some low-quality beef on the black market and decided to grind it and make meatloaf, adding some pork to the beef and grinding them together. He turned on the radio and listened to the late afternoon programming as he ground the meat. Once the meat was ground, he rummaged through some big mesh bags next to the refrigerator that held plastic bottles, jars, cans, and other things they thought might come in handy. He found an aluminum can that was the right size for the meat loaf and rinsed it with water. He filled the rice cooker with water and set it to cook. I must have looked puzzled, for he offered up that he was heating water in the rice cooker rather than the stovetop to save gas.

As he mixed minced garlic and onion into the ground meat, seasoning it with salt and black pepper, he told me stories of occasions when he had dined with foreign clients, and he reflected on how strange their eating habits were to him. He was particularly struck when he went to a lunch buffet with two Canadian businessmen. He told me that he had piled his own plate up "this big," indicating about a foot high, with "meat—beef, ham, turkey, chicken, pork." However, he was shocked when they all sat down and the two men had huge plates full of lettuce with cucumbers, onions, and tomatoes—"They were eating only vegetables for lunch. How strange!" He added that by now he had seen it enough to know that "you all (*ustedes*) eat that way." He said, "I know that it's healthier, but a Cuban just could not eat a plate of lettuce for lunch. We need meat, something substantial, real food." I told him that I had observed many Cuban meals and that I had indeed seen what he had said—most meals were meat, rice, beans, and viandas (tubers and plantains), but I had not yet seen anyone make ground meat in a can. I asked him where he had learned this technique (Garth 2019).

He told me that he had learned to cook from his mother, who, in his opinion, was an excellent cook. She taught all of her kids to cook, two girls and two boys, because she felt that cooking was a life skill everyone should have. He continued that he loved cooking because it was *una arte de inventar* (an art of invention), and he loved to take new ingredients and make them into unique dishes—something that his mother did not do; she had her repertoire and didn't really stray from it. He said that although now he just "invented" on his own, it was Nitza Villapol's television program and her book *Cocina Al Minuto* that first taught him to *inventar* in the kitchen (Garth 2014b). He stopped cooking for a minute, picked up the bag full of random bottles and cans to reveal a big, old tin cracker box. He put the box on the table, opened it, and took out a stack of pocket-sized cookbooks, underneath which was a stack of tattered pages that were all that remained of his copy of *Cocina Al Minuto*. He started flipping through the pages and found Nitza's recipe for carne prensada. He put it in front of me and explained that when he first got married to Caridad he would cook occasionally, for instance, only on Sundays or just the meat dish. However, when their son was born with special needs and Caridad became depressed and anxious about taking care of their son, JC started to cook dinner most nights. It was Villapol's book that helped JC through this difficult time. This was in the early 1990s when ingredients were incredibly scarce (Garth 2012). He spoke at length about how difficult life was for most Cubans then, but noted that his job at a local store was what saved his family. It was during this time that he really learned how to cook, how to *inventar* (invent) in the kitchen, and since things are better now, cooking has become easier and is now fun for him to take some new ingredient and "make art."

What did it mean for Caridad's sense of womanhood that her husband helped so much around the house? In turn, how did Jorge Chino's contribution to the household reflect upon his sense of manhood? How did others perceive this household? This exceptional case was actually the ideal for most women in my study, many of whom stated that they would like to be able to work outside the home and rely on their husbands to assist with household-based labor. However, both women and men negatively judge men who take on too much household labor as being effeminate and relinquishing their household authority. Even women like Reina, who believed that her husband left her because she had him do some household work, gossip about other households where women "let" men take on some of the household labor. JC's relationship with his mother, and that she was willing, even adamant, about teaching all her children to cook regardless of their gender, certainly shaped his values and sense of responsibility in the household.

Although gossip and envy of households where men help with the labor is common, in Caridad and Jorge Chino's case, the gossip did not have an envious tone. Rather, because their son was disabled, people in other households seemed to pity and feel sorry for the couple, referring to them as *pobrecitos* (poor things), who had been through too much to maintain the traditional roles of a Cuban household. On the contrary, however, Caridad and Jorge Chino did not see themselves this way at all, at least not at this point in their lives. Rather, they felt that they had found a good rhythm that balanced the household tasks with economic and social needs in a way that made their family life and their romantic relationship flourish. The fact that they were such strong socialists also helped to reinforce the idea that their way of dividing household labor was the best thing for their family and for *la patria*.

Marta

Marta, a 67-year-old retired professor of history, was thrilled to be a part of my study as a way to demonstrate her frugality and skill at stretching her pesos to feed her family. Marta lived with her husband, her two adult children, a live-in maid whom she describes as "an adopted daughter," her father-in-law, and her mother. Marta and her family were middle class and identified as white. She was the primary caretaker for her father-in-law, who was 95 years old, and her mother, who was 99 years old. In addition to her unpaid caretaking duties, Marta supplemented the household income by renting several rooms in her house at an hourly rate to young Cuban couples looking to spend some time alone together and occasional foreigners engaging in sexual transactions with Cubans. She also offered food for sale to the lodgers. She did not have a permit for this work, so both the hourly room rental and the sale of meals were illegal, but she managed to keep this business going for nearly 30 years. Her children and maid helped her with the food preparation and keeping the rooms clean.

I had initially approached Marta's daughter, Ariana, who, at age 47, was still working age and met the inclusion criteria for my study, but Marta quickly stole me away from Ariana. I found myself at Marta's side day in and day out in what seemed more like finishing school than an anthropological study. On my first day in the household Marta spent no less than two hours lecturing me on how, "Nowadays there is a lack of formal education, manners, etiquette in the family, children are spoiled and the 'deformation' is because of the way mothers raise their children." Marta took it upon herself to show me how, through her exemplary practices, a woman who is diligent and knows how to run her household can save a lot of money through meal planning and her approach to food shopping. She connected her views on women's household planning and control to "forming" children into respectable adults:

> A lazy woman will just feed her family pizza and spaghetti because it is easy, but it is expensive and does not have balanced nutrients. A woman who feeds her family pizza teaches her children that it is OK to just eat crap, that they can always have what is easy and tastes good. But a good woman will plan her family meals, taking the time to make beans, to cook vegetables in new ways, and only give her family pizza as a treat. This teaches the kids that hard work is rewarded.

Marta's vigilance over her household economy was certainly tied to run-

ning her business selling food and trying to make a profit. Due to her insistence, the entire family understood this, and her husband and children
were essential soldiers in her war against wasted time and money. They
helped by using their own social networks to scout out deals across the city
on food items, and this assistance helped to efficiently and cheaply maintain a very frugal household. This was another example of the ways women
heads of household enlist others to assist with household tasks.

Marta, although she appeared to be relaxed, had a very stressful and
highly structured daily schedule. She woke up at 6 a.m. every morning. She
cleaned up after her incontinent mother before making and serving everyone
breakfast by 7:30 a.m. After she cleaned up breakfast and got dressed herself,
she had a daily practice of taking a kitchen inventory; that is, she assessed
what foods were left, how she could put them together into meals without
buying anything, and whether or not she needed to buy additional items.
She had two refrigerators and two large freezers and constantly monitored
their contents to make sure that nothing spoiled. She then made a list of
any food items that were needed that day and the highest-priority items,
so that she and the rest of the family could start to look for deals. She gave
money to her maid to buy any items immediately needed. She kept a ledger
with all of the money coming into the house and going out of the house,
keeping track of which items were for the business and which were for the
family, as well as how the business profits flowed into the family needs.

To ensure that she got the most out of her money, Marta was sure
to use every part of the meat that she bought at the market. One afternoon she bought a pork leg and spent hours guiding me through how to
carefully butcher the meat so she could get the most out of every part.
She explained how you must carefully separate the skin from the meat,
frying the skin to make *chicharrones* (fried pig skin). You must carefully
debone the meat, so you can use the bones for soups and broth without
losing any precious meat in the butchering process. The main part of the
leg was reserved for steaks, which she sliced as thinly as possible to serve
as many people as possible. She saved all of the secondary parts to use for
flavoring beans, rice, and soups. If there was enough extra fat, she would
render the fat into cooking oil.

My days with Marta were peppered with her mantras: planificación
de la comida en el hogar es lo mas importante (food planning in the home
is the most important); variedad es sumamente importante (variety is most
important); no vivir para comer, comer para vivir (don't live to eat, eat to
live); and en mucha comida lo que te trae es poca salud, es un derroche (a

lot of food yields few health [benefits], it is a waste). These are among the many mantras she repeated to me (and to herself) daily.

Marta spent about four hours per day doing direct care work for her mother and father-in-law. With the exception of breakfast, she did not cook the household's meals but rather managed and directed others, both members of the family and hired help, to do the cooking and cleaning. She had unique and specific ideas about a balanced diet and tried to always make sure that whoever was cooking not only used the ingredients in such a way that nothing in her household spoiled, but also combined them to make meals that balance proteins and starches. For instance, she was adamantly opposed to serving protein with protein, so she would never make beans with pork in them served with ham, and she was equally opposed to serving starches with starches—as she said to me, "You will never see rice and bread together on this table." She also made sure that at least one vegetable is served with lunch and dinner, a practice somewhat rare in Cuban households.

Marta spent a lot of time cultivating social relationships with both friends and the vendors she bought food from. Whenever she was able to finish her household duties with time to spare, rather than relaxing in front of the television or sitting down to rest, she went out into the street near her house to chat with the men selling things. She would check on the prices, ask them how business is doing, and talk to them about their personal lives. She told me that she did this so that they will "keep her in mind" both for future discounts and free things, and with respect to her business. She explained that this cultivation of social and business relationships was critical for making ends meet in her household.

Making Sense of Virtuous Womanhood

In many ways Marta's feelings about her work to maintain her household are similar to those of María Julia. Both women invest large amounts of time in care of dependents, and both maintain a high level of order and control over their kitchens and households. While María Julia's vigilance focuses on perfection of appearance, Marta's pride lies in her frugality and the ability to produce a variety of different dishes for her family while spending as little as possible. These two women are characteristic of a more generalized white, middle-class ideal of womanhood that many santiagueras strive for. Marta and María Julia have shared notions of "what is right" for Cuban women, and the kinds of rewards that a "good woman" deserves, including the stable companionship of a man and well-behaved children who carry on these virtuous behaviors into the future.

For Caridad, the forms of virtuous womanhood that matter to her are somewhat different than those of María Julia and Marta. Caridad values working outside the home, has cultivated a sense of self outside of her home and role as mother and wife. She prides herself on using her workplace to make the social connections necessary to *resolver* the problems of the socialist system. She and JC have developed a flow for sharing household labor, where JC contributes to cooking, cleaning, and other household matters in ways that might be emasculating to some men and shameful for some women, like Reina. However, JC's upbringing in a household where cooking was valued as a life skill necessary for all Cubans regardless of gender, as well as the ways in which parenting a disabled son clouds the public gaze on their family with a sense of pity, and JC's comfort in his role in the household are some of the reasons that Caridad and JC evade some of the judgment that other households have dealt with.

The forms of vigilance over food and the household in these three cases are forms of virtuous womanhood that are tied to historical white colonial ideologies of womanhood. These racialized, gendered ideals were said to be in the service of protecting women from the dangers of the streets, but they also serve to maintain the boundaries of race and gender, where the proper white women is the lady of the house, but the Black woman must move through the streets to labor outside of her home. One of the implications for upholding virtuous womanhood in this way is that it renders anyone who must engage in unvirtuous behaviors, such as walking in the streets alone at night as in my own case as a researcher and in many cases of women who work long hours outside their homes, as unvirtuous and by extension less deserving of the rewards of a good life. My own experiences of being socially sanctioned for my unvirtuous behaviors and warnings over the potential negative consequences, such as being seen as a slut if I traveled alone with Esteban, demonstrate the complex social consequences that lower-income and nonwhite women have to navigate as they struggle to live a good life. Although some women may measure what is right for themselves by a different standard, socially they are still held to the standards of virtuous womanhood.

Conclusions: Food, Household Labor, and the Ideals of Womanhood

While there are exceptions, by and large as the food ration is reduced and state services diminish, the burden of work to ensure that families still eat and maintain some sort of decent quality of life is largely taken on by women in Santiago de Cuba. Despite the efforts to obtain equality under socialism, deeply entrenched patriarchal gender ideologies remain in place. Many scholars have observed that women, especially in difficult economic situations, consistently shoulder domestic work. Although most of my research participants accept this labor as a necessary part of their lives, their narratives, inflections of anger, and completely exhausting efforts in their daily lives demonstrate the ways in which this system is not adequate for providing a good life for Cuban women. If the lives of women suffer, both with respect to their household labor and paid livelihoods, the entire social system suffers. This illumination of women's daily lives demonstrates the ways in which food and gender are central to the politics of adequacy, and how changing provisioning systems have a ripple effect on other aspects of social life (Van Esterik 1999).

Yet, as we have seen with second-wave feminism in the United States, the role of cooking in women's lives and women's role in household cooking have not necessarily been cast aside as oppressive drudgery (Gilbert 2014). Food and gender are deeply intertwined (Allen and Sachs 2007; Barndt 2008; Gilbert 2014). Cooking for a family can be thankless work, but it can also be a site of "revelation and creation" (Beauvoir [1949] 2011) and an expression of care (Yates-Doerr 2014). The act of preparing and serving food to loved ones is part of the "nurturing arts" which can be a source of empowerment for women (Gilbert 2014, 21). Whether or not cooking for the family is experienced as creative and nurturing, regardless of their employment status, Cuban women are still burdened with a full load of domestic responsibilities.

This chapter has demonstrated the ways in which the ideals of womanhood are reinforced by men, women, and society at large, and how they continue to drive women to strive toward perfecting the balance between work outside the home and maintaining a perfectly clean home invariably with decent, dignified meals at the family table (Garth 2019). The discourse of virtuous womanhood and doing what is right, *lo correcto*, functions to reinforce this system of gendered labor. As food becomes more difficult to access, the relationship between food and gender becomes fraught, as gender is performed by and large through "acts, gestures, and enactments" that are central to the performance of identity (Butler 1990). If a subject, who is constructed in and through these kinds of actions, can no longer perform the actions, their very subjectivity, in this case gendered subjectivity, is undermined. By focusing on the daily practices of food preparation and acquisition in the lives of women, we see the ways in which shifts in social processes unfold as the food system changes. The cumbersome, daily household labor done mostly by women goes unseen and uncompensated, but constitutes a significant portion of the efforts made by santiagueros in everyday life to use the faltering food system and maintain the decent meal, and an adequate standard of living.

This chapter has also revealed the ways in which household-based labor largely undertaken by women is the other, invisible side of la lucha. While a large body of anthropological literature has already demonstrated that this unpaid and thankless labor often falls onto women, I revealed the ways that santiagueros reproduce this ideal gendered identity and tie it to notions of virtue. This local ideal of the "good woman" is upheld in practice through the tangible results of women's work—a clean home, well-fed children, and a well-kept physical appearance, as well as keeping and maintaining a husband (and sometimes a lover). Those who have never done it often diminish household-based labor and its difficulty. However, this labor is the mechanism for household-based *lucha* vis-à-vis efforts to *resolver* through the art of *inventar*. Although women shoulder the vast majority of household labor, other household members' efforts are not insignificant. Many male household members assist with food acquisition and some food preparation, and to varying degrees children and elder household members share in household tasks as well. This help does not diminish the virtuous status of a woman as long as she appears to be in control of the household, and the extent to which she enlists the help of others does not deter from their social role or become too emasculating for men. Nevertheless, these practices are essential mechanisms through which Cubans are able to make their faltering food system functional enough to keep food on the table. As the socialist food provisioning system weakens, these practices of household maintenance and proper behavior are increasingly seen as "the correct thing to do" and are the measure of virtuous womanhood in Santiago de Cuba today.

Although women's agency and insistence on struggle is clearly essential to the functioning of the contemporary Cuban food system, the relegation of women to the unpaid, unacknowledged sphere of the home also teeters on a form of precariousness. Important relationships hang in the balance as women struggle to conform to the idealized virtuous women trope against the odds. And whether the goal is to form the role of women in caring for the heteronormative family, or mold women into a socialist workforce, the increased burden on women's time, with the burden of formal work, informal work, and household labor, leaves them with little capacity for civic engagement and investment in the socialist project. For many Cuban women, an adequate food system would not require constant vigilance over the home and the marketplace; it would allow ease of access so that the efforts of time and energy could be placed elsewhere, whether that be the socialist project or some form of leisure.

The faltering food provisioning system increases the burden of unpaid labor on women and creates insurmountable pressure to live up to the standards of virtuous womanhood. At the same time, the perpetuation of virtuous womanhood, derived from racial colonialist values, functions to maintain forms of anti-Blackness and ideals of white supremacy in contemporary Cuban society. The centrality of virtue and respectability politics also functions to further inculcate the notion that only those who engage in the socially sanctioned behaviors of (white) virtuous womanhood are worthy of living a good life (Willoughby-Herard 2008, 2010). Instead of upholding egalitarian principles, these ideals perpetuate the idea that light-skinned Cubans are worthy of living a decent life, while those with darker skin should be grateful for the assistance of the paternalistic state, which aligns with the "Gracias Fidel" paradox discussed in the introduction.

Transitioning from a framework of virtue, the next chapter outlines the local frameworks surrounding tactics and strategies for overcoming barriers to accessing food. I illuminate the subtle differences between engaging in socially acceptable illicit activity and activity that is viewed as "not right." I reveal how these local orientations to practices of food acquisition both implicate a reliance on community and undermine social connections within the community. Nevertheless these actions are seen as necessary to access food and assemble a decent meal.

4

Community

Mickey had come down with a cold in the middle of the summer heat. Mickey was a 41-year-old, middle-class santiaguero who identified as Black and also as *moro* (Moorish) and *sirio* (Syrian).[1] He was too sick to go to work, but well enough to chat with me for hours about the changes in everyday life in Cuba during his lifetime. Between coughing fits, sneezing, and incessant phone calls, Mickey became very emotional—he started to sigh often, tears welled up in his eyes, and he began to cry—as he shared his story of living through the Special Period.

Everything had already started to become scarce, like I told you before, it was terrible. Terrible. The special period was cruel, cruel in the year 1993. I don't know if you have a lot of people who have told you this already, but it was terrible, that time, terrible. There were always clandestine things, people who worked in stores and stole things and still steal things, for economic concerns, understand? In those years [before the 1990s] the people were, they were . . .were . . . it's like—in Cuba, there is this saying: God was in the land, in the Cuban soil. Before, people had better hearts, they were more human . . . then what happened was there was an economic crisis, and the Special Period started to change the character of the Cuban people, a change of disposition. Many people transformed and started to do things, things I don't view as right, like stealing or not sharing food with their own family members. And, well, really the mind of the Cuban has suffered a lot over these things, because of the scarcities. Yes, so the Cuban way of being changed a lot because of the shortages of goods, things became scarce until everything was gone, everything, to the point where even a leaf from a tree had a value.

Mickey tearfully reflected on the ways the state economic crisis of the 1990s and ongoing repercussions have resulted in what he perceived as a shift in daily practices of food acquisition and the dynamics of social relations in Cuba. He emphasized the trauma of the worst of the Special Period and theorized that after living through that trauma Cubans have changed. In describing this change of disposition, a "transformation," and its connection to material goods and value, Mickey neatly summarized what I characterize as a perceived shift away from the practices of acquisition established under the socialist ethics of the New Man. This shifting ethics of acquisition, which Mickey glossed as people "transforming" and doing things that are "not right," has deep repercussions for social relations in Cuba.[2] Santiagueros view this as a shift away from state sanctioned ethics of consumption and acquisition toward new forms of *sociolismo*, that is, new ways of relying on community to support individual and family needs, new ways of recirculating resources into the community. In this chapter I detail how these standards get debated and how santiagueros draw on the past as they debate those standards. As access to desired foods is increasingly difficult, santiagueros grapple with their understanding that to be a decent person they must do things that might be otherwise considered indecent. Yet, they refuse to settle for indecency and inadequacy in their food consumption. Because eating in a particular way is so important that they will not waver nor accept mediocrity, instead they do other things to make it work that they do not understand as falling within the bounds of "the right thing to do." This chapter focuses on the process of reflecting, reconciling, and understanding the relationship between locally accepted practices of acquisition. These ethical difficulties reveal the ways that social relationships and the community are entangled with the politics of adequacy to show that an inadequate food system can have profound effects on the social life of a community.

In the ongoing process of the waning of the welfare state, the reduction in state subsidized foods mean that individuals must turn to their own innovative tactics and strategies in order to access basic needs. These tactics and strategies require new relational orientations toward collective activity and the public sphere. As the food system changes, Cubans have turned to more ways of pilfering from the state, hoarding, and other forms of acquisition that they question as ethical based on their own understanding of local ethics. Such practices include what Cubans refer to as a shifting stance toward sharing. While some forms of acquisition, such as small amounts of pilfering from state jobs and the use of the black market are generally accepted as necessary practices to survive, and not considered unethical, as the acquisition of goods becomes more difficult, people increasingly push the boundaries of ethical activity and sometimes turn to tactics that are more questionable, both in the opinions of their peers and in their own individual assessments.

Reliance on these practices places families and communities in complex social and emotional entanglements. Santiagueros grapple with how to still be "good people" under their collective ethical systems and normative codes despite the fact that the structure of the food system hinders their ability to acquire food in an "ethical" manner.[3] I draw upon locally defined notions of "good people" and "ethics" here based on blurred boundaries of licit and illicit, ethical and unethical. I understand this to be a local cultural system of ethics (Csordas 2013; Fassin 2008; Faubion 2011; Zigon and Throop 2014), rather than something inherent or given (Lambek 2010). While there is a relatively clearly understood set of practices that may be considered illegal but "licit" (Roitman 2006), there are also practices that are not necessarily governed by the law that are clearly unethical, just as there exist practices that are both unethical and illegal. Apart from the local laws, I draw upon my research subjects' notions of *justo* (right) and *no es correcto* (wrong), while demonstrating the ways in which the unjust conditions of everyday life may make the measurement of ethics impossible, or at the very least quite complicated. The structures of the current food system and the "traditional" ethics of consumption are incommensurate, and in order to continue eating in a "decent" manner, itself an ethically valenced notion in a different sense, Cuban consumers must shift their ethics, or contend with conflicting ethical frameworks. Because it is absolutely necessary to eat, and there are particular ways of eating that have been deemed "decent" and culturally appropriate, the shifting ethics of food acquisition and consumption play a central role in the changing experience of everyday life in the post-Soviet socialist era, which I elaborate in chapter 5. The ways in which participants reflect on ethical conundrums reveal important dimensions of the politics of adequacy. Overall santiagueros articulate a general sentiment that an adequate food system should not require that they engage in unethical practices to acquire basic needs; in an adequate system, basic food staples should be easily and conveniently accessed at all socioeconomic levels without an uncomfortable shift in ethical standards or notions of decency.

As Cuba's food system changes, actors must innovate new strategies and tactics to acquire food. There are other examples of this. Michel de Certeau's *The Practice of Everyday Life* (1984) is a part of a body of work that seeks to understand how agents, sometimes assumed to be passive and merely following rules and regulations, bend the rules to make societies more functional for them. Similarly, Scott's *Weapons of the Weak* (1985) details the ways in which subaltern subjects overcome forms of hegemonic domination through small, daily practices. Certeau's framework of "ways of operating," helps to illuminate the importance of understanding practices of acquisition through tactics and strategies to make meaning of individual positions within the contemporary global food distribution system. Using this framework, tactics and strategies are the specific types of practices through which people maneuver through or around state structures in order to acquire enough food to keep rates of hunger extremely low in Santiago. Strategies are the processes by which an individual agent acquires what they need through the official state system by way of carefully calculated under-standings of institutional rules and social norms for using the system. In the case of food, this might include acquiring the maximum amount of food on the ration before turning to more costly food purchases. Tactics, on the other hand, are practices through which agents find loopholes or weak points in the official system, often by breaking or bending the institutional laws and social norms in order to fulfill needs. An example of a tactic might include buying and selling on the black market, or unofficially trading foods.[4]

As discussed in chapter 2, Cuban state discourse on ethics is imbued with Che Guevara's socialist narrative of *el hombre nuevo* (the New Man), and Cubans have accepted many aspects of this ideology in their own indi-vidual ethical ideals. Self-sacrifice for the good of the collective was central to the ethical redrafting of the New Man: "Individualism, in the form of the individual action of a person alone in a social milieu, must disappear in Cuba" (Gerassi 1968, 115). The Cuban *conciencia* was changed through explicitly political goals and revolutionary programs (Blum 2011). Although many Cubans are frustrated with the inadequacies of the faltering socialist provisioning system, they continue to have a deep-seated emotional attach-ment to this ideology as part of what constitutes contemporary Cubanidad. Building on these concepts, Denise F. Blum proposes that in contemporary Cuba it is essential to consider what she calls *doble conciencia* (double con-

sciousness), which is a dual morality central to the changing sociopolitical context of Cuba today, where Cubans simultaneously attempt to both
"uphold the traditional moral character" of Cuban identity and undermine
it through their changing actions (2011, 18).[5] In the post-Soviet setting,
actors now must innovate practices in order to make ends meet, and these
strategies and tactics may not be part of what was previously considered to
be ethical behavior.

These strategies and tactics are used by families to determine how to
access basic needs and get by as state provisioning diminishes. They are able
to "get by." Both strategies and tactics require careful calculations of risk
and relations with the state and the law, as well as nuanced understandings
of how citizens of that state will judge the ethics of such strategies (Certeau
1984). At the same time as their practices and tactics are changing, my
research participants uphold what they conceptualize as "traditional" ethical framings of their actions as the right way to behave even though these
framings are incommensurable with the needs of individuals to procure
foods under the current food system. Ethical dilemmas surrounding the
role and agency of individual action with respect to their community and
the state often lead people to reflect on their own understanding of ethics
and what this means for Cuban socialism. The ways they grapple with these
ethics and reflect on the meaning of the perceived shift in social relations
is intertwined with the moving power of state institutions, global forms of
distribution, and the forms of socialist governmentality that exert power
over and impact individual lives and social relations in Cuba.

Unpacking Tactics and Strategies: Pilfering and *Resolviendo en la Calle*

Drawing on the stories of Monika, Regina, Elvira, and Armando and
their households, in chapter 1 I described the lived experience of searching
for food in the context of Cuba's faltering food provisioning system. This
experience is stressful and exhausting, and the way out of it is not always
clear. Some of the options that people turn to in the face of food scarcity
include pilfering from the state or buying and selling items on the black
market, also known as *resolviendo en la calle* (resolving in the street).

As it becomes increasingly difficult to satisfy basic needs through official state channels, like the rationing system, many santiagueros say that
they feel they are left with no option but to pilfer from the state or use the

FIGURE 12. Street Vendor. Source: Author

black market. Looking across socioeconomic status and neighborhoods, the 22 Santiago families that I studied were all users of the black market. From reliance on the lowered prices of black-market meat pilfered from state cafeterias, to the purchase and resale of sacks of grains from security guards at state warehouses, every family seemed to be involved at some level. For each of them, there is a fine line between engaging in these activities in acceptable ways and the subtle shift to unethical acts. These practices are also entangled. Among my research participants there were several people who reflected on the common practice of pilfering goods from state and nonstate workplaces for their own household use and for resale. Through pilfering they supply the black market. State employees might pilfer food items to feed their families, to sell directly to the public, or as an ingredient or component in something they add value to and then sell to the public. For instance, a baker might pilfer some flour and leave the bread rations a little short, using it to make their own dough at home, or sell it to someone else who needs flour, who may also have their own small side business making cakes or other baked goods to sell to the public.

Cecelia is a 54-year-old, middle-class, white santiaguera. She works as a *bodeguera*—the person who runs the ration station where dry goods are distributed, known as the *bodega*. Cecelia is a beloved member of her community who has worked in the same bodega for nearly 30 years. Cecelia is the older sister of Amalia, who was engaged in the search for corn to make hallacas in the introduction. I observed Cecelia's loving relationship with her clients over the course of a week in her ration station and during my time studying her household, and came to understand the multiple dimensions of her work as both an agent of the state and a member of a community. Cecelia and those in positions like her are the nodes that connect the state with civil society. According to Cecelia and my conversations with some of her clients, those who receive their rations at Cecelia's bodega view her as someone who is on their side, helping them out as much as she can within the limitations that the state puts on her and the supply of ration food.

Cecelia earns a modest salary and works long hours six days a week. To make ends meet, she told me that feels that she must also maintain her own unlicensed side business selling things out of her ration station while she works as a state employee. Cecelia uses myriad practices to pilfer foods from her ration station without her customers or bosses saying anything. These include a trick involving placing her thumb on the scale to make the amount look like more than it is; after weighing the foods for each family, she leaves just a bit in the basin as she dumps the rest into their bags. She keeps that little extra bit of rice, beans, sugar, etc., and then later in the month when there are none of those things left in the ration she sells the extras out of the same ration station at a price higher than the subsidized one, but lower than the peso market price. She only sells this pilfered food to trusted consumers who come to her regularly for it, and they are aware of how the food is acquired. Her long-standing relationship with the community and her willingness to recirculate this pilfered food to them, rather than keep it for herself and her own family, has led to an established relationship of trust and a form of reciprocity.

Cecelia is connected to an extensive network of black marketeers who pilfer foods from ration warehouses and resell them. Although she does not participate in this specific activity, her cooperation often results in monetary or in-kind kickbacks. While I was observing her work, I saw her receive one such in-kind donation. One morning just before seven, as she was opening the bodega, a young man arrived with a 55-gallon drum of tomato puree in the back of a truck. He told her it was all hers to sell, but that it was going to go rancid in a day or two. She did not ask questions, but grabbed her dolly and quickly helped him load it into the bodega. Without pausing she wrote in big letters on her chalkboard, "¡HAY PURÉ!" (There is [tomato] puree!) and placed it in the doorway. She instructed me to go fetch her sister who lives up the street and tell her and Cecelia's nephews to come right away. In addition to selling the puree to her regular customers, she worked with her sister and nephews to mobilize a small network of *socios* (acquaintances) and family members who might be interested in selling tomato puree out of their homes, which, although illegal without a permit, is extremely common and can be very profitable. Within an hour several santiagueros showed up with buckets to fill with her puree. Because they were trusted friends, they would be able to take the puree and pay her only after they had sold it. I was fascinated by how quickly they were able to move this puree into households across the city, making a small profit at each step. When I asked Cecelia where the puree came from she shrugged and said "el estado" (the state), seemingly uninterested in its origins.

Cecelia's position as a bodega operator places her at the interface of the community and "the state." Here the state is "imagined," in the sense that it is not clear what level of government is referenced, and there is not a clear, coherent entity of reference (Anderson 1983; Gupta 2012b). At the same time, the historically unchanging sitting government is often understood as an embodiment of the state in Cuba. However, in the way that Cecelia alludes to the state, there is also the very real entity that exists in the socialist infrastructures, such as the ration station, a state pharmacy, or clinic, that allow for the provisioning of food and other goods and services. As a bodega operator, Cecelia is both an agent of the state and a member of the community.[6] In her under-the-table, *por la izquierda,* work she simultaneously undermines the state and its efforts to distribute basic needs to its citizenry, and she serves her community by ensuring that food does not perish and is distributed to people so that they can consume it rather than having it go to waste. She embodies the state as an actor, while undermining the idea of the state and its effects (Abrams 1988). Cecelia sees her under-the-table actions as virtuous and a central part of ensuring that her community has adequate food. Here pilfering from the state serves community needs; the lines between civil society and the state blur as Cecelia, at the interface of the two, the point of contact between the state distribution system and the neighborhood, undermines the state system in order to make it work for people.

Like Cecelia, Ramira, a low-income 34-year-old who self-identifies as *mulata,* also pilfers from her state job. However, Ramira's pilfering is less centered on creating channels for a wider distribution of food and much more focused on feeding her own household. This type of pilfering and use of food in the home is more typical than Cecelia's broader distribution and money-making strategies. Ramira lives in a humble two-bedroom first-story home in Chicharrones with five other adults and two young children, and struggles to maintain her family's lifestyle. Ramira's home includes an ample living and dining room at the front of the house, but the back half of the house has been divided into several very small bedrooms. There are four rooms, and one household member, Ramira's uncle, sleeps on a narrow cot stored in the hallway. At the end of this hallway the house opens to an enclosed patio where they store water tanks and have two corrals for pigs, chickens, and goats. This is also the area for household laundry, a task mostly done by Ramira's daughters. Ramira's two daughters each has a child of her own. Her older daughter lives in the house with her husband, Francisco, and daughter. Her younger daughter is single and lives in the house with her one-year-old son. Ramira's daughters are not employed outside the home. As the only person working outside the home, Ramira has a lot of responsibility for the household; she must bring in income and also provide critical access to the scarce resources that she can access through her job.

Ramira works as a server in a state-run cafeteria on the other side of the city in Sueño. Because of the amount of food she is able to pilfer from her job and the connections she makes with others to acquire food both on and off the black market, Ramira's household food acquisition hinges on her employment at the restaurant. Through this and other channels, Ramira is responsible for nearly all of the household food acquisition. She picks up the ration goods before or after work and acquires the household's remaining food during her work hours at the state-run cafeteria . Her uncle is the only household member who sometimes eats outside of the home; other than his occasional meals elsewhere, all four adults and two children eat three meals a day at home. Ramira often eats one of her three meals a day while on her shift at work. Because of her job Ramira rarely has to buy food at the market; however, she or her daughters will occasionally buy food from ambulant vendors that pass by the house as the need arises. Like some other very low-income households in my study, Ramira and her family rarely venture outside of their neighborhood to acquire food, and most of their food purchases are made within steps of their front door, with the exception of what she acquires through work. As Ramira, Carla, and Regina (introduced in chapter 1) all explained to me to varying degrees, this choice to stay close to home was in part due to their ability to rely on the nearby vendors to cut them deals and sometimes offer them free items. Also they were often caring for young children, often their grandchildren, and needed to stay close to the house throughout the day. They did not have many options for nice clothing, and it was a social standard to dress up to walk through the city. Social norms allowed them to remain in their house clothes to walk just a few doors down or a block away to make a purchase. This means that they were limited in their food options to those ambulant vendors that happen to pass by on a given day and to what was available at the local ration station.

In the case of Ramira's household, they were able to maintain some variety in their diet because of the food items she was able to bring home from work. She was careful to delicately balance how much she pilfered from her state job. She took a steady amount of food home, not too much or too little, as either would cause a change in the restaurant's supplies and draw unwanted attention from her boss and the other employees, who likely were also pilfering on the job. She also only took what could fit discretely in her backpack so as not to draw attention to herself at work or on her commute home. She reflected on these tactics of food acquisition as necessary for her family to eat:

> Yes, this is how we eat, stealing from work, and then we use our salary to make it enough for the household. I want to make more money, to start my own business on the side. I am a good cook and I could take the ingredients from work. But I have to keep this job because it gives me access to things and it's secure. If you get sick you still get paid, but if you are hustling on the street and you get sick then you can't sell things and you don't make money. Those youth who just sell in the street, well it's not good, it's not bad, but what's bad about it is that they don't have enough aspiration for their lives, it's ok because they get some money. But they get caught, get things taken away, and then they have no education or job to rely on.

Ramira alluded to a certain ethics of pilfering here. She distinguished her own activities from others who engage in similar activities, but with no "aspiration for their lives," with "no education".[7] This points to another dimension of ethical conduct and the practices of acquisition. Here, the types of overarching motivations that one has in striving toward a "better," but still ethical, life are seen as good motivations for pilfering, while self-interest is not. Therefore, if Cecelia's pilfering is virtuous in that it serves so many in the community, Ramira's is acceptable as the mode through which she provides for her family's needs. These two forms of acceptable pilfering are to be distinguished from those that are "not right," which has its own competing ethical frameworks.

Socios and *Palanca*: Reliance on Social Networks and Community

Given the complicated food acquisition system and the overwhelming difficulties faced by poor families in Santiago, how do socially marginalized, resource-poor families manage to get food on the table? I found that the two fundamental things that hold this system together are: (1) reliance on a network of socios—friends, family, neighbors, coworkers, and godparents, and (2) willingness to *resolver* (resolve) problems via illegal channels. Not only are these the fundamental ways in which santiagueros make ends meet, but they say that their uses of and movement within these practices have shifted in recent years.

The term *sociolismo* (a classically Cuban tongue-in-cheek play on the word *socialismo)* is used to describe the nature of the cooperative system the revolution created, in which social networking became the critical means for people to acquire the basics for daily life. The sociolismo system of cooperative interdependence has existed in Cuba since the 1960s and continues to this day. Reliance on a network of socios (literally, associates), a term that most generally means acquaintance, but also includes friends, family, neighbors, coworkers, and godparents, is essential to make ends meet in Santiago. Together the declining food rationing system and the dual currency economy resulted in an increased importance of social networks, both on the island and off, for acquiring basic needs. Through veiled language referencing sociolismo, resolviendo, and luchando, among others, Cubans are often invoking a double meaning of these terms that includes a critique of the socialist state and a way to blame the political leaders that are not adequately providing for the Cuban people. The work of maintaining networks of socios is crucial to accessing material goods in Cuba. This work has a gendered nature to it, as women are more likely to maintain social networks near the home, while men are out "in the streets" and venture across a larger geographic area to build and maintain their network of socios.

Through maintaining a large network of socios one can attain *palanca* (leverage) or connections. Through palanca, santiagueros are able to access goods and services that might be closed off to them without strong social networks. However, someone's palanca usually remains within their social network, and the sorts of things that one is able to access are determined by the amount of resources within it. An example of palanca might include having a friend or socio who works at a nightclub and can get you in without paying cover or having to wait in line. Cecelia's network of distribution is filled with palanca at every turn. With respect to food acquisition, palanca is particularly important for people who access food on the black market where social connections are crucial for access in general and especially for accessing higher quality or scarcer items. For instance, one must have good socios and a certain degree of palanca in order to acquire beef regularly on the black market.

Luchando La Vida

Luchando la vida, struggling for life, is a ubiquitous phrase in Cuba. It has multiple meanings, among them, the more literal expression like

FIGURE 13. Buying Garlic. Source: Author

"just trying to get by" or a veiled reference to using the black market. A somewhat more complex way of thinking of luchando la vida is to see it as "filling the gaps of the state" which can no longer provide for the citizenry as it did previously and as it continues to promise. As Sean Brotherton has noted with respect to Cubans' use of the healthcare system:

> Individual citizens draw on the metaphor of *la lucha* (the struggle) to describe their actions in a way that is similar to *la Revolución's* historical use of Cuban independence fighter Jose Martí's notion of *lucha* and *sacrificio* (sacrifice). Martí's ideas, shaped by a political idealism, sought to create a political utopia based on lucha, and stressed unity and morality over individual rationality and self-interest. However, the impact of the economic crisis on the primary health care system has meant that many individuals no longer feel concerned with the overall objectives of the revolutionary project, that is, the maintenance of the collective good, defined as putting state objectives ahead of individual wants and desires (2005, 21).

It is common for Cuban consumers to comment and reflect on their own individual forms of luchando la vida and how these practices impact household and social dynamics. In practice, for many of my research participants, luchando la vida is not just about acquiring things through illegal or unethical channels, but it becomes a metaphor for the complex emotions wrapped up in the practices that individuals must undertake in order to meet their individual needs, while attempting to have the least negative impact on the collective good—it is all *una lucha*, a struggle. While it is true that the vast majority of Santiago families use the black market in one way or another, some are faced with varying degrees of difficulty as they navigate the black market. Others face ethical dilemmas when they must turn to the black market to acquire food and other goods in order to make ends meet. These ethical dilemmas vary from reflecting in general on the meaning of black-market activity in the socialist state, to contemplating one's own activity and whether it has gone too far.

Mayelín, a young, white-identified woman born in the 1990s, reflected to me on the tensions between need and desire as she debated the ethics of black-market activity. Mayelín was about six months pregnant and at home on bed rest due to high blood pressure when I studied her household. She did not talk much, and her mother-in-law had asked me not to talk to her too much, as I might inadvertently cause her stress, which she believed could raise her blood pressure. One day Mayelín and I found ourselves alone at home, so she started to make small talk with me. She offered up a saying I had heard a lot in Santiago: "Here in Cuba it's either eat well, or dress well." She elaborated that in her mind the cause of the problem was low state salaries and the extreme difficulty of succeeding as an entrepreneur. I gently pushed Mayelín to elaborate about how people manage to get by if salaries are not enough to both buy food and clothes. She responded, "Well, Cubans have to eat well and they have to dress well. There is no option not to do either of those, so we do it by luchando la vida."

I asked what she meant by "luchando la vida" and she spelled it out quite clearly: "They steal (*roban*). They steal things from the state or whatever or whomever they can to use or sell [stuff]." This understanding of luchando la vida resonates with Brotherton's analysis of the ways Cubans see themselves as filling the gaps of the state. However, it also opens up the possibility of stealing from the state or luchando la vida in a way that goes beyond filling the gaps of the state to, for instance, serve only individual desires.

Contemplating the use of the black market and the role of filling the gaps of the state provides a window into the ethics of exchange in times of scarcity. Cori, who lives with his sister Carla, reflects on these types of practices that skirt the boundaries of ethical conduct and their role in contemporary Cuban society:

> This exists everywhere . . . For example, if I go to the Plaza de Marte now and I try to hustle some newspapers or something, to resell them for five cents more than I bought them for, even if the people from the state see me they won't say anything because it's—there's always going to be this activity. You are just going to be one person losing five cents, and I am going to make a 1,000 pesos and with that I can actually do something, you can't do anything with your five cents. So it's the way it is, it's how we get ahead, most of those people losing five cents don't even think about it.

Cori continued:

> You have to do something to get by, look for possibilities, abilities. Businesses, selling, buying, try to find some supplement to the salary so that you can buy things. And it's hard work, this counts as working too, you have to work with others, find resources, stealing or not, I don't know, but if there is a ship unloading boxes of chicken, someone is going to have the skills to get a box of that chicken and sell it in the street. Whether I do it or you do it, it's going to happen.
>
> Hanna: That's how food gets into people's hands?
>
> Cori: No, that's how money gets into people's hands, you have to take food out of the state system, because it isn't working, it doesn't provide enough, and you have to generate money with it. Now we need money, if the state is not providing enough, we need money to buy things, so we have to steal from the state and that makes it provide even less, which just means we need more money to buy things so the stealing continues. That's the truth, that's how we survive.

Here Cori reveals his own personal justification of black-market activity and why he thinks that it is necessary for the functioning of the current food system. From his point of view, black marketeers provide the legwork to make the system work. The black market, then, is how money and goods "get into people's hands," circumventing the inefficiencies of the state system and alleviating a labor burden from the state in exchange for individual profit-making and state loss. For Cori, this work to make the state provisioning system more functional is fundamental to survival. It is both a virtuous act that helps keep the system going and a self-serving act to make profit off the inefficiencies of the system.

Like others, Cori reflects on an intricate system of well-thought-out tactics and strategies that make the state system work. Cori describes the functioning of a post-Soviet socialist governmentality that tacks back and forth between formal state systems and the informal mobilization of social networks. These forms of "improvisation under conditions of adversity" (Ferguson 2015, 94) function to both overcome the inadequacy of the socialist distribution system and to ensure that socialism continues chugging along as the revolutionary goals of getting food on the table are achieved even if by other means. Importantly, Cori also includes the notion that even doing something that is self-serving can be virtuous, which is a part of many santiagueros' perception that there has been a shift away from orienting serving collective needs to include individual profit.

Building on his reflections on the blurry ethical boundaries of pilfering and reselling foods at a higher price, Cori connects these ethical quandaries with Cubanidad and the role of the Cuban state. He stated:

> We have this idea that we have to rise up, to overcome and ironically we get this idea from the state, *el comandante* Che Guevara [said to Fidel Castro] "Don't trust, or don't follow the politics of the economy too much, forget about imports and try to create your own nutrition, because your country your people have it in them naturally." That's what he said and we do have it in us, we naturally jump over problems and find solutions to feed ourselves.

Here Cori connects the *doble moral* of Cubans today with Fidel Castro and Che Guevara's framing of how the Cuban state should interact with the global market. Cori expresses some of the deep-seated logics of Cuban socialism, which are now being pushed by the current Cuban government—the good socialist does what it takes to make the system work. Cori continued:

> If he [Fidel Castro] had listened to this advice, instead of relying on the Soviet Union, we [the country] would have developed. But he didn't pay attention to Che, he just relied on the state and economic relationships with the Soviets and look where we are now. Now it's too late for us to build our agricultural system. We don't have the luxury of planting trees and waiting for them to grown now, we will starve while we are waiting.

So we've learned lessons from this, we don't pay attention to the political
rules and we just do what we need to do to get by.

Cori layers on a critique of the state provisioning system, pointing to the
ways in which inefficiencies cause problems. This sentiment illuminates
Cori's sense of the politics of adequacy, that an adequate food system would
not have such inefficiencies, the people would not "starve while waiting."

I followed up on these points by asking: "How do you apply these
principles or ideas in your everyday life?" Cori responded:

> I have worked in gastronomy since the 1980s. I have always taken food
> from my jobs, and it doesn't hurt anyone but the state. I sell things to
> the public to satisfy a need, and I am also part of the public, so I have
> needs as well, and that is the money that comes from selling those things.
> I sell beefsteak now, it's something everyone wants, [and] I make people
> happy. I always have at least three or four steaks in my house for the
> family to consume at any time. But there is always a boss, and sometimes
> that boss is more skilled than you are or there are angry people trying to
> preserve the triumph of the revolution. But it's not about who preserves
> the revolution, it's about the laws of life in a group of people. Here we
> are, like for example playing dominoes and someone says there's no
> money, let's rob a bank and someone else is going to say you're crazy, and
> others will say no no, *compadre*, count me out: it's not the right thing
> to do. It's known that it's wrong, but in other things we agree they are
> OK even if the state says it's not.

Illuminating where santiagueros perceive a shift in the ethics of acquisition, distribution, and consumption, Cori unravels some of the complex
layers of the shifting ethics of acquisition as the long-standing ethics of
socialist consumption move in and out of alignment—sometimes acquiring goods with particular tactics can be seen as a way of upholding the
revolution, other times these acts undermine it. Cori reflects on the strategies that are a calculation of power relationships between the state and the
people, and how such strategies are ethically justified. There are still some
clear boundaries of "the right thing to do," even as one becomes increasingly desperate and the shifting ethics of acquisition feel like a slippery
slope; an act like robbing a bank still seems preposterous and is clearly not
a part of living a good life, socialist or not.

As much as Cori and others work to justify and explain why some
seemingly unethical acts are indeed virtuous and necessary to keep the so-

cialist system functioning, not everyone agrees. During my interview with Yaicel, also a member of Carla's household introduced in chapter 4, her friend Flavia stopped by to say hello. As Yaicel was completing her thoughts, Flavia interrupted her interview to make sure that I knew that not everyone agreed about the ethics of pilfering. She said:

> No, it's not necessary to steal, and what's more important is that it's not necessary to always have new clothes! Wear the same clothes you wore last year. Look, right now I could sell food out of my front window, but think about the time and the effort and the stealing that I have to do in order to do this, and without a *patente* [license] it's illegal. Why would I do all of these things, these stressful things when I can just learn to be happy with what I have? But there are too many Cubans who don't want to work, or don't know how to work honestly, and they just want to have more and more stuff so they steal, or they sell their bodies, without any ethics, and feel like its OK because that's the only way they can get these amounts of stuff.

Like Cori's example of robbing a bank, Flavia framed illegal food vendors as people who are only motivated by material objects, new clothes, more clothes, who are willing to go to extreme measures that are also clearly in the realm of "not right." She links stealing to prostitution (selling their bodies) and notes that people are doing these things "without any ethics." For Flavia, there is a clear demarcation that any illegal acts motivated by material accumulation are not right.

Also reflecting on the connections between individual actions and a broader community ethics, Matitis, a 41-year-old low-income *mulata*-identified woman working as a maid in a middle-income home in the city center, rattled off a set of Cuban refrains that she felt pertained to the food situation; for her the crux of the problem is a loss of ethics and a loss of Cuban character:

> No, it's not that the food is expensive, it's that the salaries are low and that *el cubano* is very materialistic, very obsessed with consumption. We always want to have new things, more and more and more and more. People who have the good sense to think and plan, people who organize their lives will have enough to feed their families.

Interjecting with a clear stance against the rise of materialism, Matitis highlights that it is virtuous to "plan" and "organize" in ways similar to the women detailed in chapter 4. While Matitis is clear in her ethical orientation, this assertion that the origins of the problem lie somewhere else, in this case another ethical orientation to materiality, gives a sense that ethical orientations to new forms of food acquisition are still not clear. This unmooring of ethics leaves the ethics of food access up for debate and contemplation; indeed this untethering of ethics is likely part of why so many of my research participants openly reflected on this topic.

While many people blame the government's lack of oversight for the problem of pilfering, it is not clear whether more government oversight would result in better or worse food access. Those who work within the system, like Cecelia and Ramira, have concluded, like Cori, that pilfering is necessary to make the system work. On the acquisition side, some consumers try to combat this situation by bringing their own scales to weigh their foods, while others combat it by building strong relationships with food vendors and trying to establish an honest, trust-based relationship. This augments the need for strong social networks in times of scarcity. However, the successful hustler is always innovative and finds new ways to trick the system, so it is nearly impossible for users to always stay one step ahead of these professional hustlers. Furthermore, users cannot interject to stop the pilfering that happens at earlier points in the food system.

Luchando la Vida Versus Getting Ahead

Like the many viewpoints on ethical consumption reflected upon by Flavia and Matitis, there are more distinctions between engaging in unethical activities to a more-or-less virtuous end—to get by, to fight for life, etc.—versus engaging in unethical means to arrive at unethical ends, such as "getting ahead." This distinction helps to illuminate the ways in which the socialist ethic of egalitarianism is still important for santiagueros despite the questionable ethics of most people's tactics. In Cori's narrative, the acts of reselling pilfered goods for profit is not only part of making the struggling provisioning system work but also as a way of getting ahead. He justifies this as necessary for survival, but in the following case of Lisandra and Rudy, getting ahead is a way to live a better, more luxurious life at the expense of the collective. This form of pilfering to get ahead has different ethical interpretations than those that pertain to the actions of Cori.[8]

Lisandra and Rudy: A Case of Upper-Income Household Food Acquisition

Lisandra, 59 years old, and Rudy, 61 years old, live in a newly built modestly sized home in an upper-class Santiago neighborhood. They have been married for 34 years and have two adult children; Miguel, their 33-year-old son, lives at home with them and Sandy, their 35-year-old daughter, lives in Spain. Sandy married a Spanish man who frequently visited Cuba as a tourist; she has lived in Spain for ten years and sends large sums of money, about 100 euro, home to her parents each month. With these remittances Lisandra and Rudy were able to move out of their old neighborhood, San Pedrito, a lower socioeconomic area, and into their current home and neighborhood. Lisandra identifies as *mulata*, and Rudy identifies as Black. Their son Miguel identifies as *jabao*—defined as having light but not white skin, with wavy or curly hair. Both Lisandra and Rudy earn income informally. Lisandra sells homemade juices and candies out of her house, and Rudy owns a motorcycle that he rents to people by the day.

Lisandra does all of the household food-related tasks, including all of the food acquisition. As she puts it: "Limpiar todos los días, cocinar todos los días—es el destino de una mujer cubana." (Cleaning every day, cooking every day—it is the destiny of a Cuban woman). Rudy dedicates his time to fixing things around the house and working on the motorcycle. Like others, Lisandra's food acquisition is thoroughly planned and budgeted. She does all of her additional meat, fruit, and vegetable shopping on Saturdays at the weekend farmers' market one block from her home. She rarely buys food items at CUC stores and does not purchase foods from ambulant street vendors; because she recently moved to the area she does not trust the vendors here because she does not know them.

Lisandra and Rudy never have to borrow food or money from friends or family; however, they have had a hard time dealing with the number of friends and family members who want to borrow from them. Due to their physical relocation to a nicer neighborhood and their shift in economic class, they have a wide social circle within lower socioeconomic classes and fewer friends who are well off. Because of these changes they have been faced with dilemmas surrounding how much they can help out their friends and family financially. They have explicitly decided to stop lending money or goods to anyone and developed an explicit policy to never offer anything more than water to guests, refusing any requests for coffee, snacks, or meals. When they moved into their new home, they renovated the space so that there was a small front living room in which to receive guests that would shield their eyes and imaginations from the objects of wealth inside. This was both to protect themselves from people who might take advantage of their situation by asking to borrow too much and to protect them from people who would possibly report them to the authorities.

In addition to the food acquisition practices described above, Lisandra and Rudy regularly purchase large amounts of rice on the black market, so that they are able to keep bulk quantities and do not have to buy so often. This illegal purchase is made through a connection with a bodega employee. Several times per year a 100-pound sack of rice is delivered to their home just before sunrise. The rice, stolen from the rations of their neighbors, is nearly one-tenth the cost of buying additional rice off the ration and helps to solve the problem of unpredictable shortages for this family. In an interview Lisandra reflected on this situation to me:

> Sometimes it is difficult when I start to hear "There is no rice! There is no rice!" neighbors tell me that they didn't get their ration this month; others come to me asking to borrow rice. It's hard because I know that the rice I have makes it harder for them to get rice, but it is what I have to do to get ahead. We have the possibilities to buy rice like this and it saves us the money and trouble of getting the ration rice.

Faced with the discomfort of knowing that her black-market activity directly and indirectly causes her friends and neighbors strife, Lisandra expresses a feeling of remorse but still justifies her actions as "the only way to get ahead." Lisandra's situation is one where the alternative to *not* participating in the black market creates stress and financial strain. In order to escape this and move toward achieving her life goals, she chooses to buy rice on the black market.

Similar to the questionable ethics of acts motivated by excessive materialism and the desire to get ahead, hoarding illegally acquired food for personal consumption rather than reselling it, giving it away, or sharing it is considered to be "not right" by many Cubans. This distinction between getting by and getting ahead is important, as it demonstrates the boundaries of ethical conduct and illuminates the ways socialist ethics remain present as part of people's desire to maintain Cuba's socialist provisioning system. This is a gray area of community ethics. It is hard to determine where the line between getting ahead and getting by lies, but households that are clearly on the side of getting ahead will eventually be called out by their neighbors, friends, and family as "not right."

"We each have a cabinet with a lock": Not Sharing with Family

Pilfering from the state and by proxy from faceless community members is a widely known part of life in still-socialist Cuba. In rare instances, families also have to combat pilfering within their own households. Sharing food between family members and within households is part of the commonly understood ethics of feeding in Cuba; as the previous chapter elaborated, it is a central part of gendered household dynamics and social forms of care. When food is systematically not shared between family members, for many Cubans there is a sense of "moral breakdown" (Zigon 2008) that comes to light in the moments where people grapple with the tensions between the need to eat and moral obligations to one another (Zigon 2007). In these moments of moral breakdown santiagueros are able to reflect on the unmooring of what they conceive of as their socialist ethics in a realm where it is unclear at all whether certain practices are necessary, acceptable, or instead something that is "not right." For example, Regina's household, detailed in chapter 3, developed a system to address the fact that food seemed to regularly go missing from the household. As I noted previously, Regina's household has 24 people officially registered in it, and although only eight people regularly eat there, several other household members come through the house each day. Regina and others often found that the food that they were counting on would go missing throughout the day. Although her own family members likely ate the food, Regina felt that she needed to be able to rely on maintaining some basic food staples available for meals. To resolve this problem she and her brother built six small cabinets with locks on them to store food and other valuable items, so that those six adults could ensure the reliability of their food supply.

When she explained this to me, Regina lamented having to put locks on cabinets in her own home. She reflected that in the past they were able to share food items within the household, but as their economic reality became difficult, borrowing with the intention to return a similar item in the future slowly shifted into stealing. This developed into a situation where brothers and sisters, mothers and sons really wanted to share food but felt that they could not trust the other family members not to steal from them. The family reflected on the locked cabinet system as sad, shameful, and unfortunate, but at the same time they felt it was the only solution to be able to retain the food items that each person had purchased.

As Mickey stated toward the beginning of the chapter, in many Cubans' reflections "people had better hearts" before and "they were more human," and santiagueros believe that food scarcity has led people to do things that they do not view as right. This notion that things used to be better is a reflection on the fact that during previous eras food was abundant, easily accessed, and therefore shared among friends and family without a second thought. This is in contrast to a shift after the Special Period, where scarcity of many goods has led people to reorient to food as something of (monetary) value, which they are more careful about sharing with others. For Mickey and many others, to not share food among family, ostensibly the most important and most closely knit social unit in Cuban society, is a deeply disturbing social manifestation of the loss of a traditional orientation to family and community. The locked cabinet system in Regina's household is one of the ultimate signs of the moral failings of the Cuban food system, reflecting how deeply inadequate this system is as families are no longer able to share food and trust one another.

Conclusions: Social Relations and the Shifting Ethics of Consumption

This chapter focused on the social dimensions of the politics of adequacy by turning attention to ways in which Cubans reflect on the ethical issues surrounding their tactics of food acquisition. The social dimensions are characterized by sociolismo, the system of cooperative interdependence, palanca (leverage), and access to the social networks. One of the clearest effects of the changing Cuban food system on social relations is in the shifting ethics of food acquisition. This shifting ethics and rise in the use of "unethical" tactics is one indication of the inadequacy of the current food system. The changing food system leaves Cubans faced with the dilemma of needing to eat but only being able to access food by way of unethical practices. In this chapter I revealed how Cubans problematize the ethical conundrums they find themselves in as they must take part in unethical practices to acquire basic needs, and what this means for their lives.

Several research participants have alluded to certain practices that were simply "not right," from not sharing food with family members, to unethical forms of pilfering, to "getting ahead." These forms of food acquisition might include certain unethical forms of pilfering from the state, which is to be distinguished from those that are considered to be acceptable. For instance, Ramira makes the distinction between the two, characterizing those that are "not right" as done by people "with no aspiration for their lives" or "no education." I interpret this characterization as the distinction between those who carefully plan and calculate when it is necessary to pilfer from the state versus those who do it carelessly and excessively for their own personal benefit, drawing attention to themselves and jeopardizing everyone else who is linked to their practices. In another case, in Regina's home, the situation where it is necessary to lock one's food in a cabinet to prevent household members from eating it is another clear sign of a breakdown in the long-standing forms of social relations that Cubans have come to expect. The data demonstrate the ways in which Santiago families are constantly tacking back and forth between tactics and strategies, skirting the edges of ethical practices. Along with their actions, their reflections on the social meaning of their actions also tack back and forth, establishing a loop of logic to reflection on a shifting ethics of acquisition. If they must engage in unethical activities to get by, this is evidence of the deep inadequacies of the provisioning system.

This breakdown is caused at least in part by the faltering food system. When food has long been communal and at the very least shared at the household level, to see food scarcity reach the point where members within a household begin to lock their food away from their own family members is a clear transition in social relations that is connected to the inadequate food system. In this context food can no longer be the locus of care for family and friends. It can no longer cement social bonds. Then, others reference the unethical dimensions of getting ahead, which signal a different stance toward acquisition than the ways in which people use illicit channels just to get by; getting ahead may be taking this too far. Unethical practices of acquisition used for getting ahead are among the practices that contribute to the growing inequalities in post-Soviet Cuba, and these growing inequalities are part of what make many Cubans uneasy about their changing reality. Getting ahead undermines the socialist distribution system, favors individual or nuclear family priorities over community, and signals an orientation to the collective that is not a part of the socialist ideal. The existence of these forms of consumption create a sense of insecurity and uncertainty about Cuba's future and is a sign of the precariousness of particular ideologies of Cuban decency and good character that have been refined under socialism. The jeopardization of such fundamental aspects of Cuban life illuminates another dimension of the politics of adequacy here. For most Cubans, an adequate food system would not require compromising ethical standards for acquisition and orientations to family, friends, and collective needs in this way.

These shifts in the ethics of food acquisition affect Cubans' deep-seated ideological orientations to collectivism over individualism, a change that significantly impacts social relations. A lingering desire to maintain socialist ideals persists in the background of these practices that vacillate between facilitating and undermining the socialist state. Some of the narratives presented here illustrate santiagueros' feelings of frustration and ambivalence with the shifting definition of the scope of ethical consumption practices. As I outlined in chapter 2, socialist Cuba's nationalist ideologies include an established orientation to the collective that has historically been prioritized over individual desires with respect to consumerism. With the food scarcities of the Special Period, as people turn toward more reliable, concrete social networks, many are forced to choose between collectivism and more self-oriented consumption decisions. Paradoxically, as the state system falters, consumers must increasingly rely on collective activity and work within the public sphere in order to be able to fulfill their individual basic needs. Social networks for consumption expand and contract in different ways: some consist of only close family while others expand across neighborhoods to distant friends and relatives. Santiagueros and people across Cuba also increasingly rely on the black market for food access. This is another form of increasing collective activity. However, the increase in collective activity does not necessarily indicate a particular ethical stance—reliance on social networks and community resources may be in the interest of serving individual or familial needs only. On the other hand, there are clear moments of conscious reflection on collective need documented here. As Cori observes, there are many ways in which ethical values are not commensurate with the current reality. There is a breakdown happening here that opens a space for ethical reflection (Zigon 2008, 2007). The types of reciprocal exchanges via the legitimate market as well as the black and gray markets are part of an elaborate ethics of exchange that santiagueros often interpret as virtuous and necessary to maintain their ideal way of life.

Looking across socioeconomic status and neighborhood, this shifting ethics of acquisition is not happening in the same ways across demographics. In this context lower-income families rely more heavily on borrowing and lending within their families and communities, and networks of fictive kin, thus increasing reliance on the collective and building community in particular ways. Although the increasing reliance on social networks is nearly ubiquitous in Santiago de Cuba, the realities of relying on social networks rather than an adequate state provisioning system have resulted in new inequalities and exacerbated existing inequalities. For those in low-resource settings, this means that the networks upon which they rely for their basic needs are also resource poor, meaning that there is less to go around in the communities with the most need. Those with a higher socioeconomic status are able to draw on a privileged set of resources to get by, and some, like Lisandra and Rudy, may take this too far, verging into unethical territory by trying to get ahead.

In Mickey's opening quote to the chapter, he very clearly articulates a course of events that have taken place in Cuba since the Special Period. He begins by reiterating and detailing, as many others have told me, the forms of struggle, of suffering, that Cubans went through during the worst of the Special Period. This is the context he provides to explain why Cubans have had a "change in disposition" and why the "mind of the Cuban has suffered." Cubans today are transformed by their practices of acquisition and are thus shifting their own ethics of interacting with one another. Nonetheless, because the socialist ethics of equality and an orientation toward the collective good still have salient meaning for most Cubans, these shifts in community interaction bear significant meaning on the ways in which Cubans conceptualize themselves as decent people, living a good life. While this chapter has focused on the ways in which community life has been impacted by a changing ethics of acquisition, in the following chapter I turn to the individual and reflect on the ways socioeconomic changes in Cuba impact individual subjectivity as well as the ways in which this changing ethics of community interaction affects individual subjectivity.

5

Breakdown

On July 28, 2010, I was challenged to *madrugar* (to stay up until sunrise) during one of the final days of the annual weeklong Carnaval celebrations. Santiago de Cuba is home to Cuba's most famous Carnaval, and santiagueros and Cubans across the island anticipate the annual celebration throughout the year. The festivities culminate in the celebration of the 26th of July, the date commemorating the attack on Santiago's Moncada Barracks in 1953 by Fidel Castro and the 26th of July Movement before he was exiled to Mexico where he regrouped to plan the Cuban Revolution. However, for most of the households I worked with, the most important part of Carnaval was a chance to relax and have fun.[1] During the celebration, local offices close and the majority of santiagueros are not expected to work; even those who do not participate in the street festival are able to spend the time relaxing at home. For others, it is the only time of year when the state subsidizes beer and provides street food vendors for round-the-clock partying.

That year Carnaval fell while I was studying Carla's household. Carla, introduced in chapter 1 and 4, was the head of a household consisting of four generations. The younger members of the family, Yaicel and Yordanis, along with their significant others, all in their twenties, had been celebrating Carnaval in full force that year—going out each night around 10 p.m. and not returning home until 7 a.m. to sleep away most of the day. They had been doing this for more than seven days, and while I had been joining them each night, I had yet to stay up until sunrise. Accepting their challenge, on the last night of Carnaval that year I promised I would stay with them until dawn. We had been drinking the cheapest state-subsidized beer—watery and with little carbonation, it functioned to keep us hydrated and just barely intoxicated if we sipped it all night long. We had moved from the Santa Úrsula neighborhood party area, the hottest spot to party that year by all accounts, to the most crowded party area in a neighborhood called Sueño. There we ran into another set of friends and our night was reinvigorated, as we had hoped. We shared five-peso street pizzas, and continued to drink state-subsidized beer, while we danced away our sleepiness.

Just as the dark sky began to slowly brighten, the DJ played the hit song of the summer, "El Cachito" ("A Little Piece") by Kola Loka, a reggaeton group from Santiago de Cuba that had recently gained national and international fame. Those of us left in the streets dancing sang along with the song, belting out its words together. Our small group stopped dancing to watch a man near us, red-faced and sweaty from a night of drinking and dancing, begin to cry as he belted out the words. His tone shifted from innocent fun to palpable pain:

> Ahhhhh yo lo que quiero es un cachito pa' vivir
> Dame un cachito mi cielo pa' ver si yo soy feliz
> [. . .]
> Un cachito de cualquier cosa pa' yo ser feliz
> Puede ser un refresquito gaseado o un cucurucho de maní
>
> Ahhh what I want is just a little piece to live
> Give me a little bit my love to see if I am happy
> [. . .]
> A little bit of anything so I can feel happy
> It could be a soda or a tube of roasted peanuts.

The man threw his head back, stretched out his arms, and belted out the lyrics toward the sky. With tears streaming down his face, his singing turned into yelling and became angrier and angrier. My group of friends completely stopped dancing and, as the song ended, Yordanis looked at each of us and said, "Ya vámonos" (That's enough, let's go). The group split up and we walked toward our respective neighborhoods. While we were walking, I asked Yaicel why she thought that man was so emotional over that song. She said:

> After being here for so long you must understand it by now. We just
> want a little piece, *un cachito*, to feel happy. That little piece can be love,

which is sometimes what the song is about, or it can be a soda, or for the
humblest people, just the possibility to buy some peanuts. Sometimes
we just can't take it anymore. It's enough to make you go crazy, to break
down and cry in the middle of Carnaval, the best time of the year. But
when you know it is over tomorrow and you have to go back to life, you
just wish your life was not always a struggle.

To go from the joys of the height of celebration to a contagious feeling
of desperation and exasperation is a ubiquitous part of life for many santiagueros. The nexus of emotions that contemporary Cubans feel in the
face of the struggle of their daily lives, amid the contradictions of hopes,
desires, and disappointments surrounding the social and political structures in which they are enmeshed, has ongoing repercussions for the lived
experience of post-Soviet socialist Cuba. Struggling along, day in and day
out, has become exhausting; there appears to be no end in sight, and some
grow weary.[2] Indeed, as Yaicel's grandmother Carla elaborated in her reflections on her life, life for many Cubans has long been characterized by
relentless hard work. Yet, despite these intergenerational struggles with the
difficulties of everyday life, people continue to push forward, striving to
live a good life. Weighed down by the standards of the past, what one is
able to achieve in this new context does not necessarily meet local ideals of
a good life. People cling to what appears to be lost or fading away. Local
notions of decency carry a lot of weight for assessing the good life, but
when decency is nowhere to be found, it becomes clear that the good life is
slipping away, and feelings of guilt, shame, and uncertainty creep in. This
has a deeply affective hold on santiagueros. The inability to achieve a decent standard of living spins into a cycle of questioning and renegotiating
how people perceive their social position in relation to imagined pasts, an
idealized present, and an anticipated future. Seemingly small acts in everyday life serve as a constant reminder of this loss; when you cannot even
get a little bit of something you want, it may signify that things are falling
apart. Santiagueros fear that they are losing themselves. The precariousness
of everyday life calls in to question local considerations of humanity, of
Cubanidad. Indeed, Cubanidad is life as they know it.

Building on the connection between food and identity, I want to turn
to the social and emotional dimensions of the politics of adequacy, or forms
of distress that manifest as people struggle through living with an inadequate
provisioning system. These forms of distress that people live through are not
necessarily permanent states; indeed they are juxtaposed with great amounts

of joy, humor, and celebration. In this chapter I analyze how Cuba's chang-ing food system impacts individual lives, social positions, and interpersonal relationships (Good 2012; Good et al. 2008), and how (in)adequacy can give rise to certain forms of existential fragility (Jenkins 2015). Food access becomes a node linking individual and collective experience. The ability to consume a decent meal, access a dignified cuisine, and sit down to a meal together become an "inhabitable space" in which santiagueros are able to "live out their existential imperatives" (Willen 2014, 84), including self-care, social relations, and sustaining the practices that ground their lives. In post-Soviet Cuba, the emotional experience of the political subject is necessarily postcolonial. Building on the political dimensions of the poli-tics of adequacy laid out in the previous chapters, in this chapter I turn to the ways in which "politics" in late-capitalism, and in this case post-Soviet socialism, can produce and sustain particular emotional reactions and in turn how the ongoing effects of these forms of distress are experienced by individuals (Mankekar 2015).

To illuminate this connection, this chapter focuses on breakdowns. The breakdowns addressed here are characterized by moments when my research participants enter a highly emotional state, often one of anger or sadness. These breakdowns often happen when santiagueros face the fact that their ideas about the way that their lives should be do not align with the life they experience. The breakdowns tend to be moments when this frustration comes into their consciousness. Although a breakdown may last for a long time, people often bounce back from them. While I consider each vignette to be some sort of breakdown, the breakdowns are somewhat different in character. Some are about the moments when people feel that they "can't take it anymore," when the daily struggle has worn on them so much that they have an emotional breakdown. Others, like the man who breaks down during Carnaval, or the sudden market closure that Monika experienced in chapter 3, involve moments that trigger someone to realize how difficult things have been for them, that the life they are living is not what they had dreamed for themselves. One might break down and just eat cake for lunch when one cannot access the food one wants. Or a breakdown might be experienced while talking about the difficulties of food access and the accumulation of the moments of breaking down and eating cake or pizza. Additionally, a breakdown could be a realization that as times have changed, so have people and their behaviors. These emotional breakdowns can have a contagious effect, causing those who witness them to feel uncomfortable and possibly have a breakdown of their own. Strong anger or extremely sad emotional displays are not common in public spaces, and this breach of social norms can have an effect that reverberates through other people. Indeed, some people in Cuba go to great lengths to emotionally prepare themselves to hold it together in public (see Garth 2013).

These forms of breakdown are often moments when santiagueros realize that the content of their daily lives is out of sync with their vision of what they are striving for, their concept of a good life. These are moments that can be experienced as an "impasse" a sense of being stuck, unable to launch forward into the realization of a dream life (Berlant 2011). That stuckness also reverberates through the breakdown, and the pain of the stuckness can be soothed with forms of immediate gratification, like a piece of cake or a slice of pizza. In the moment of the breakdown, people are forced outside of their taken-for-granted way of being in the world and forced to reconcile the aspects of their lives that are incommensurate with their idealization of life.

Food and the Mind

Omara and Eugenio are a well-off couple married for 19 years, living in an old aristocratic neighborhood—Vista Alegre. Omara worked as an accountant in a state factory and Eugenio was in the military. Although they live in a large, old house now, their family did not come from wealth; Omara's parents had been given this property in return for their service to the socialist revolution. She and her husband, 15 years her senior, were devout socialists with two adult children, Cristina and Yasmanis. While they had more economic resources than others in Cuba, they still struggled to make ends meet and find all of the food that the family needed. In reflecting on this situation, Omara told me that she was tired, deeply deeply tired, and she just wanted to rest her mind.

On the breezy patio of their lovely colonial-era home, I sat down with both of them for our final interview after I had spent two weeks studying their household. Omara served cold beers to me and Eugenio. They were the only family in my study well off enough to keep cans of cold beer on hand and drink them even when it was not a special occasion. As Omara drank her beer she started the interview on her own:

> Omara: My daughter is interested in diet and nutrition, and she wants to study this, but she is crazy. I tell her "but here there is no nutrition."

Eugenio: Why you going to study that, when here there is no food? She has her issues, she is not living in reality. She went crazy.

Hanna: What exactly made her crazy?

Omara: The same stress of the same things, the same everyday needs, you understand? The same stress you have when you need to buy something and you can't have it.

Hanna: That made her go crazy?

Omara: Huh? Of course it did! Because this life is all in accordance with the capacity of each individual, but there are people who, who they get sick and, and. . .

Eugenio: Because there are people who year in and year out it is the same thing, start a new year, end a year, start a new year, end a year—looking for things. It is the same, the same, the same, the same, and we don't see a way to get out of it. All minds are not equal, and for some these things, this, this always looking for things that you can't find, it is too much. On top of other problems, and complications, and hurricanes, and your house falls down, and you don't have water, and there is no food, there is no food, there is no food . . . If there is a primordial thing here, it is food. You start to ask what am I going to eat today, what am I going to eat today, and tomorrow what am I going to eat? You go to the market with your 200 pesos and you get back to your house and you say "what did I buy" you say "I earned 200 pesos and I came back with nothing" . . . for me, nutrition, eating, is fundamental because you have to eat three times a day every day, you need to sustain yourself so you can work. But you also have to sustain your mind, you have to know that you are eating well, and know that you can get what you need.

The interview continued going off on some tangents, but later Omara brought us back to the topic of food.

We are taking care of my grandmother who is 93 years old and she can only eat soup—three times a day, soup. We have to find the ingredients for homemade soup and sometimes we cannot find what we need. But we have to; we cannot give her the soup in packages—that will kill her. So we struggle to make soup.

These examples of struggling to assemble soup, of "going crazy" about the idea of nutrition and feeding yourself, are central to the politics of adequacy; these conversations reflect Cubans' understanding that an adequate food system would not lead them to "go crazy" or struggle in these ways.[3] There is a sense that people have in mind a particular type of cuisine that they want to consume—that they "need" and feel they have the right to consume, but when they go out and try to get all of the ingredients to put it together they cannot do it; either they do not have enough money because the ingredients have skyrocketed in price, or the ingredients are not available. They characterize this as a struggle, as something that provokes feelings of stress, and some feel that they are "going crazy." In a setting where there is little to no problem with hunger and malnutrition, we can see the ways in which food is more than mere physical sustenance; here it is also consumed to sustain the mind, to be assured that things are alright.

While families assemble things to eat based on what is rationed to them, or what the state sells in subsidized markets, foods referred to as "whatever appears," most families have particular ideas about what meals should consist of and which ingredients are essential for assembling a proper meal. Despite their efforts, many cannot assemble everything necessary to consume meals that meet their standards. These families are constantly struggling to acquire the ingredients necessary to assemble a decent meal. They are struggling to fit what they have always done into a shifting context, and while it may work on a case-by-case, meal-by-meal basis, it results in levels of stress and anxiety that make everyday life exceedingly difficult. Across social class, the ability to access particular foods, then, goes beyond physical health vis-à-vis sufficient nutrition, to include existential nourishment of the mind and whole being.

Similar to the stresses of food acquisition that Omara and her family face, María Julia, introduced in chapter 1, where I described the horrors that María Julia felt after receiving spoiled or very low-quality products from the ration stations, felt that she had no control. The inability to turn elsewhere leaves patrons like María Julia feeling extremely frustrated and stressed out about how they will acquire food that meets their standards of quality. On several occasions while studying María Julia's household, she became extremely angry while talking to me about food. In one such instance, I was asking her about why rates of obesity appear to be on the rise in Cuba. I pointed out that Cuban cuisine has always been relatively high in fat and high in carbohydrates, and I asked María Julia what she thought had changed. She was agitated and replied:

> There used to be other options . . . before you could . . . Look, before, like I told you at the beginning, before there were options. When I was

a girl and my mother and father went to look for produce, there was always something available. We ate vegetables with our meals, we had that tradition then. But now, who can afford that? What you can buy [with your salary] might last you one day. Do you think that we could afford to go to the vegetable market everyday?

I asked her what people have begun to consume more of instead of vegetables, and she replied.

Wheat, flour. It is cheap. Think about it, how much does a pizza cost? A cake? Two pesos. It is wheat. It kills your hunger, fills you up but it does not nourish you. You know the other day at the work cafeteria in Vista Alegre they only served plain white rice, no sauce, no beans, nothing. So what do people do to feel satisfied, they go to the street and buy a two peso cake. That makes you feel better.

María Julia started to get very agitated and began yelling.

Then at the end of the day, after having eaten nothing but a small cake all day, you get to your house and eat a full days worth of food at six in the evening and then go to sleep from exhaustion. That doesn't make you fat!? That doesn't make you fat?! and gives you ulcers! I have an ulcer!

She stood up from the table abruptly, pulled up her shirt, and pointed at her stomach, yelling loudly over and over again that she had an ulcer. I asked her to calm down and stop yelling. Remaining in her standing position she became even more angry:

Stop yelling!?! You don't understand me! You don't understand what I am saying! No! People are sick here with anxiety and they start eating crap!! Do you hear me Hanna?! People are sick with nerves and anxiety and it makes them sick!

María Julia was so upset that we had to end the interview. She sat down, and her mother brought her some warm jasmine tea. She and I sat in the rocking chairs in the living room and listened to a Juan Luis Guerra CD to try to help her calm down. We both apologized to each other, and I thanked her for her willingness to explain things to me, telling her that just seeing how upset she was talking about food access had clarified the gravity of the situation.

To move from talking about the lost tradition of eating vegetables, to yelling about an ulcer, to self-soothing with loud music and rocking chairs, this cycle of emotion that is palpable in María Julia's interview is precisely the emotional spiral that she describes herself and others going through. Frustrations with the seemingly never-ending daily struggle of searching for ingredients, struggling to piece together meals, facing sudden changes in the state-provided lunch at work are central to the lived experience of food access in Cuba. In turn, eating cake to soothe anxiety and stave off hunger, or "resting the mind" as Monika did in chapter 1 (see also Garth 2013), becomes part of the emotional and social process for dealing with the frustrations of the food distribution system.

In these interactions the precariousness of a stable state of mind and well-being come to light. It is highly telling that these moments of reflecting on the food system, thinking through the processes of acquiring food, a seemingly mundane daily activity, result in breakdowns. In this context it is the Cuban state, a political apparatus that distributes food to the population, which delivers just enough to prevent hunger and malnutrition, but not enough to stop extreme levels of stress and anxiety for Cuban consumers. In addition to stress and anxiety, the changing food system can also elicit feelings of depression and hopelessness as the following narrative from Manuel illuminates.

Manuel was 38-year-old, Black-identified, low-income santiaguero. The younger brother of Regina, introduced in chapter 1, Manuel lives in a small unlit, windowless, cinder-block room with a leaking tin roof that is attached to his sister's home. They share a toilet and water. In 2011 I sat with Manuel in his room to talk about Cuban life and the food system. As my eyes adjusted to the dark, I fumbled with my recorder while he cooked a piece of ham and an egg on an electric hot plate on his cracked cement floor. In a corner of the room along the crack in the floor greenish water pooled. As he sat on the floor and ate his very simple lunch, he reflected on the ways in which access to resources and forms of inequality affect contemporary Cuban life:

> People have lost all of their beautiful traditions, like sitting down to dinner as a family each night . . . it's totally lost because the mental development (*desarrollo mental*) has completely changed. The world has changed, love is harder, love is more difficult to find now, and already, friends are not true friends. I ask myself why . . . it appears that the world has turned upside down, moved backwards, regressed . . . People don't know what's happening, like Adam and Eve, they eat the forbidden fruit—they do it out of necessity. I see it as necessity, but it is also hopelessness. This is very big, people don't know what to do, and then

they are desperate to achieve what someone else has, they want to be on par with someone who has more means than them, but they can't be on this level. Everyone has to wait until their moment comes, there are people who reflect and understand that, and there are others who say, "When is my turn? My turn never comes, so I have to take it." So they lose the confidence and sincerity of many people, the friendships that were in the neighborhoods, people shared, everyone equally, and now it is all lost. Now even families are falling apart, everyone becomes independent; the union of the family is gone.

The process of social change that Manuel glosses as a "loss of tradition" was a common topic of reflection among my interlocutors in Santiago. As I have discussed, santiagueros are observing that the "character of the Cuban people has changed." Manuel also reflects on the breakdown of ethics and responsibility that come with the shifting forms of acquisition that santiagueros must undertake. The national-level changes to the Cuban provisioning system have created emergent forms of uncertainty and stress surrounding food acquisition, and the ability to consume a decent cuisine, shifting the ways individuals experience everyday life. These political economic changes have exacerbated inequalities for people in Cuba with darker skin, women, and those who experience various other forms of marginalization. The changes Manuel observes are tied to shifts in the ways Cubans experience everyday life in the post-Soviet period, shifts not unlike those experienced in postcolonial and neoliberal contexts all over the world, where the unsettling of long-established systems requires a shift in daily practices of life. The changes have led locals to think of their everyday life as a struggle. Wrapped up in that struggle are tensions that may lead to psychological and social breakdown through the loss of ethical relations, and the maddening process of searching endlessly for something that seems to never appear.

People experience the present via the ways in which they infuse memories and ideals into personal and communal experiences of present situations and events. These ways of interpreting such experiences are articulated and expressed through local discourses surrounding a decent cuisine. The "beautiful traditions" like sitting down to dinner as a family are part of what I found to be a normative view of what constitutes "the good life" for many santiagueros. There is a strong attachment to remembered pasts and idealized traditions that are disappearing in contemporary life. These reveries not only work as "free and pleasurable movement across space and time" (Varma

2016, 59), they also provide grounding for anticipatory futures. Manuel's dire living conditions and his reflections on his life illuminate the ways in which individual experiences of the present are also always social and political. When spaces indexical of the good life appear to diminish, there is a growing sense of panic surrounding the links between the changing structures of everyday life, peoples' sense of self, and how one becomes or remains a "good person." It is through these practices that many santiagueros cultivate and maintain their sense of self. Furthermore, it is by and through the relational practices surrounding food that santiagueros establish their subjective understandings of what it means to be a good person and a good Cuban. However, conducting these everyday practices is increasingly difficult as political economic structures hinder the ability to create such scenes in everyday household life.

This explains, at least in part, why so many of the families in my study go to such great lengths to acquire a decent and idealized cuisine, rather than simply fulfilling their caloric needs with other available foods. One example was detailed in chapter 1, with María Julia and Elvira's dissatisfaction with eggs as their protein source and Elvira's insistence on eating rice rather than pasta or another starch. My research participants exerted overwhelming efforts to acquire particular foods and consume them in particular ways as a means of holding on to traditional modes of life even though these efforts may have threatened their well-being in other ways. Lauren Berlant's work illuminates the importance of understanding the hold that objects of desire, such as a decent cuisine, can have on people's sense of who they are, arguing that this sort of "binding to modes of life . . . recasts the object of desire not as a thing (or even as a relation) but as a cluster of promises" (Berlant 2011, 16). In the case of my research, a meal, family dinner, dish, or particular ingredient may hold this level of promise. Santiagueros cling to "beautiful traditions of the past" as a way of giving shape to their own social positions in the present.

The tradition of family dinnertime is a ritual that, for many, establishes a sense of security with respect to the passing of time and constant change. Sitting down collectively to a daily meal is a regularly punctuated assurance that everything is not lost and that there is some hope for the faltering Cuban system. For many, mealtime is a secure time and space that people can rely on remaining relatively constant. This is a space for care of the self. But when the daily therapy of dinnertime is interrupted, suspended, or disappears entirely, that sense of security is lost and the temporal arc continues to move toward an unknown telos. Manuel eating alone in a dark room is a striking sign of things gone wrong. Is this the future? The insecurity of the unknown future heightens people's anxiety around maintaining a decent cuisine. Further, if the mood changes, the event changes.[4] Even if meals are consumed as a family and traditional cuisine is a common occurrence, this sense of precariousness, struggle, and urgent clinging to these moments tempers the comforting feeling and sense of security associated with family dinners. People are aware of and uncomfortable with how rare and difficult these moments are. Dinnertime is rendered a site of struggle, protest, resistance, and no longer a space of soothing assurance of the self; instead dinnertime underscores the struggle of daily life. Even as families sit down to traditional Cuban dinners, the struggle to acquire foods and the ways in which those moments seem to be fleeting creates "a sense of out-of-syncness" (Berlant 2011, 91) with local notions of what it means to be Cuban, and what it means to be a good person and to live the good life.

Not only are certain material goods and foods thought to be necessary for creating the spaces where cultural identity and individual sense of self are maintained, but the practices through which those goods are acquired, the modes of acquisition, are also associated with local ideals of what it means to be a good person. This is critical for the politics of adequacy. However, rather than finding comfort in the maintenance of tradition, the forms of anxiety and fears that arise from the threat of losing tradition often make the meal a site of contention and struggle (Berlant 2011). Manuel continued to expand on his feelings that Cuban traditions have been lost and Cubans today have changed. He said:

> The old way no longer exists, there is a new generation, and most of the people who have taught us how to be [Cuban] have disappeared. All those people who had the discipline, all gone and now those of us who are 40, 50, 60 years old have entered a new era, a new phase. But we could not, the youth have slipped through our hands, we have lost them with all of these catastrophic changes that have happened in the world. We could not make the youth think the same way that our parents did. [The youth] can't see, they can't see and even if you want to instill in them you can't. Say you're a politician and someone who wants, who doesn't want to educate themselves, they say to you "Hey old man, you're old." I mean, I am not old, I am the same as you, I dance the same as you, and [wear] the same clothes. . .well not the same clothes, not those American brands . . . because I have a strong conscience and I won't change who I am because I am a [Cuban] countryman. I am a realist,

I have my two feet fixed on the ground and my thoughts are fixed too.
I don't live in the air like those guys. . .they live in a fantasy world too
big to fall, too big, they don't adjust—they don't adjust to the system,
every day they are more and more ungrateful more, as I see it they have
lost friendship, true friendship is our great loss.

Manuel contrasts his generation with that of his more "disciplined" el-
ders, who have left his generation in charge of the unruly Cuban youth of
today. He references "catastrophic changes" that have led the youth to slip
through the fingers of his generation. For Manuel, while his generation
is firmly grounded in the reality of the fleetingness of material goods, the
younger generation of Cubans have been influenced by changes across the
globe in the circulation of material goods, media and technology, and the
movement of people and ideas, leaving them with the false sense of identity based on the forms of "commodity fetishism" that Manuel alludes to
and an inability to value close interactions with others.

Food as an Entitlement and Locus of Care

Manuel's notion of the tensions between discipline and chaos are palpable
in food acquisition. Through disciplined planning the decent meal is possible; without discipline people are unable to care for their families and
selves properly. Food *allocation* can be seen as a particular locus for discourses of nurturance and discipline. People link food allocation to local
ideas of individual responsibility to the family, as well as notions of the
state's duty to the people. These are also forms of care that are often linked
to neoliberalism and the welfare state respectively, but come together here
around one object. The ability to create and consume a decent meal as a
family has become a symbol of an ideal socialist life and the modern and
responsible socialist subject, loyal to the collectivist goals of the state.[5] This,
of course, does not mean that socialist subjects are not "self-governing,
self-fulfilling, self-empowering individuals and communities" (Sharma
and Gupta 2006, 47). It simply means that through the decent meal, the
socialist subject is nurtured, tethered to the socialist state, and grounded in
a particular imagined postcolonial community. When the decent meal is
absent, these groundings and tetherings loosen and open up the possibility
of some other connections between the subject and systems of power.

The making of the decent meal in turn disciplines the socialist subject. The foods allocated by the government and the appliances provided

FIGURE 14. Manuel's Feet on the Ground Outside His Home. Source: Author

for preparing them direct Cubans to structure their food preparation and other tasks in particular ways. As I elaborated in chapter 1, people must pick up their rations at three different places—bodegas, placitas, and carnicerías—and the various other locations where they must travel to get the nonrationed foods they consume. This creates particular temporal and spatial constraints. They do not know ahead of time what will be available at what prices, which necessitates a constant vigilance that directs human behavior in particular ways. Vigilance over the household requires full attention, leaving little time for other activity. Slippage, a loss of vigilance, may cause people to cling, to grab hold, and to insist on maintaining a particular way of life. They do the work that had been the job of the paternalistic state and struggle through the difficulties.

There is ongoing change and unpredictability surrounding any particular practice of food acquisition at any time. As illustrated in chapter 1, for most of my research participants, change is a viscerally experienced uncertainty and instability in everyday life. The mundane activities of everyday life are a constant reminder of this perpetual uncertainty. Tasks as simple as finding the ingredients for breakfast keep Cubans in a state of panic, unable to predict the effects of their actions, thus perpetuating the reach of Cuban state power. The state, in other words, through its very changeability has managed to make itself present within the most basic activities of daily life. State power and its uncertainties have permeated even the most basic daily tasks, shaping the lives and social relationships of santiagueros, and further changes are on the horizon. As much as we think them to be anomalies, uncertainties are a fundamental part of our lives. Arthur Kleinman contends that uncertainties "make life matter" (2006, 1).[6] Cuba's shifting food provisioning system is similarly thrusting Cubans into situations in which they are faced with dilemmas that give rise to larger questions about what it means to live a good life. What kind of life is worth living?

Although the paternalistic socialist state is seen as the ultimate provider in Cuba, in practice, spaces of care are most often located in the household. The decent meal becomes a space for both caring for kin and for care of the self. This space of care converges ethics with people's sense of who they are in the symbol of the meal. There is both an ethics of care in providing for others and an ethics as a "practice of freedom" for caring for and staying attuned to one's own sense of self.[7] These practices establish the conditions necessary for the "possibility of moral *experience*" (Csordas 2014, emphasis my own; see also Zigon and Throop 2014), or what I am calling "ethical *work*" at the locus of adequacy. The task of ethical work is "to establish the right relationship between intellect and character in the context of practical affairs" (Rabinow 1994, xxxiv).[8] The notion that a lack of nutrition might make Cubans "go crazy," as we saw in the opening vignette, is an expression of this point, turning our attention here allows for understanding of the "hidden and sometimes fraught articulations" of human need (Garcia 2014, 53). That is, it requires effort to maintain one's sense of self, and it is imperative to attend to regular daily needs, which include not only accessing sufficient nutrition, but also a decent meal that upholds one's sense of dignity and cultural identity. Merely eating to survive is not enough; Cubans feel that they must eat in particular ways to maintain their whole sense of sociocultural self. Furthermore, this is connected with the histories of Cuban orientations to the collective and the ideologies of anti-imperialism that have developed in Cuba since independence, as discussed in chapter 2. The desire to maintain culinary traditions and the insistence on a decent cuisine are ideological orientations that hold steady in the face of constant disappointments in the face of the changing Cuban political economic system. To insist upon a decent meal is also a way of acknowledging its loss.

Returning to Manuel's reflections on the changing ethics of food acquisition in Cuba, he states, "I ask myself why . . . it appears that the world has turned upside down, moved backwards, regressed . . . people don't know what's happening, like Adam and Eve they eat the forbidden fruit, they do it out of necessity. I see it as necessity, but it is also hopelessness." His words reflect a deeply emotional interpretation of individual and collective experiences of change in Cuba that is shared among many of my research participants. These changes in ethical ideals become compounded and tied up with other social issues in the imaginaries of people like Manuel. He continues (as quoted above):

> Everyone has to wait until their moment comes, there are people who reflect and understand that, and there are others who say, "When is my turn? My turn never comes, so I have to take it." So they lose the confidence and sincerity of many people, the friendships that were in the neighborhoods, people shared, everyone equally, and now it is all lost. Now even families are falling apart, everyone becomes independent; the union of the family is gone.

Many santiagueros experience the post-Soviet era as stagnant. They feel a sense of stuckness, and the ways they discuss their feelings about a shared historical present reveal that the struggle for a decent cuisine is a profoundly political struggle that is experienced as a type of identity crisis.[9] There is an overall sense that at least since the Special Period everyday life in Cuba has not improved, but it feels like this cannot be true, as we see noticeable improvements in daily life everywhere from the workplace to public spaces to the use of technology in homes. Many feel that the promises of the revolution have never come to Cuba, and the rest of the world has moved on. There have been so many reforms, so many opportunities, and yet no matter how hard they try, santiagueros still must struggle to make their lives better. The knowledge that things are changing, that new things, like microwave ovens, have arrived in Santiago and that one can buy or sell cars and property is part of what gives people hope that things will improve. However, the experience of the present as stagnant juxtaposed with previous dreams of a better life yield to layers of discontent with the present. This discontent with the present leads some santiagueros to dream of the good life, juxtaposing remembered past periods of abundance and imagined moral unity with dreams of the future.[10]

Remembered Pasts

The deeply emotional process of struggling for life every day in Cuba can often invoke past periods of emotional struggle, such as the Special Period. For instance, after discussing his troubles with fixing his crumbling house in 2011, and his memories of only eating ice during the worst of the Special Period in 1993, Julián stopped, realizing how many years he had been going through these struggles. He looked me straight in the eye and said: "Do you ever just want to weep into your mother's chest?" Tears welled up in his eyes, and he continued, "Sometimes when it is all too hard, I remember the comfort of my mother's breast as a small child, feeling safe there in her arms. Uninhibited crying, and a deep sense of protection. Sometimes I just want to be able to do that again." When the struggle becomes too much, people often reflect intensely on their lives, on who they have become. They may long for a different state of the present by invoking the past.

In times of trouble, food is a source of comfort. Food is a refuge where we turn to rekindle our sense of self. Through foods that are particularly closely linked to our identities, in this case rice, beans, viandas, and pork, among other things, food becomes a reflection of the self. We are what we eat. A dish can be a signifier of our cultural identity, and as we ingest food it literally becomes a part of us, becoming our bodies. In some instances food consumption can serve as a reinforcement of selfhood. However, in other cases food consumption can be unsettling—when the actual substances or the circumstances under which it arrived before us do not align with our physical and psychological needs for our food consumption. Here an inadequate provisioning system has given rise to a shift in practices of food consumption, in this case based in part on global food distribution patterns, and as practices of food consumption move away from how people envision their lives to be, in turn they question who they have become.

Conclusion: Struggling for Life in Post-Soviet Socialist Cuba

The constant need to struggle causes some, like Julián, to feel exasperated. However, the concept of struggling for life, luchando la vida, has multiple meanings and interpretations in Cuba today. The forms of luchando la vida discussed in chapter 4, struggling to make ends meet and struggling to make the faltering state system functional, are also related to the notion that luchando la vida means to struggle for life, to struggle to maintain a good life with a decent standard of living. To struggle in this way, *siempre en la lucha*, always in the struggle, is about having the self-respect to never let the difficulties of the socialist state plow through your sense of self and the good life. This struggle is central to the politics of adequacy and in turn the Cuban ethics of struggling for a good life as part of the Cuban ethos of what is right, illuminates to us the importance of understanding cross cultural struggles for adequacy. To maintain the struggle for a good life serves both individual quality of life and holds the state to a certain standard, working to uphold and strengthen the socialist state as well. The possibility of a better life propels people forward.

In the post-Soviet era, Cuban households are embattled between needs and desires, an increasingly fraught locus of struggle to maintain a decent quality of life impelled by memories of past periods of scarcity and fears of what sweeping economic reforms may bring in the future. Through these tensions and the vicissitudes of emotion that arise from such struggles, subjects may shift their practices of appropriation and meaning making, searching for new spaces of care and cultivation of the self (cf. Foucault 1988b, 1998). The meal, decent or not, is a tangible physical and social space for the cultivation of national and cultural identity, as well as connections to family and care for the self. It is also a manifestation and symbol of the collision between local desires and the transnational forces, like the global industrial food system, so deeply entrenched in Cuba. When signifiers like the decent meal and the family dinner become too difficult to grasp, or begin to signify something else entirely, and the social meaning that these social practices hold is not reinscribed elsewhere, people begin to question the meaning of their lives and who they are as people. In the case of Cuba, the realization that one is no longer regularly consuming the meals so deeply linked to identity results in an aperture that offers a glimpse into the realities of change and uncertainty. For some, this aperture sets in motion of sense of panic, a vociferous desire to maintain traditions and everything that they signify. Like Eugenio's description of the compounding of life difficulties—hurricanes, blackouts, and a constant feeling that there is no food—some santiagueros find themselves spinning around and around the same problems. The realization of this spinning can set off a feeling of panic, a desire to make it all stop, to get off the ride, to be somewhere else, but they cannot leave.[11] They may feel powerless. In the midst of pervasive powerlessness, clinging to the decent meal and all of the forms of struggle entailed there becomes a source of solace, a form of agency to maintain normalcy. At the same time this insistence on the decent meal creates considerable stress and anxiety. As Manuel illuminates, the affective dimensions of this struggle also include anxiety about the future and feelings of loss.

Struggling implies individual work toward improving life conditions, toward reflection on the ways the past and present collide with possibilities for the future. In his reflection on life in Cuba today, Manuel points to hopelessness as the cause for "the world turning upside down" and people doing things that are "not right" out of "necessity." Hopelessness and anticipation are entangled with fear and anxiety over the future. Manuel's characterization of the present demonstrates a loss of hope, the weakening of certain social ties, and existential uncertainty (Allison 2012, 2013; Mankekar 2015). Although to some hope appears to be lost, the move to struggle through difficulties implies some kernel of hope for a better life.

While suffering may "drive people to despair" (Parish 1996, 2), struggling implies a somewhat different relationship to the self. For some, the struggle is too arduous and appears to have no end in sight. As in the case of Cristina detailed above, and others, it can be maddening. For others, it offers a chance to reflect on the possibilities for their lives and for making meaning out of a collective identity, such as Cubanidad.[12] Like Manuel, these santiagueros ponder the cumulative effects of shifting ethics and the loss of traditional practices, wondering what it means for Cuban-ness writ large if everyone is different from how they used to be.

This chapter reveals Cubans' reflections on what an adequate provisioning system should be and the ways in which the inadequate food system impacts their everyday lives, leading to a cumulative effect on their social relationships and understandings of their own individual social positions in relation to others. For most of my research participants, an adequate food system would not lend itself to struggling or suffering in this way. Rather than give in to complete hopelessness, Cubans invest in a politics of adequacy, an insistence that living a good life is possible and that through an adequate provisioning system they must be able to access the basic entitlements necessary for that decent, dignified life that they deserve.

Conclusion
The Politics of Adequacy

On October 25, 2012, Santiago de Cuba was struck by Hurricane Sandy. The disastrous 124 mph (200 km) winds killed 11 residents and damaged over 170,000 homes, or nearly half of the local residences and the majority of public buildings. There was an estimated $2 billion USD in damages. Initially, brigades from all over Cuba were sent to help santiagueros recover from the storm. However, in the longer term, materials and labor for rebuilding homes and public buildings were scarce and difficult to access. Efforts to rebuild Santiago after Sandy were slow and steady, with plans to build and repair through 2019. It is clear that the damage of Sandy has forever changed Santiago de Cuba's landscape.

While Sandy was clearly disastrous for Santiago, the support pouring into the region in the aftermath has had some benefits for the city. The United Nations Development Program stepped in to assist. As part of the hurricane recovery and in celebration of the 500th anniversary of the city, Santiago received a new sea wall at the Bahia and improvements to the parks along the Paseo de la Alameda. New play structures for children were installed, and the Club Nautico restaurant was given new life. The principal shopping street, Enramadas, was completely refurbished, from the new cobblestone pedestrian-only street to the many new businesses that have sprung up along the street spanning from Plaza Marte to the newly refurbished Bahia.

My research participants and others have told me that these improvements provided a sense of relief, a sense of hope that things were getting better. Things seemed to be going so well in Santiago that a friend from Havana claimed that Habaneros were travelling to Santiago as tourists to go shopping and enjoy the new sights. Yet, in many ways these "improvements" only impacted leisure activities and did not seem to have a significant effect on the struggles of everyday life. Despite these improvements, the forms of food scarcity described throughout this book continued to be a daily source of stress for households in eastern Cuba. For example, in 2015 there were shortages of chicken in the rations and no chicken available on store shelves. María Julia told me of the ongoing stresses of food scarcity in 2015. She said: "There was no chicken in the rations or in the [unsubsidized] markets in [December and January], and even into the summer chicken was hard to find." She also remarked that, in addition to the chicken scarcity, there were changes in the food provided by her son's school: "And don't even talk about the school food, it is grave. Some days the children do not eat at all [at school]. Before [the school] always provided lunch and a snack. Imagine how much money and time I have to spend now!"

María Julia had always counted on the free lunch and snack provided by the state at her son's public school, but she was faced with the new tasks of either sending him to school with a packed lunch or finding time to leave work to prepare and serve him lunch. She viewed either option as a heavy burden on her time and money. This situation, in addition to the uncertain availability of meat products in the city, is just one example of the ongoing forms of stress that Cubans deal with related to food access.[1]

During my visit in summer 2017, María Julia warned me not to be fooled by all of the improvements along the central shopping street, Enramadas, and down by the Bahia; these were "only facades," and "if you look down the side streets, you will see the same pot holes, the houses falling down, people fretting over where their next meal will come from, and wondering when more water will arrive as their household tanks quickly empty." I interpret María Julia's analysis of the situation as another way of calling into question the politics of adequacy, of reflecting on what is an adequate foundation for living a good life.

In this book, I have interrogated and theorized the notion of adequacy, what makes a food system adequate, and how that facilitates the possibility of living a good life. The data that I have drawn upon to theorize adequacy reveal the dimensions of food consumption that matter beyond the caloric content. The politics of adequacy lie within Cubans' ongoing insistence on alimentary dignity and the right to the decent meal. This book began with

Amalia's search for corn, a story that reveals the everyday reality of food acquisition and touches upon many of the themes addressed throughout this book. Like Amalia, santiagueros continue to search for the foods that they desire in attempts to put together decent meals and maintain alimentary dignity, and they continue to insist upon their right to an adequate food provisioning system.

Since the 1960s, the Cuban government has poured resources into ensuring the equal footing of those who had been disenfranchised throughout the previous centuries. In the early years this was an imperfect effort to determine what was adequate for Cubans to thrive. While Cuba has maintained exceptional population-level health and social indicators, since the 1990s services and resources from the state have been slowly withdrawn and Cuban individuals, families, and communities have been forced to work together to maintain those excellent indicators. While levels of malnutrition and hunger are still extremely low, the daily work of food acquisition, including great deals of time, energy, and stress, is an essential factor impacting health. The forms of unpaid and unrecognized daily labor, so often shouldered by women and made more difficult by prejudice against dark-skinned and otherwise marginalized Cubans, also undermine well-being in ways that are not so easily captured by statistics or superficial analysis. Therefore, although some indices might give the appearance that Cuba's food system is adequate, a deeper analysis of the politics of adequacy, exploration into local concerns over basic needs and entitlements, and the day-to-day struggles that people face reveal the dimensions of inadequacy in Cuba's food system.

The fall of the Soviet Union and subsequent period of financial hardship in Cuba—the Special Period—was the impetus for an avalanche of changes, unpredictability, and insecurity that continue to be experienced in Cuba today. These events not only set off an economic crisis, but also unleashed a crisis of political and cultural identity: what did it mean to be among the few remaining socialist republics after the fall of the socialist world power? As the former Soviet and other Eastern European republics launched into postsocialism and China's ongoing market reforms moved it ever closer to a new form of socialism, Cuba lost its subsidized trade and was left with few allies. While Cubans often have a strong sense of identity apart from their political identification, this global shift in the socialist world left many wondering what the impact would be on their identity as socialists and anti-imperialists. However, as I illuminated in chapter 2, the socialist ethics of the New Man and the postcolonial formations of Cubanidad would

:he Cuban socialist state and Cuban citizens weary of the forms of ism that prevailed nearby. Cuba would not enter a postsocialist era but moved toward an emergent form of market socialism in the post-Soviet era. While Cuban socialism is unique and this form of political economy isolates Cuba in many ways, the slow demise of the socialist welfare state and changes we see in everyday life on this island are not unlike those in the rest of Latin America and across the globe. As I discuss in chapter 2, the ethics of struggling for Cubanidad are also deeply entangled with ideologies linking food and agriculture to Cuban identity. Struggling for a decent meal is a way of struggling for Cubanidad. As Manuel phrases it in chapter 5, "The world has turned upside down." This wavering sense of political identity and lingering questions of who Cuba would ally with and what this means for deeply entrenched anti-imperialist ideologies planted the seed for an unraveling of political subjectivity in the post-Soviet era. This crisis opened up a space for a new emergent sense of self and for the development of new post-Soviet, socialist subjectivities.

As food access shifts and there continue to be difficulties in accessing culturally appropriate foods, Cubans face a form of culinary discontent. Amid the many uncertainties of changing times, Cubans also face the possibility that the foods they have long been accustomed to will not be there, like the corn for Amalia's hallacas. There is food to fulfill caloric need, but not "real food" that one might enjoy eating and be proud to serve to others. The long-standing connection between food and identity means that as "real food" is more difficult to access, Cubans call into question their own understandings of personal subjectivity and social relations, as they note the ways in which aspects of the self are damaged by the faltering food system. In the case of Amalia's hallacas, the connection between food, nostalgia for the past, and memories of loved ones hangs in the balance. Food is deeply linked to identity, and when that connection is ruptured, the ways in which food consumption articulates with care of the self and individual understandings of selfhood can also come unhinged.

Difficulties in food acquisition, always shaped by political, economic, and social forces external to our selves, can cause shifts in subjectivity, which is negotiated through discourse or actions (Butler 1990), such as the insistence on eating in a particular way or endlessly searching for desired foods. Santiagueros have continuously adapted new tactics and strategies for food acquisition; however, despite their efforts to struggle through difficulties, their ideals are rarely achieved. The failure to eat in a manner that is locally defined as dignified and decent can lead to a "moral breakdown" (Zigon and Throop 2014), through which some santiagueros observe and articulate a shift in their subjectivity.

The struggle for a good life is not just a way of upholding and striving for Cubanidad; the insistence on living a good life and the ability to continue consuming a decent meal in the face of the changing food system is also a form of resistance to state power and a way of talking back to the state (Schwenkel 2015; Gupta 2012a). We might also call this a form of refusal (Simpson 2014).[2] In Amalia's case her insistence on searching for corn, and her unwillingness to simply prepare something else for the occasion, is a clear example of this kind of refusal. However, efforts to maintain a decent meal, including the many layers of what it means to know what food is good for you, reach far beyond resistance to include fundamental aspects of how people grapple with social change.[3] The seemingly small actions of everyday life hold the capacity for agency among ordinary people, and in the lived experience of change, people face new forms of stress and uncertainty that rattle their senses of self.

Since the early 1990s, the ongoing state of change has not only created a sense of uncertainly; it has also given rise to a sense of hope that positive change is on the horizon, hope that life in Cuba will get better, and that more Cubans will be able to live a good life. Santiagueros tend to strive for a better life even though their daily experience is often not very hopeful.[4] These efforts toward the work to require that the state uphold its promises to provide the basic entitlements necessary for living a decent life is a struggle that is central to the politics of adequacy. The politics of adequacy is one way in which Cubans continuously assert their rights and desires to be legible political subjects who will not be dismissed.

This contemporary moment of change in Cuba, while giving some hope, also lends itself to certain degrees of uncertainty and an ongoing state of anxiety for many Cubans. The stories detailed throughout the book reveal some of the generational differences in the ways that people interpret contemporary Cuba; some of the older generations of Cubans remember when access to basic goods and services was much more difficult than it is now. For lower socioeconomic status families, during the years preceding the 1959 revolution, fear and uncertainty were normative and more intense than they are under today's socialism, where at least some basic entitlements are still guaranteed. However, these older generations also remember different forms of past abundance. They cite memories of eating meat with every meal, drinking fresh cows' milk daily, and the ability to buy any number of goods in stores before the socialist revolution. They remember fresh corn for hallacas during two different seasons. It is important to note though that the pre-revolutionary experience was highly differentiated by race, class, and region. Like this generation, those who were born at the start of the revolution remember difficult periods in the early 1960s and reflect fondly upon the years of relative abundance during the height of Soviet material aid in the 1970s and 80s. Many of the santiagueros who participated in this research long for the relative abundance of those years, reminiscing about the days when they could walk into the "parallel market," a set of unsubsidized markets that were popular in the 1970s, and buy canned meat from Russia as an ideal time in their lives. This past haunts the present with the lingering awareness that something better was possible.

There appears to be a commonly held notion among Cubans of a link between periods of material abundance and strong social values and the ability to have strongly bonded social relationships. Many santiagueros today remember nearly everything as being better before. In their memories of the past, things were easier to access, people were more kind, families were closer, and socialism functioned well in hindsight. My research participants contrasted this past with the contemporary moment where material goods, including food, are increasingly difficult to access, people are not genuine but *interesado* (self-serving), families no longer sit down to dinner, and food is not made with love. The question arises as to whether Cuban socialism, the basic premise of what it means to be Cuban, and the ethics of the New Man are falling apart before our eyes.

This somewhat hyperbolic interpretation of the conditions of everyday life in Cuba is, exaggerated or not, a common enough set of perceptions that it has become a daily topic of conversation in homes across Santiago de Cuba. Regardless of how true it is that the past was better than the present, many people are experiencing the present period in Cuba with a deep sense of personal and social crisis, and some panic about what to make of it all. Cubans, like many others experiencing the effects of globalized capitalist distribution, are taking a moment now to pause, to reflect on the present, which indicates that the path toward whatever the future may hold for Cuba will not be without fractures and challenges. In doing so, they reflect on the ways in which changing material realities will impact the way that they live.

What does it mean when we slowly lose our ability to practice or enact the daily rituals that we believe to be essential to who we are as people? For many groups of people, in Cuba and elsewhere, access to the basic ingredients that it takes to practice daily habits and ceremonial rituals, such as sitting down to dinner with family or cooking a cherished family dish, are critical aspects of living a good life. When those essential components of habitual life become scarce and people must struggle along through their lives, Cuban families spend less time together. Unable to gather around the table, they may find themselves alone in a house full of people, disconnected and in some cases, such as Regina's locked cabinets, no longer able to trust one another.

Nevertheless people must go on; they must eat. There are pragmatic responses to the changing food system. In order to eat, in many households one person must dedicate their full time and energy to food acquisition, preparation, and clean up. Those with enough means can hire someone to do this for them. Others may have a retired family member take on these tasks. For many families, as detailed in chapter 3, this increased work to access food is shifted onto women, who either continue to work the triple jornada (triple schedule) at home, at work, and maintaining necessary connections in the community, or do not work outside the home. As patriarchy reigns, and women retreat into the domestic sphere, the value of women's labor is not attached to the wage-earning jobs many of them had in the first three decades under socialism, and the value of their work becomes less tangible and tied up with the social value of decency, the need to be a "proper" woman and maintain a "proper" home.

The idealization of domestic life and the values of decency and dignity that must be upheld by women are then infused into the ideal, decent meal that *should be* served for lunch, or the hallacas that *should be* a part of a celebration. In uncertain times, the decent meal comes to represent an ideal family life, a functioning social system, and an overall good life. This ideal, though extremely difficult to achieve, has become the standard to which household cooks aspire. The insistence on maintaining the decent meal is a form of clinging to the known past rather than an unknown future. The decent meal, thought of as traditional, also becomes symbolic of the social and political values that are associated with the good old days. The lack of the decent meal, and the need to resort to eating "crap" or inadequate meals, is a frightful symbol of what the future might hold for Cuban households, a symbol that sends some frantically searching for food and others into a state of moral panic.

Not all who search for food have the same experience; some are confronted by the barriers of prejudice and discrimination with varying levels of surmountability. The continued prejudice against Cubans with dark skin color makes it more difficult for them to access food by way of the formal channels at ration stations, markets, and stores where they face varying degrees of discrimination. Even more difficult, accessing food on the black market and through other informal channels is a system built on social networks and relationships of trust, where dark-skinned, queer, and otherwise marginalized Cubans are discriminated against as their very being is erroneously linked to criminality and distrust. Inequality plagues the food distribution system from the local to the global level, in formally institutionalized ways and in the daily microinteractions necessary to acquire food.

Dimensions of Adequacy

This book has addressed the relationships between food distribution and the politics of adequacy, food acquisition and the faltering welfare state, as well as the contemporary assemblages that often link subjectivity and these state provisioning systems. Through these frameworks we can better understand why shifts in food access have such a profound effect on most Cubans, and in turn, we can use the study of food consumption to understand these key issues within the social sciences. For instance, the everyday struggles of households in contemporary post-Soviet, still socialist Cuba are an essential part of how we understand global capitalism and the history of globalization (Gupta 2012a). These stories from the marginalized city of Santiago de Cuba illuminate the ways in which the long-reaching arms of global capitalism penetrate the lives of the subaltern despite the protections of a socialist welfare state. The global food industrial complex is rife with inequality. The capitalist undercurrent of the politics of distribution dictates that those states and corporate entities with sufficient cash flow, power, or ability to take on national debt will determine the ways in which food products ebb and flow through households across the globe. Natural disasters or national politics can create surges in the price of basic food staples—corn, soy, wheat—to the extent that low-income countries, those like Cuba that cannot make many food purchases on credit, must simply do without these staples. Household cooks must adjust their meal plans, either with bold innovation at the stove top, or by turning to low-cost imported foods—pizza, spaghetti, and packaged foods. And yet, in Cuba these packaged imports are not low cost for the average consumer earning around 20 dollars per month. The logic of these global and local shifts applies to exports as well. When an increase in the price of coffee on the global market means the Cuban government must divert its national supply to make money on the international market, Cuban families simply go without coffee for weeks on end. Although Cuba has long been entrenched within global capitalism, the socialist state has served as an intermediary between global capitalism and individuals through a socialist welfare state.

Whereas in other parts of the world the rise of transnational capitalism has led to a breakdown of the role of the nation-state and the deterritorialization and globalization of "the economic" and "the social," in the context of post-Soviet, late-socialist Cuba, the state still serves as the central provisioner of individual needs, and the ideologies of nationalism still unite Cubans across the island. Even though the ingredients that make up the ideal Cuban meal enter the country via long-established international trade routes, few of the household cooks in my study were aware of where their food products come from and the ways in which the products of global capitalism flow through their homes.[5] However, most Cubans are aware of changes in state-set food prices, shortages, and changes in the state-based ration. The focus on food acquisition adds a critical dimension to our understanding of global capitalist distribution, even in the context of socialist Cuba, by way of the analysis of production, distribution, and consumption.[6]

However, the marcoscale focus on distribution misses the full story. The politics of adequacy provides a framework for understanding the ways in which the politics of distribution permeate the everyday lives of households across the globe. In our contemporary world, where the ingredients that make up the foods we eat may traverse the globe several times, travelling thousands of miles in a web of economic transactions so complex that we cannot trace the origins of our meals, the connection between food and subjectivity becomes highlighted; the meanings of our consumption practices are called into question, debated, and reinterpreted. In other words, a politics of adequacy framework allows us to understand the changes to macrolevel food distribution by locating the impact on real people at the moments when food actually hits the table, or not. The Cuban context, part of a larger Caribbean discourse of *mestizaje*, is one where "traditional" foods have always come from elsewhere, and the creation of a national cuisine has been likened to the idyllic view that people of different skin colors, religions, and cultural practices can come together to create the vibrant flavors of a stew, ingredients all jumbled up into something delicious. At the same time, this mixed heritage tradition has been deeply national and territorial for the past few centuries. However, this idyllic view of the making of traditional foods in the context of modern global commodity flows may not have an endless extension into the future.

Adequacy matters. Nestled between abundance, including rising rates of obesity in Cuba, and the insufficiency of hunger and malnutrition, lies a gray area of precarious survival. Struggling for life. Luchando la vida. In this gray area the boundaries of what is necessary, and what is adequate, are called into question, renegotiated, and rationalized. To survive we only need the most basic things, but to live a good life, we require more. For contemporary santiagueros, an adequate food system would include: affordable and convenient access to culturally appropriate or "traditional" food, which includes not having to traverse the entire city to find basic ingredients, and not fearing steep price increases that render ingredients unaffordable; dietary variation and accessibility to various proteins, fats, and carbohydrates; a guarantee of freshness and the ability to consume foods without fear that they have spoiled or may lead to illness; and the ability to assemble all of the components of a decent, dignified meal. Adequacy matters for the very definition of a good life.

My second area of concern in this book has involved the changing welfare state. As the welfare state declines and entitlements disappear, it is important to pay keen attention to the politics of adequacy and the ways in which people can slip from doing just fine into precarious existence. Even in the post-Soviet era, socialist Cuba is still fundamentally a welfare state. Furthermore, contemporary Cuba is also a *welfare society*, "a social system in which welfare assumptions are an organic part of everyday life" (Robertson 1988, 222; see also Lin 2004, as cited in Murphy 2015).[7] Therefore, despite the decline of the welfare state and drastic reductions in social entitlements, the ideology of the welfare society remains in place for many Cubans. In some contexts, like the United States, the notion of welfare is thought of as the need to rely on government assistance rather than one's own hard work and is often perceived as shameful. This is not the case in socialist Cuba. Most Cubans see welfare and the elaborate entitlement system as a basic right, and most fundamentally as a form of social protection that guarantees the basic needs of everyone, establishing a basic level of equality and keeping Cubans out of dire poverty. In this system, welfare is established through a system of entitlements—a legally guaranteed right to some benefit—and includes food rations, education, and health care, among other things. In addition, the Cuban socialist welfare system subsidizes utilities, including electricity, gas, and water, so that minimal use of these necessities is extremely inexpensive. Despite ongoing problems with state systems, low-cost transportation and other structures are also in place to make daily life less burdensome.

These basic entitlements have been the cornerstone of Cuban socialism. However, after the collapse of the Soviet Union, the Cuban state has not been able to maintain the robust welfare system, and many of the basic entitlements that were guaranteed in the 1980s have not returned even after the worst of the Special Period was over. For instance, rolling blackouts and brownouts have been used intermittently to save electricity. The Cuban food system is one of the areas that have faltered since the loss of Soviet material aid. Unlike the problems with some other entitlements, the shifting access to food appears to affect people in more personal and fundamental ways. Although a rolling blackout may be annoying and elicit complaints, it does not appear to foster the same forms of panic and outrage that the loss of access to foods elicits. Food consumption is so fundamentally tied to identity and the flows of daily life that shifts in food access can have profound personal and social effects. In chapter 3, the cases of Elvira, María Julia, and Marta demonstrate the centrality of a good meal in the Cuban household, and the forms of care and gendered subjectivity implicated in what many Cubans view as the virtuous task of feeding a family well.

My third area of concern in this book has been the ways food consumption is deeply linked to subjectivity and how shifts in food access impact individual subjectivity and social relationships. As access to the goods people have long counted on shifts, and it becomes more difficult to obtain the things they feel are necessary to maintain their quality of life, some people may begin to panic over what this means for their present and future, questioning whether the crisis of the present even has the possibility of becoming a future. This is illustrated in chapter 1 by Monika's need to "rest her mind" after discovering that the market she preferred to use had been bulldozed to the ground, by Elvira's desire to always have rice with her meals, or by María Julia's insistence that a meal should always include meat. Adequate systems matter for maintaining physical health, mental health, and long-standing social and familial dynamics.

The Caribbean has been a site of modern, translocal subject formation, bringing together elements from transnational contexts and local settings, since the colonial period, when the flows of goods, people, and ideas to and from the Caribbean already necessitated a concept of place like translocal that encompassed the global and the local. In the postcolonial era, this translocal subjectivity has been taken up by many groups of people in the region. Many Cubans see themselves as vibrant mixtures of the various groups of people who came to or influenced Cuba. Contemporary consumption practices are tied to this history of translocal identity. Consumption and desires to consume in particular ways, therefore, are not necessarily part of the neoliberal imaginary of late capitalism; rather they are part of a long-standing translocal identity that has been developed since colonialism and independence in Cuba. Longing to consume in these "traditional" ways imbues the present with notions of the remembered past as a way of thinking through and making claims about contemporary subject positions through and in spite of changing consumption patterns.[8] Particular forms of consumption are crucial parts of identity and subject formation. This post-Soviet, socialist orientation to consumption locates the individual within a long history of ideologies of independence, anti-imperialism, and Cubanidad, all of which continue to be deeply entrenched within global capitalism through the global industrial food system. As distribution systems shift, ideologies may not change at the same pace; this can lead to a rupture in the way that people connect their consumption patterns with their sense of self. As access to basic needs becomes more precarious, consumers call into question what constitutes enough, what is adequate, and even what it means to be Cuban in this day and age.

This book has revealed the ways in which the faltering welfare state and the reduction or elimination of entitlements can impact individual subjectivity, social relationships, and exacerbate existing inequality. We see how prejudice impacts food access in chapter 1 through the ways Regina is constrained by fear of discrimination in her search for food, and the ways homophobia restricts the social networks through which Rodulfo, Armando, and Carlos can acquire food. The notion of the politics of adequacy can be extended to frame other forms of entitlement beyond food access, such as questions of what constitutes a basic standard for housing or education in cross-cultural contexts. A detailed understanding of the politics of adequacy with keen attention to those voices that are often not heard will augment our understanding of the processes by which people slip into poverty and other forms of precarity.

As this research in post-Soviet Cuba demonstrates, the waning of the welfare state disproportionately impacts women, people of color, queer people, and other disenfranchised populations.[9] There will be secondary and tertiary effects of reductions in basic entitlements. Some of the stories included in this book may allude to such impacts; for instance, as working-age Cubans increasingly take on second jobs or side hustles in the newly legal small business world or still illegal black-market channels, how does this impact their household presence? Are grandparents increasingly relied on for childcare as parents work more? Will the social importance of the decent meal mean that those who are unable to achieve it will be further marginalized? Will these ideals only be available to those who are already among the privileged classes with access to what is necessary to create a decent meal?

In Cuba specifically, as market mechanisms are increasingly incorporated into the current version of state socialism, we must continue to analyze how the increasing influence of multinational corporations and changing importation patterns impact people's everyday lives and how they see themselves. There may be a potential shift from the state sector and state bureaucracy serving the needs of the people to the state serving the needs of corporations and being driven by profit rather than the needs of Cuban households. In turn, keen attention to such shifts and the impact of rising rates of inequality is also necessary. As welfare states dissipate and new forms of distribution emerge, a focus on the politics of adequacy allows for a deeper understanding of local notions of need, entitlement, and how institutions, communities, or other entities make access to those needs possible. Expanding our understanding of adequacy to include the process by which individuals and communities determine what their basic needs are in their own cultural-historical frameworks is necessary to grasp the ways development and distribution impact individuals, families, and communities across the globe.

In the 2000s and 2010s, while I conducted this research there were sweeping changes to many aspects of everyday life in Cuba. In addition to changes in Cuba's leadership for the first time since 1959, a number of political-economic changes affected daily life for some Cubans. For instance, at the beginning of my research in 2008 the use of personal cellular phones was legalized, in the middle of my long-term fieldwork in 2011 the purchase and sale of vehicles and homes was legalized, and later the first public wi-fi spots opened in 2015. Under the presidency of Barack Obama limits on remittances to Cuba from the US were lifted,

FIGURE 16. A Decent Meal, 2017. Source: Author

and billions of dollars have flowed into Cuba. In 2014 Obama and Raúl Castro announced steps toward normalization of relations, reestablishing embassies, swapping political prisoners, easing the embargo, and increasing travel from the US to Cuba. In 2010 under the leadership of Raúl Castro new laws expanded the legalization of small businesses and encouraged Cubans to become entrepreneurs. Yet, even with these monumental shifts that took place while I conducted this research, as María Julia's grievances at the beginning of this chapter reveal, my trips to Cuba have still been characterized by very similar conversations to those I have had since 2008: scarcity of particular food items, rising food costs, and struggling to piece it all together into a good life. While some people might be inclined to assume that changes such as the use of cellular phones, public wi-fi, or a new president would mean improvements in food access, many of my research participants have not found that to be the case. And yet, although food acquisition is still characterized by difficulty and struggle, the decent meal is achievable, and knowing that it is possible is part of why santiagueros continue to strive for it. In August 2017, I revisited long-time Cuban friends who, after hours of scouring the city for ingredients over several days, were able to put together the decent meal (see figure 16). The meal was complete with deliciously prepared beefsteak, hand-cut french fries, *congri*, a salad with cucumber, tomatoes, and avocado, and even freshly made *hallacas*.

Notes

Introduction

1. Unless otherwise noted, all proper names are pseudonyms. In some cases details that may reveal identities were also changed. For instance, a person's occupation may be slightly changed to ensure anonymity. This practice is used to protect the identities of research participants and reduce any potential physical, social, psychological, or political harm from participating in this study. This research was conducted under Institutional Review Board (IRB) approval from University of California, Los Angeles.

2. *Hallaca* is sometimes spelled *ayaca*.

3. Corn is assumed to be native to the island and was a principal staple of the Ciboney Indians, who are considered to be a faction of the Western Taíno of Cuba. Hatheway (1957) provides an elaborate account of the history of corn in Cuba.

4. The market was opened on December 31, 1859, and was previously known as Mercado Concha and Mercado Aguilera. In the early 1930s, a fire destroyed the original building and it was reconstructed in 1932.

5. Scholars have referred to post-Soviet Cuba as: "late-socialist" (Henken 2006; Hernández-Reguant 2004; Fernandes 2006; González 2016; Stout 2008; Tanaka 2011; Weinreb 2009), "para-socialist" (Frederik 2012), and even "neoliberal" (Perry 2016). Others have simply labeled it "post-Soviet" (Brotherton 2012; Humphreys 2012). Although I have used the term "late-socialist Cuba" in some previous publications (Garth 2009), I now refer to Cuba as "still socialist." I contend that the ongoing redistributive economy and the extent to which welfare entitlements are still in place clearly indicate that Cuba is still socialist, and, like Frederik (2012), I do not necessarily think that Cuba must inevitably become a typical capitalist economy or neoliberal state, hence the hesitation to label it "late" in some teleological sense.

6. However, see Carney's *The Unending Hunger: Tracing Women and Food Insecurity across Borders* (2015) for a nuanced analysis of the relationship between the economics of food acquisition and cultural dimensions of food consumption in the United States.

7. For further discussion see Fischer 2014, and Fischer and Benson 2006.

8. Cuban anthropologist Fernando Ortiz distinguished the terms *Cubanidad* and *Cubanía* (1947). It is likely that he drew upon Miguel de Unamuno's (1927) distinction between *Hispanidad* and *Hispanía*. Unamuno preferred the term Hispanidad as an inclusive referent for all people who share the Spanish language and Spanish cultural affinities even if they are not Spanish. Unamuno's use of Hispanidad is thought to be inclusive of various

races. Ortiz used the term Cubanidad in a similar way to capture the shared sense of identity and inclusive racial variety found in Cuba. According to Frederik (2012) "the term Cubanidad was coined by Jose Antonio Saco, a political scientist and philosopher, who used the term to distinguish Cuban identity from that of Spain and the United States. Saco's definition was created from the criollo perspective, leaving out the centrality of African and indigenous cultural presence" (2012, 279). Therefore instead of using the term Cubanidad, Frederik follows Kapcia in the use of Cubanía, which according to Kapcia (2000) "refers to ideology and the teleological belief in Cubanidad" and includes the sense of dissent and revolution that are part of the post-revolutionary period (ibid., 6–7). Following Ortiz (1940) and Pérez Firmat (1997), I use the term Cubanidad in most of this book as both the "general condition of Cubans" and to capture that sense of Cuban nationalism that I find santiagueros often use to define themselves against the United States, much in the way that Saco originally used the term (Gonçalves 2014). That is, Cubanidad includes a sense of Cuban identity linked to place and the nation-state. I acknowledge the problematic elements of the historical meaning, i.e., that the notion of Cubanidad tends to exclude Black and indigenous identities as a part of what it means to be Cuban. See also Bodenheimer 2015.

9. In the past few decades a growing amount of scholarship has focused on various aspects of Cuba's food system since the 1990s. Cuba's post-1990s turn to pesticide-free agriculture and the rise of peri-urban farms have drawn a lot of attention. The work of Fernando Funes Monzote, Cuban agronomist and farmer at one of Cuba's most famous peri-urban farms, is at the forefront of this literature (Funes Monzote et al. 2002). Premat (2012) has written on urban gardens in Havana. Wright (2009) has written on the ways in which Cuban agricultural adaptations after the Special Period might offer productive lessons for other countries in the era of oil scarcity. While this work is important for understanding local agrifood movements and forms of food sovereignty, it does not address the relationship between this relatively small amount of locally produced food and the majority of what is consumed on a day-to-day basis in Cuba.

10. In 2008, just before the data collection for this research, the Cuban press announced that 84% of all food consumed in Cuba is imported (USDA 2008).

11. While we often think of the collective redistribution of wealth as a fundamental part of socialism, there are many forms of redistribution in capitalist societies as well. Moreover, in contemporary socialist societies, consumers still earn money with which to buy goods in addition to the services they access via redistributed wealth. The histories of Cuba's agriculture and food systems, and the ways they are aligned with revolutionary ideologies of egalitarianism, are related to a particular politics of distribution, as I will show in greater detail in chapter 2.

12. In orthodox Marxism, labor power is the source of all value. The ability to labor, or labor-power, when transformed into a commodity, which can be bought by a capitalist, has a particular use-value, namely that it creates value. That use-value may yield a surplus value. Those who work for their labor are thought of as the proletariat, as opposed to the bourgeoisie who may have inherited their wealth. Marx and Engels also describe a class of people called the *lumpen-proletariat* who, for a variety of reasons, are not consistently suc-

cessful at working for pay; we might also call these people *the precariat* (Ferguson 2015, 44). Besides the precariat, those who dedicate their labor to the domestic sphere, such as women bearing and rearing children, are another category of nonwage earners. These nonwage earners, regardless of the moral valences surrounding the reasons they do not work for pay, are part of what Nikolas Rose has observed to be categorized as a "social" concern (1999).

13. In addition, babies and children younger than four receive one twelve-ounce can of fortified fruit puree (*compota*) per day, and from zero to seven years old all children receive one liter of powdered milk per day. Children from seven to fourteen years old receive one liter of soy yogurt per day. Around 2000, the Cuban state began allocating rice supplements for people over 60 years old, and additional rice for children from zero to fourteen years old. There are also meat products in the ration; these are distributed at a carnicería. Each registered individual receives six ounces of chicken, six ounces of fish, and either eight ounces of ground meat with soy, eight ounces of bologna, or ten ounces of additional chicken per month depending on availability. Eggs are also distributed at the carnicería. From the first to the fifteenth day of the month there are five eggs available per person that cost 15 cents each. From the fifteenth to the last day of the month, there are five eggs available per person for 90 cents each. Each item arrives on a particular day in the first half and second half of the month, and that item can be picked up beginning the day it arrives until the next shipment comes. Each ration station has a chalkboard indicating when the items will arrive. Many people pick up each item on the day it arrives, both because they need it and for fear that they might miss out on their allotted amount (due to spoilage or pilfering).

14. This economic breakdown was due in large part to economic reforms in the USSR, then Cuba's major trade partner, under *perestroika* which began when Gorbachev took over in 1985 and continued to worsen until the disintegration of the USSR in 1991.

15. Caloric intake per person was measured as the total per capita amount of food available after subtracting the food allocated to the tourism industry and losses due to distribution and cooking. These measurements were conducted by the National Institute of Hygiene, Epidemiology, and Microbiology from 1980 to 1999 (Jiménez Acosta, Porrata, and Pérez 1998). The Food and Agriculture Organization of the United Nations also provided data on per capita food availability by dividing total calories available for human consumption by the total population consuming the food supply during the reference period in 1995 and 2001 (Franco et al. 2007).

16. Broadly speaking, a black market is a market of goods or services that operates outside of the official state system. Black-market exchanges are common all over the world, where officials, individuals, and other entities pilfer items and sell them. Black-market systems of exchange have been particularly salient in socialist settings (del Real and Pertierra 2008; Dunn 2004, 2005; Porter 2008).

17. For more discussion on the notion of precarity and precariousness within anthropology, see Allison 2012; Biehl 2005; Garcia 2010; Molé 2012; Muehlebach 2012, 2013; Stewart 2007, 2012.

18. This stands out from the ways in which Yurchak (2005) has characterized the postsocialist transition in Russia, where Yurchak demonstrates that Russians felt that things had

remained the same and imagined that they would remain the same forever. This made for a jarring transition to postsocialism.

19. For further discussion of the tactics Cubans use to circumvent barriers within the official state system, see also Andaya 2014 and Brotherton 2005. In other socialist contexts, see Kligman 1998, Ledeneva 1990, and Salmi 2003.

20. As some local intellectuals in Santiago say, if Havana is the New York of Cuba, then Santiago is the New Orleans.

21. Part of Santiago's orientation to the Caribbean rather than the rest of the island has to do with the histories of migration to eastern Cuba from the rest of the Caribbean. For instance, the Haitian Revolution had both immediate and long-lasting effects for Cuba, especially for the eastern part of the island, where most Haitian migrants were located (Johnson 2012). Beginning in 1791, the slave rebellion in Saint-Domingue sent a wave of fear through the other Caribbean colonies, and during the course of the Haitian Revolution over 30,000 white refugees migrated to Cuba. (For further analysis of the complexities of narratives of Haiti and Haitian history see Ulysse 2015.) Many arrived in Santiago and other parts of Oriente (the region with the closest proximity to Haiti), bringing slaves with the intention of starting new plantations (Viddal 2013). Free Black and *mulato* people also fled to Cuba from Haiti, again mainly to Santiago and Guantánamo (Millet and Brea 1989; Viddal 2006). Many of these new migrants drew on their coffee expertise from Saint-Domingue, establishing new plantations in the Sierra Maestra mountains; some of these remain operational today. Haitians migrated across the Caribbean at several points in history (Louis 2014). Between 1913 and 1931, more than 500,000 Haitians entered Cuba (James, Millet, and Alarcón 1992). A smaller, but still significant, population of migrants came to Cuba from the British West Indies in the early 1900s (Queeley 2015). Many migrants worked on plantations in the eastern provinces (Viddal 2013). Many of the Haitian laborers who came to Cuba in the 1900s were eventually repatriated to Haiti, often leaving behind children and younger relatives in Cuba (Rolando 2014).

22. Santiago's aura of Caribbeanness more easily situates the city and the scholarship of the city within a "global Caribbean" context (Slocum and Thomas 2007). The Caribbean has been characterized as the first modern, or global, region (Maurer 2004; Mintz 1998; Slocum and Thomas 2003) and as a "master symbol" for many scholarly analytics in circulation since the 1990s (Khan 2001).

23. Laurie A. Frederik translates *guajiro* as "hillbilly" (2012, 5).

24. The term *subaltern* is used to refer to those who have been excluded from the dominant political structures of a society. Spivak (1988) has critiqued the use of the term to refer to the oppressed more generally, and Spivak underscores that it does not broadly apply to anyone who has been discriminated against, or who does not have access to everything that they wish. I use the term here to refer to the notion that santiagueros not only suffer from inequalities with respect to other Cubans, but also lack social capital due to years of institutionalized racism and regionalism within Cuba.

25. For an account of contemporary life in the Cuban countryside see Frederik 2012.

26. In Santiago de Cuba, discussions of racism in Cuba are still sensitive topics. The concepts of prejudice and discrimination, however, are more commonly discussed. For

further discussion of race in Cuba, see Tomás Fernández Robaina's *El Negro en Cuba* (1990) and Carlos Moore's *Castro, the Blacks, and Africa* (1988).

27. Here and throughout the book I try to use the term *Black* as a descriptor for African-descended Cubans and their traditions. The term *Afro-Cuban* is also used by some scholars of Cuba, but its use has been critiqued as a hegemonic use of a Western construct that is not often used in the local context. Indeed, I rarely heard santiagueros refer to Black Cubans as *afrocubano,* and it was much more common to use Black or "negro" to refer to both people and practices associated with Africa and the diaspora. (See also Bodenheimer 2015; Helg 1995; de la Fuente 2001, 2011; Moore 1988; and Fernández Robaina 1990).

28. The celebration of Carnaval has very deep historical roots and has taken on important political meaning. Celebrated since the 17th century, *Los Carnavales* are held in late July each year. Cuban Carnaval is not the typical pre-Lenten festival held in many Spanish, French, and Portuguese colonies, but rather is derived from the Fiestas de Mamarrachos, which were held on St. John's Day (mid June), St. Peter's Day (late June), St. Christine's Day, St. James the Apostle's Day, and St. Anne's Day (all in late July). For more information on Santiago's Carnaval see Wirtz 2014; Bettelheim and Ortiz 2001; Nunley and Bettelheim 1988.

29. The following list was created by Paul Ryer (2008) based on his observations of skin color categorizations in Cuba: *blanco* (white); *blanco lechoso* (milky white skin); *albino* (albino); *blanco blanco* (a very blonde person, a truly white person); *rubio* (literally blonde, means same as above); *castaño* (chestnut-colored—fair skin and dark brown hair); *trigueño* (literally wheat-colored: a person with olive-white skin and dark but straight "good" hair); *blanco Cubano* (Cuban white, as opposed to "really" white; it implies an underlying racial mixture); *chino* (a person of Asian appearance, usually trigeños, but appearance of the eyes is critical); *jabao* (light but barely not white skin, wavy or curly hair); *capirro* (a person with "bad" but blonde hair); *azafrán* (with freckles, reddish-brown skin, curly red hair); *sirio* (to describe Ethiopians or East Africans—black with fine features and "good" hair); *mulato* (medium dark skin, either "bad" or "good" hair); *yucateco* (from the Yucatan—to describe Cubans of indigenous/mixed or Mayan appearance); *mestizo* (a person with caramel colored skin, with "good" hair); *indio* (dark skin, straight hair); *moreno* (literally dark brown between indio and moro); *moro* (literally moor, dark dark skin with straight or curly black hair); *prieto* (dark, may be used in place of negro); *negro* (dark skin, "bad" hair); *azul* or *negro azul* (blue, persons with skin so black they have a bluish quality); *fosforescente* (similar to azul literally phosphorescent); and *ñato* (dark skin, flat nosed—to denote an "African" nose). This exhaustive list of skin colors that Cubans use to describe themselves and one another illustrates the ways that descriptions of skin color and other phenotypic features are common and important features of social life. In my research, beyond the basic categories of *blanco, mulato,* and *negro,* most often I heard people use color categorizations including rubio/a, castaño/a, trigueño/a, chino/a, jabao/a, mestizo/a, indio/a, moreno/a, moro/a, prieto/a, and ñato/a.

30. I began doing this research during the global economic crisis of 2008. This had a large influence on the initial direction of the research. Food prices increased dramatically between 2007 and 2008 around the globe. Given Cuba's heavy reliance on food imports, food supplies were also low in Cuba that year.

31. I first traveled to Cuba in 2001. I have conducted Cuba-related research since 2005 and began this specific focus on Cuban food in 2007. Preliminary fieldwork was conducted in 2008 and 2009. Long-term fieldwork was conducted in 2010 and 2011. Later, follow-up trips took place in 2016, 2017, and 2019.

32. Children were not interviewed, but their lives and their food consumption needs were an integral part of all other aspects of the research. For more information on child-hood in Cuba, see Casavantes Bradford 2014.

33. While I was conducting research in Cuba, I always had an officially licensed *casa particular* (guest house) where I was staying. During fieldwork, I moved to four different casa particulares in various parts of the city to facilitate my fieldwork and get to know different areas better. Although I always had an official casa particular, in some cases I would stay in the household that I was studying for the duration of the study period; this was the case with the households outside of the city as transportation each morning and evening was not possible.

Chapter 1

1. I opted to keep *mulata /o* in italics denoting that the word is in Spanish, to mean a person of mixed Black and white heritage. I do not use the English *mulatto*, which is an offensive term now thought of as a racial slur. For more explanation of racial categories in Cuba see introduction, note 29.

2. Caldosa, a Cuban stew, has long-standing social importance in Cuba, and is tradi-tionally served at parties and celebrations. Historically the dish was prepared in a com-munal fashion: a fire was built in an outdoor communal space and the stew was prepared over an open fire. Community members would contribute the various ingredients for the stew—yuca, potato, squash, plantains, sweet potatoes, chayote (an edible gourde that tastes like a cross between a squash and a melon with a potato-like consistency that makes it stand up well in soups), chicken or pork, and common Cuban spices.

3. Chard is not required in caldosa, but some Cuban cooks include variations in their recipes. For more on recipe adaptations in Cuba, see Garth 2014b.

4. Culantro and oregano cubano are very common herbs in Cuban cooking. Culantro (*Eryngium foetidum*) is also known as Mexican coriander. It is not the same plant as ci-lantro (*Coriandrum sativum*), although some say it has a similar, but much stronger taste. Oregano cubano (*Plactranthus amboinicus*) is a large succulent herb plant with a strong flavor well-suited to seasoning meat. The plant also has widespread medicinal properties.

5. *Mamey colorado (pouteria sapota)*, also known as *sapote* or *zapota*, is a very sweet fruit found in the Caribbean, Mexico, and Central America. The variety found in Cuba today is red and fleshy inside.

6. For more on resting and disconnecting the mind, see Garth 2013.

7. I heard people refer to this dish of white rice with a fried egg on top in this way several times in my research. One explanation behind the name is that if a woman prepares such a simple dish of rice and eggs it must mean that she has been off in the streets with other men rather than spending her time cooking for her family. The other explanation is that sex workers commonly consume this dish in the early hours as a combination of breakfast and

dinner after they have been working all night. Either way the name has clear misogynistic undertones.

8. For further exploration of the elimination of the socialist welfare state in the context of the former Soviet Union and Europe, see Yurchak 2003.

9. However, regardless of class, dark-skinned Cubans also experience racialized forms of prejudice and discrimination. For instance, see Roland 2011.

10. The government also feared that in the hands of Cuba's enemies, racism could be manipulated to weaken the nation by driving a wedge between Black and white Cubans.

11. *Congrí* is technically the correct spelling and pronunciation of the word, which refers to black beans and rice. It is common among lower-class Santiago households to refer to the dish as *congris*.

12. Based on household members' self-identification and the household asset elicitation, the 22 households in this study were categorized into low, medium, and high socioeconomic status (SES). Seven (31.8%) are characterized as low, six (27.3%) are medium, and nine (40.9%) are high SES. High-income households are somewhat overrepresented in the sample due to the fact that members of these households were more likely to have time to participate in the study. Strong efforts were made to include low- and middle-income households in the sample. The low SES households tended to also live in neighborhoods characterized as low-income in Santiago, including Chicharrones, Desey, San Pedrito, Los Pinos, and parts of the city center. All families who were classified as low SES also had a majority of household members who self-identify as Black, and the second most common self-identity in these households was *mulato*. The upper- and middle-income families in my study all lived in high- or middle-income neighborhoods: Vista Alegre, Sueño, Terrazas, Santa Bárbara, Portuonda, and the city center. These families identified their skin color in diverse ways, both across and within households. Households consisted of varying numbers of individuals. The smallest household had two individuals and the largest had nine. The average household size was five. Low-income households were more likely to have a greater number of individuals per household than middle- or high-income households. In total, there were 107 individual members living in 22 households.

13. In my observation Regina has grown accustomed to having to prioritize certain family members over others when acquiring and preparing food. Many of the young adult household members are readily able to acquire food through their jobs or in the homes of their significant others, so she does not worry so much about them. She told me that she does sometimes worry that she does not eat enough herself and that she is too skinny.

14. For an elaboration of family structures in Cuba, see Andaya 2014; Núñez Sarmiento 2001.

15. For an elaboration on the role of women in acquiring and preparing household food, see chapter 3.

16. Andrea J. Queeley has observed a similar phenomenon among the African-Anglo-Caribbean diaspora in Cuba. She refers to this as the "narrative of social mobility" (Queeley 2015, x).

17. Interview in 2011.

18. For an in-depth discussion of cross-cultural experiences of satiation, see Throop 2009.

19. There is a growing body of work on food insecurity and mental health/well-being. For instance, see Cole and Tembo 2011; Dewing et al. 2013; Hadley et al. 2012; Hadley and Crooks 2012; Nanama and Frongillo 2011; Maes et al. 2010; and Orr 2013.

20. Interview in 2011.

21. This experience is similar to what a tourist might see while staying in a *casa particu-lar* (guest house), which usually employs at least one person to assist the business owners.

22. Certeau begins his discussion of strategies and tactics by locating particular types of behaviors in space. He describes such spaces as the place of work or leisure (1984, 29). In many settings food acquisition lies somewhere in between these two places—it is certainly not leisure, but not formal work either. However, most of the Cuban families in my study would likely categorize food acquisition as a form of unpaid labor. I argue that this notion of spaces and places includes products and the geography of their distribution, as well as the situation of consumers in that geography. These are more than just products but also part of "a repertory in which users carry out operations of their own" (ibid., 31). Still, it remains to be asked what the consumer makes of these products and the ways in which consumers use their time. For instance, do consumers adjust to what is available or make demands that the market adjust to their needs?

23. For Certeau (1984) this would fall under "tactics" which do not obey the law of place, that is, they are not defined or identified by place. Whereas strategies are able to produce, tabulate, and impose space, tactics can only use, manipulate, and divert spaces. Certeau goes on to note that, for example, colonized people have been subjected to the colonizers' laws, but although they accepted their subjection, they made particular uses of the laws, subjected them from within, so that they metaphorized the dominant order and made it function on another register.

Chapter 2

1. From my US-based perspective, this glorification of Hatuey is a problematic, racist production of the image of the "noble savage," which perpetuates the image that indigenous people are magic and superhuman. For further reading on the problematic appropriation of native images and designs, see Trudelle Schwarz (2013).

2. All of my research participants were given an opportunity to self-identify their own race or ethnicity. The category of mestizo often refers to mixed European and indigenous ancestry in many parts of Latin America. However, in Cuba the term mestizo usually means "mixed ancestry," which may include any mixture of European, Black, Chinese, Indigenous, or other ancestry. Geo is likely to have some combination of European, Black, and Indigenous ancestry, which could be why he chose to identify as mestizo rather than *mulato*, which just references Black and European mixture.

3. See Dawdy 2002 for an extended discussion of the concept of native Cuba.

4. Cuban *ajiaco* is similar to a dish called *sancocho* in Colombia, Ecuador, Peru, Costa Rica, Panama, and the Dominican Republic. In Cuba the word *sancocho* refers to household food scraps used as pig feed.

5. In this same piece, Ortiz (1940) defends tobacco, which he aligns with Cuban nationalism, and criticizes sugar, which is aligned with imperialism and world exploitation of

Cuba. Derived largely from Cuban national hero, Jose Martí, Ortiz's perspective on nationalism influenced his view that the capitalist sugar economy was not inevitably global. Ortiz thought globalism to be artificially imposed, caused by a lack of regulation within Cuba. Ortiz's central focus was within Cuba; he used sugar and tobacco to show that economic causes have social effects (Santí 2002).

6. The ideology of mestizaje, racial and cultural mixing, has a long history in Latin America and the Caribbean. In the Caribbean the term is simply used to connote racial mixing. It is loaded with colonial and contemporary aspirations to improve Caribbean society by whitening the population, with the goal to diminish Africanness in terms of phenotype as well as cultural expression. See also Yelvington 2001 and Hernandez-Reguant 2005.

7. The engine of the slave food system was the conuco, a name derived from the plots traditionally used by indigenous people in the region, which refers to the small plots of land that slaves were allowed to use for their own food cultivation (Ortiz 1985). Because Taínos were the only agriculturalists on the island before conquest, it is believed that the cultivation of these plots began in eastern Cuba (Esquivel and Hammer 1988). Enslaved people in Cuba typically planted their conucos using slash-and-burn methods. Typical crops included maize, cassava, sweet potatoes, taro, squash, beans, fruits, spices, and sugar cane for making *guarapo* (fresh cane juice). Larger fruit trees, such as plantains, mangos, and avocados, were planted near the house for shade (Esquivel and Hammer 1988).

8. My research methods for this study included a household asset elicitation, which I used in conjunction with self-reported socioeconomic status to categorize the families that I worked with as low, middle, or high socioeconomic status families. Although I am referring to socioeconomic status rather than class in the Marxist sense, I use terms like *middle class* in writing and speaking about these families because those are the terms they use to refer to their own social position. The terms in Spanish were: *clase baja/clase humilde, clase media, clase alta/gente con posibilidades.*

9. Pressure cookers are an essential part of Cuban household cooking. Pressure cookers are preferred for slowly cooking beans, tubers, some meats, and other foods that require softening. The socialist government has encouraged the use of pressure cookers as a way to save energy, in particular gas used for cooking. The state has distributed free or subsidized pressure cookers across the island in various programs since the 1990s.

10. The term *viandas* in Cuba is a classification of starchy foods that include various types of tubers, including yam, sweet potato, *yuca* (Manihot esculenta), and *malanga* (Xanthosoma sagittifolium), as well as plantains.

11. In the early 1960s, the government consisted mostly of members of the 26th of July Movement.

12. At the start of my research in 2008, the monthly ration per person included: 5 pounds of white rice, 10 ounces of beans, 1 pound of refined sugar, 3 pounds of raw sugar, 1 kilogram of salt, 4 ounces of coffee, 250 milliliters of oil, and a roll of bread per day. Meat products consisted of 6 ounces of chicken, 11 ounces of fish, 10 eggs, and 8 ounces of ground meat mixed with soy per month.

13. The initial iteration of market measures was a Soviet-style *sistema de dirección y planificación de la economía* (SDPE) (System for Directing and Planning the Economy). SDPE

attempted to establish greater autonomy for firms with incentives for them to increase production—"not a material incentive per se, but rather what Zimbalist calls an internal incentive, whereby workers internalized the goals of the firm or the larger economy" (Gordy 2015, 99).

14. During the 1970s and 80s, 85% of trade was with CMEA, 70% with the USSR, and 95% with socialist countries (Gordy 2015, 166–167).

15. Such projects included a nickel processing plant and nuclear power plant (Burki and Erikson 2005).

16. Damian Fernández argues that these ideological shifts were part of the development of a "political religion" in Cuba, through which the government built an "affective discourse" relating Cuban moral action to Cubanidad and la patria (2000, 67). Unity and community harmony were emphasized as a part of the moral character of the "political religion" of Cuba. Fernández emphasizes the affective side of Cuban politics, calling the revolutionary transition an "affair of the heart" (2000, 2).

17. Along with the legal possession of US dollars, dollar stores called *tiendas de recuperación de divisas* (stores for recuperating hard currency) were established for Cubans and foreigners to buy imported goods; at that time these shops were mainly patronized by "Cubans with family in the diaspora" (Gordy 2015, 171). The idea was for the government to acquire as much hard currency as possible through these measures and to then use it to alleviate shortages in other areas. Prior to these reforms the possession of hard currency was a crime according to penal codes of 1979 and 1987. See also Garth 2014a and Tankha 2016 for further description of the symbolic meaning of the dual currency system in Cuba.

18. In October 2013 it was announced that the currency was to be unified with the Cuban peso, *moneda nacional.*

19. In response to lingering food shortages during the Special Period, a formal government initiative facilitated the creation of several types of community gardens (*huertos populares, huertos privados, autoconsumos,* and *organipónicos*). Four basic forms of urban gardens were officially promoted during the Special Period: (1) *Huertos populares* (popular gardens) are private gardens cultivated on state land by individuals or communities. The produce serves the gardeners and their families and is sometimes sold to the public. Gardeners make all decisions as to what and how to produce; (2) *Huertos privados* (private gardens) are individual or family gardens on private land; produce from these serve the family or are sometimes sold to the public. Gardeners make all decisions; (3) *Autoconsumos* (self-cultivation plots) first emerged in the early 1980s to supply the state farm canteens from their own resources. During the Special Period *autoconsumos* were extended to any institution or workplace such as a school or factory. The garden is cultivated by the group and is typically located on an unused plot of their property; occasionally an organization will obtain state land located elsewhere when there is no land available; (4) *Organipónicos* are intensive production gardens that emerged during the Special Period, functioning as model gardens to diffuse techniques to the agricultural community (Deere 1995; Premat 2012). However, these gardens have declined and do not seem to have a significant bearing on contemporary food consumption in Cuba, especially outside of Havana (Funes et al. 2001).

20. For more on dual morality and *doble conciencia* in Cuba see also Andaya 2014; Brotherton 2012; Simoni 2015; and Wirtz 2014.

Chapter 3

1. I want to stress that gender is not binary. In Cuba, there are myriad ways of expressing gender identity. This chapter focuses on a particular form of gendered identity that is linked to the notion of a "good woman" or a "virtuous woman." A person who expresses this gender identity can be female or any other biological sex or gender. In my study, the majority of people who strove to be "good women" in this way also identified as female.

2. There is no singular category of "woman" in Cuba. To be clear, the notion of a "good Cuban woman" is a social construction that is an ideal rarely met in reality. I do not attempt to create an "undifferentiated category" of Cuban women here, but rather recognize that gendered identities are constructed through various intersectional subject positions (Brenner 1998, 19).

3. For an in depth analysis of masculinity and the daily lives of men in the Caribbean see Thornton 2016.

4. I want to emphasize here that, while I do not believe that heterosexism and upholding "traditional" male and female gender roles is true for all households, the vast majority of the families in my study upheld heteronormative gender roles in their households. Most people saw masculinity, a trait found in both women and men, as linked to providing for the household economically, and femininity, also a trait found in both men and women, as related to caring for and maintaining family and domestic space. Masculinized activities "in the street" should not be construed as mere laziness or not "contributing to the family" but as forms of socialization that often yield benefits for families. For further discussion of the detrimental effects of seeing males, particularly Black males, as "trouble," see Sojoyner 2016.

5. For a comparative view of other parts of Latin America see Menjivar 2011.

6. A key imperative of the revolution was to help women enter into the workforce, because involving women in socially productive labor was key to their "emancipation," according to Marxist thinking. In order to achieve the revolutionary goal of equality, the Cuban state implemented social policies focused on eliminating the structural dimension of social inequality. For Fidel Castro, women were key to the success of the revolutionary movement: "It is evident that women need to participate in the fight against exploitation, against imperialism, colonialism, neoliberalism, racism, in two words: the fight for national liberation" (Castro 1974b, 9).

7. For an in-depth discussion of the ways in which women's lives were improved in the early years of the socialist revolution, see Cole and Reed 1986.

8. Fidel Castro's sister-in-law, Vilma Espín, ran the organization. Espín described the role of the FMC as "aimed at winning over more and more women, uniting them and with them building a conscious force on behalf of the revolution" (Espín 1975, 94). The FMC still exists and consists of neighborhood, regional, municipal, provincial, and national units. A Cuban woman's participation in the FMC is taken to be an indication of her acceptance of the revolution.

9. Before the revolution there were 194,000 women working in Cuba, about 70% of whom were employed in domestic labor (Castro 1974a). In 1974 there were three times as many women working, and over half a million of those women were working in the sec-

tors of production, services, and administration, and women made up 25% of the working population (ibid.). While the percentage of women working in the military was 13% in 1974, women only made up 6% of the functionaries in the socialist party (ibid.). These numbers continued to rise over time: by 1985 women were 38% of the labor force, and in 1993, just after the fall of the Soviet Union, that figure jumped to 41%(Safa 2005, 324).

10. The FMC had also already established Cuba's national day care system. Inaugurated in 1961 in Havana, there are now approximately 1,000 state subsidized, full-day childcare programs in Cuba, providing care for 184,000 children. However, these state services are only available to women who are officially working.

11. The Special Period of the 1990s brought many of these programs to a halt. Nevertheless, women have remained a crucial part of the workforce. By 1999, women made up 66% of Cuban professionals and technicians, and as a group they had attained higher educational levels than men. Furthermore, to get a more accurate picture of women's rates of employment it is important to remember that increasingly, professional women are leaving state-sector jobs for higher paying work in tourism and unofficial jobs on the black market that pay better.

12. In 1992, a special charter on equality was added to the Cuban Constitution. Article 42 explicitly prohibits discrimination based on sex. Article 44 states that "men and women have equal rights in economic, political, cultural and social endeavors as well as within the family. The Cuban state guarantees women the same opportunities and possibilities as men, so that women can achieve full participation in the development of the country" (Gaceta Oficial). Article 295 of the Penal Code (Ley No. 62 (1979)) also provides for sexual equality. Well before this, under Fulgencio Batista's 1940 Constitution, discrimination based on sex was prohibited. Women gained a critical step toward equality with this measure, which also called for equal pay for equal work.

13. This is due in part to the fact that men are more likely to have higher paying jobs, chiefly in the managerial sector (Núñez Sarmiento 2001).

14. Berto is not included among the 22 households represented in my study. I did a separate interview with him.

15. Although Reina was not included in my 22-household sample, her perspective reflects that of many other female study participants.

16. She is only able to do this because her brother, who lives in Spain, sent her a laptop. She doesn't have internet at home but is able to do a lot of her typing work at home.

17. However, see Boehm 2012 for further discussion of the ways in which these sorts of household practices are still gendered divisions of labor.

Chapter 4

1. In Cuba there are multiple forms of blackness that people invoke as their identity. Here Mickey identifies as *moro* which is literally *moor*, defined as having "dark dark skin with straight or curly black hair" (Ryer 2008) and *sirio* a term used "to describe Ethiopians or East Africans—black but handsome with fine features and decent hair" (Ryer 2008). On a related note, Andrea Queeley (2015) fully explores the concept of the multiplicity of Blackness in Cuba, through her work with people of British West Indian ancestry on the

island. She notes that the ability to have an international affiliation may give these Black Cubans a higher social status.

2. I would like to add two points of clarification here. First, I am not trying to demonstrate that there has been an actual transformation in Cuban character; instead I am documenting the ways in which Cubans perceive, describe, or experience a shift. Second, the type of ethics that I am talking about here in terms of what kinds of behavior and actions are deemed right and wrong is not to be confused with the type of ethics related to notions of decency and propriety that I discuss throughout the book. Nor do I want to collapse the aesthetic dimensions of food consumption into the type of ethics that I am writing about in this chapter.

3. For further discussion of "conflicting systems of moral and ethical behavior," see Gupta 2012, pp. 80–81, which delves into some of the issues related to studying corruption ethnographically and the fact that "any discussion of corruption necessarily assumes a standard of morally appropriate behavior against which corrupt actions are measured" (Gupta 2012, 80).

4. These unofficial practices of everyday life stand in contrast to the forms of corruption and pilfering that may happen among Cuban party-state officials (cf. Verdery 1996). I do not conduct research on corruption and pilfering among party officials, and I am not able to discuss how these forms of acquisition impact the socialist state. Verdery (1996) has extensively discussed the ways in which high-ranking party-state officials used their positions of power to hoard, pilfer, and siphon resources from the state in various ways in the Eastern European and Soviet socialist contexts. She argues that this was the principle cause of inefficiency in state socialism that ultimately led to the fall of Soviet and European socialism. Gupta (2012) has documented the ways in which corruption at all levels of a state bureaucracy can lead to the complete breakdown and dysfunction of state systems in capitalist settings as well.

5. For more on dual morality and *doble conciencia* in Cuba see also Andaya 2014; Brotherton 2013; Simoni 2015; and Wirtz 2014.

6. For an extensive discussion of bureaucracy and agents of the state, see Gupta 2012.

7. For further discussion of Cuban notions of the proper way to engage in illicit activity, see Stout 2014.

8. See also Scott 1985.

Chapter 5

1. For an analysis of the official and unofficial Carnaval celebrations in Santiago de Cuba see Wirtz 2014; Bettelheim 2001.

2. The term *struggling along* was used by Robert Desjarlais (1994) in recounting the experience of one of his homeless, mentally ill interlocutors in New York City.

3. As far as I can tell the use of *crazy* here is simply a colloquialism for struggling to make sense of the difficulties of everyday life. There is no evidence that Cristina had a serious mental health problem, other than potentially anxiety, stress, or depression, and it is not clear if she even experienced any of those.

4. I am drawing on Berlant (2011) here.

5. It is also important to note that in many cases there are "unequal biopolitical investments" between different groups of citizens (i.e., fewer investments are made in communities of color than predominantly white communities), which results in an "uneven distribution of resources" (Ong 1999). This uneven distribution further exacerbates the tensions between needs and desires under conditions of scarcity.

6. In writing about moral experience, Kleinman distinguishes between "values" and an understanding of what has the most meaning for us versus something that is "good" in the ethical sense of what is right and wrong (2006, 2–3). He states, "Ordinary experience frequently thrusts people into troubling circumstances and confounding conditions that threaten to undo our thin mastery over those deeper things that matter most" (ibid., 4).

7. For Foucault, ethics is a "practice of freedom" central to the processes of taking care of oneself and knowing oneself (Rabinow 1994, xxv). Ethics and subjectivity are tied to politics here, in the sense of "governmentality," as in the "life of the city" and the moral codes or ethical practices tied up with that life. To understand the ways in which ethics and subjectivity are interconnected we must pay keen attention to "the way in which the individual establishes his relation to the rule and recognizes himself as obligated to put it into practice" (Foucault 1985, 27). Drawing on Kant, Paul Rabinow illuminates Foucault's reflections on ethics and subjectivity: "It is through the obligation to work on ourselves that we may discover a proper relationship to the Enlightenment—we will 'dare to know'" (Rabinow 1994, xxxii). While contemporary Cuba is certainly not the Enlightenment, my research participants share similar understandings about the relationship between their own understandings of who they are as people, their personal and communal ethics, and Cuban society today.

8. Most generally Foucault characterized the practice of ethical work as "problematization"— "to define the conditions in which human beings problematize what they are, what they do and the world in which they live" (Foucault 1985, 10). A central part of the ethical work of problematization is the act of "self-distancing," which is "an exercise of detaching and examining parts that need to be cared for and ultimately repaired or replaced" (ibid., xxvii). Similar to the Foucauldian argument, many Cubans are familiar with and still believe in Che Guevara's concept of the New Man, which underscored the importance of work for the collective as a part of one's individual moral development (see also Gordy 2015).

9. Stephen J. Collier (2011) has also written about stuckness in the context of post-Soviet Russia. In this case Collier refers to the problems of being stuck with the same old infrastructure that was designed for socialist distribution systems and is not optimal in neoliberal or postsocialist contexts (2011, 212–215). Collier draws this term from Michael Storper (1995). Cuban stuckness is inclusive of Collier's definition, but also extends more broadly to include their inability to travel away from the island legally, as well as the lack of advances in infrastructure, planning, and provisioning.

10. I am inspired here by Steven M. Parish's (1996) discussion of moral fantasy in the face of disappointment. "Discontents inspire moral fantasy, a reimagining of the world. This reimagining can take many forms which yet have a kind of underlying unity: there are dreams of justice, reveries of revenge and reversal, the musings that define aspirations, the poetics of utopia and the value-statements of social critique." (Parish 1996, 2).

11. Cuba has historically had very strict exit visa regulations. The exit visa, known as the *tarjeta blanca* (white card), was put into place in 1961. Few Cubans were able to legally travel abroad even if they had enough money to pay for the process. Since January 2013, an exit visa is no longer formally required and the need for a letter of invitation from the host country has been waived; however, Cubans who wish to travel abroad must have enough money to pay for a passport and acquire an entry visa to the country they plan to visit. Many of the santiagueros in my study could not fathom having enough money to accomplish such a task. The Cuban government reserves the privilege to restrict travel for the purpose of national security or defense as well as the right to preserve the human capital of the country. It is unclear how these policies have been upheld. Passports may not be issued to citizens who are dissidents. Cubans who are able to travel abroad must return to Cuba within 24 months or they forfeit their property, and rights to social security, free health care, free education, and the ration.

12. I am drawing from Parish (1996) here: "People struggle to interpret history and society in the light of a sense of moral possibility and necessity, framed in terms of their cultural ethos and experience. Such discourse rejects what is, the way society is; it appears to define what might be and what should be, putting culturally imagined possibilities into conceptual play, pitting actuality against ideals, defining aspiration and hopes that may be felt with a certain intensity, however unreal they are in practical terms. What people imagine might be and should be are key aspects of human consciousness" (Parish 1996, 2).

Conclusion

1. Quote also published in Garth 2017.

2. Audra Simpson (2007, 2014) has developed the notion of "refusal" in the context of the anthropological study of indigenous communities. Refusal for Simpson is a way of pushing back against particular forms of power and sovereignty that do not align with the needs and identities of a particular group. I think this concept of refusal can be extended here, to include the refusal of particular commodities, the refusal of impositions from outside the community, and the refusal to call unaccepted forms of eating "real." See also McGranahan 2016; Simpson 2007; Simpson 2014.

3. For further discussion of resistance and the opening of new political spaces in post-Soviet contexts, see Schwenkel 2015. In particular, Schwenkel draws upon Bennett (2010), Latour (2005), and McFarlane (2011) to demonstrate the ways in which an assemblage of actors might interact with state bureaucracies in more agentive ways than the literature usually portrays. In a somewhat similar way, I am analyzing the realignment of Cuban households with the state as a provider of food. The insistence on a decent meal is a form of agency here as well. However, as Schwenkel discusses, the role of capitalism in Vietnam creates a particular kind of governance where state bureaucracy is enmeshed with emerging forms of capitalism. This emergent from of "rule by sentiment" that Schwenkel (2015, 211) describes in Vietnam, which has also been taken up by Akhil Gupta (2012), is not necessarily the case in Cuba at this time. The Cuban state has not completely shifted from serving the people to serving corporate needs; rather the state seems to be simply struggling to make good on its promises. However, it is important to continue research in this area

to monitor whether the Cuban state begins catering to corporate interests as marketization increases. See also Ferguson and Gupta 2002.

4. For further discussion of hope and subjectivity, see Parish 1996. Similar to what Cubans experience, Parish writes, "Tacitly, at least, we imagine a world that might better embody our hopes and values, and believe that our human world has some meaningful order, that our actions mean something, even when our sense of reality does not provide evidence for these hopes and wishes" (1996, 3). Relating to hope in the face of devastation, Parish notes that: "Even as they are 'sealed in the crushing objecthood' created by the images others have of them (Fanon 1967, 109), individuals struggle to define themselves and their place in society, from the inside out, contesting the way they are socially constructed, trying to recreate culture to make meaning for themselves" (ibid., 8).

5. There were a few exceptions to this. It was commonly known that rice and pasta were unlikely to come from Cuban farms. Also, some of my study participants were aware that Cuba imported chicken and other products from other countries. Those who were aware of importation rarely knew where those products came from.

6. As Akhil Gupta has noted, "The efflorescence of historical studies of food in the last two decades strenuously reject a version of history that privileges the last quarter of the 20th century as a watershed in the grand narrative of globalization" (2012, 36). There has been a clear trend in food studies to consider the *longue durée* of global flows in foodways. This type of lens on foodways also allows for greater generalizability of work in the area. The lives detailed here are necessarily part of a larger picture of a global history of consumption and global commodity flows.

7. Following Keith Murphy (2015) in his analysis of the Swedish welfare state, I argue that Cuba is a welfare society. The forms of ethical and social commitments to the socialist welfare state in Cuba described in chapters 3, 4, and 5 in particular are illustrative of the belief in the principles of welfare.

8. See also Fischer 2003.

9. Some scholars have already begun this important task. See Bodenheimer 2015; Helg 1995; de la Fuente 2001, 2011; Moore 1988; Fernández Robaina 1990; and Wirtz 2014 on race in the contemporary period. See Allen 2011; Bejel 2001; Cabezas 2009; Fernandez 2010; Fosado 2004; Fusco 1998; Hamilton 2012; Hodge 2001; Saunders 2009; Saunders 2010; and Stout 2014 on gender and sexuality in Cuba today.

References

Abrams, Philip. 1988. "Notes on the Difficulty of Studying the State." *Journal of Historical Sociology* 1 (1): 58–89.

Agard-Jones, Vanessa. 2013. "Bodies in the System." *Small Axe: A Caribbean Journal of Criticism* 17 (3 (42)): 182–192.

Alexander, M. Jacqui, and Chandra Talpade Mohanty.1997. *Feminist Genealogies, Colonial Legacies, Democratic Futures*. New York: Routledge.

Allen, Jafari. 2011. *¡Venceremos?: The Erotics of Black Self-Making in Cuba*. Durham, NC: Duke University Press.

Allen, Jafari, and Ryan Cecil Jobson. 2016. "The Decolonizing Generation: (Race and) Theory in Anthropology since the Eighties." *Current Anthropology* 57 (2): 129–148.

Allen, Patricia, and Carolyn Sachs. 2007. "Women and Food Chains: The Gendered Politics of Food." *International Journal of Sociology of Food and Agriculture* 15 (1): 1–23.

Allison, Anne. 2012. "Ordinary Refugees: Social Precarity and Soul in Century Japan." *Anthropological Quarterly* 85 (2): 345–370.

———. 2013. *Precarious Japan*. Durham, NC: Duke University Press.

Andaya, Elise. 2014. *Conceiving Cuba: Reproduction, Women and the State in the Post-Soviet Era*. New Brunswick, NJ: Rutgers University Press.

Anderson, Benedict. 1983. *Imagined Communities: Reflections on the Origin and Spread of Nationalism*. London: Verso.

Appadurai, Arjun. 1990. "Disjuncture and Difference in the Global Cultural Economy." *Theory, Culture & Society* 7: 295–310.

Aristotle. 1976. *The Nicomachean Ethics*. Translated by J.A.K. Thomson. New York: Penguin.

Barndt, Deborah. 2008. *Tangled Routes: Women, Work, and Globalization on the Tomato Trail*. Lanham, MD: Rowman & Littlefield.

Beauvoir, Simone de. 2011 [1949]. The Second Sex. Translated by Constance Borde and Sheila Malovany-Chevallier. New York: Vintage.

Behar, Ruth, and Deborah A. Gordon, eds. 1995. *Women Writing Culture*. Berkeley: University of California Press.

Bejel, Emilio. 2001. *Gay Cuban Nation*. Chicago: University of Chicago Press.

Beliso-De Jesús, Aisha M. 2015. *Electric Santería: Racial and Sexual Assemblages of Transnational Religion*. New York: Columbia University Press.

Bennett, Jane. 2010. *Vibrant Matter: A Political Ecology of Things.* Durham, NC: Duke University Press.

Berlant, Lauren. 2011. *Cruel Optimism.* Durham, NC: Duke University Press.

Benjamin, Medea, Joseph Collins, and Michael Scott. 1984. *No Free Lunch: Food and Revolution in Cuba Today.* Princeton, NJ: Princeton University Press.

Bettelheim, Judith, ed. 2001. *Cuban Festivals: A Century of Afro-Cuban Culture.* Kingston, Jamaica; Princeton, NJ: Ian Randle Publishers/ Markus Wiener Publishers.

Biehl, João. 2005. *Vita: Life in a Zone of Social Abandonment.* Berkeley: University of California Press.

Blum, Denise F. 2011. *Cuban Youth and Revolutionary Values: Educating the New Socialist Citizen.* Austin: University of Texas Press.

Bodenheimer, Rebecca M. 2015. *Geographies of Cubanidad: Place, Race, and Musical Performance in Contemporary Cuba.* Jackson: University Press of Mississippi.

Boehm, Deborah A. 2012. *Intimate Migrations: Gender, Family, and Illegality among Transnational Mexicans.* New York: New York University Press.

Bonilla, Yarimar. 2015. *Non-sovereign Futures: French Caribbean Politics in the Wake of Disenchantment.* Chicago: University of Chicago Press.

Brenner, Suzanne. 1998. *The Domestication of Desire: Women, Wealth, and Modernity in Java.* Princeton, NJ: Princeton University Press.

Brotherton, P. Sean. 2005. "Macroeconomic Change and the Biopolitics of Health in Cuba's Special Period." *Journal of Latin American Anthropology* 10 (2): 339–369.

———. 2008. " 'We have to think like capitalists but continue being socialists': Medicalized Subjectivities, Emergent Capital, and Socialist Entrepreneurs in Post-Soviet Cuba." *American Ethnologist* 35 (2): 259–274.

———. 2012. *Revolutionary Medicine: Health and the Body in Post-Soviet Cuba.* Durham, NC: Duke University Press.

———. 2013. "Fueling la Revolucion: Itinerant Physicians, Transactional Humanitarianism, and Shifting Moral Economies." In *Health Travels: Cuban Health(Care) on the Island and Around the World,* edited by Nancy Burke, 127–151. Berkeley: University of California Medical Humanities Press.

Browner, Carole. 2000. "Situating Women's Reproductive Activities." *American Anthropologist* 102 (4): 773–88

Browner, Carole, and Ellen Lewin. 1982. "Female Altruism Reconsidered: The Virgin Mary as Economic Woman." *American Ethnologist* 9 (1): 61–75.

Buraway, Michael, and Katherine Verdery, eds. 1999. *Uncertain Transition: Ethnographies of Change in the Postsocialist World.* Lanham, MD: Rowman & Littlefield.

Burke, Nancy J., ed. 2013. *Health Travels: Cuban Health(care) On and Off the Island.* Berkeley: University of California Medical Humanities Press. .

Burki, Shahid Javed, and Daniel P. Erikson, eds. 2005. *Transforming Socialist Economies: Lessons for Cuba and Beyond.* New York: Palgrave MacMillan.

Butler, Judith. 1990. *Gender Trouble: Feminism and the Subversion of Identity.* New York: Routledge.

———. 1993. *Bodies That Matter: On the Discursive Limits of Sex.* London and New York: Routledge.

————. 1997. *Excitable Speech: A Politics of the Performative*. London and New York: Routledge.

Buyandelger, Manduhai. 2008. "Post-Post-Transition Theories: Walking on Multiple Paths." *Annual Review of Anthropology* 37: 235–50.

Cabezas, Amalia. 2009. *Economies of Desire: Sex and Tourism in Cuba and the Dominican Republic*. Philadelphia: Temple University Press.

Caldwell, Melissa. 2002. "The Taste of Nationalism: Food Politics in Postsocialist Moscow." *Ethnos: Journal of Anthropology* 67: 295–319.

————. 2004. "Domesticating the French Fry: McDonald's and Consumerism in Moscow." *Journal of Consumer Culture* 4 (1): 5–26.

Carby, Hazel V. 1992. "Policing the Black Woman's Body in an Urban Context." *Critical Inquiry* 18 (4): 738–755.

Carney, Megan A. 2015. *The Unending Hunger: Tracing Women and Food Insecurity across Borders*. Berkeley: University of California Press.

Casavantes Bradford, Anita. 2014. *The Revolution Is for the Children: The Politics of Childhood in Havana and Miami, 1959–1962*. Chapel Hill: The University of North Carolina Press.

Castro, Fidel. 1974a. La revolucion tiene en las mujeres Cubanas hoy dia una impresionante fuerza politica. Ediciones Politicas: Editoral de Ciencias Sociales, La Habana.

————. 1974b. Discurson del comandante Fidel Castro en el acto de claurura del seguno congreso de la federacion de mujeres cubanas, la habana, 29 de Nob de 1974 Ano del XV Aniversario de la Revolucion 17–23.

————. 1980. *Informe central al Segundo congreso [del Partido Comunista de Cuba]*. Bohemia. December, p. 59.

Certeau, Michel de. 1984. *The Practice of Everyday Life*. Berkeley: University of California Press.

Certeau, Michel de, Luce Giard, and Pierre Mayol. 1998. *The Practice of Everyday Life*. Vol. 2, *Living and Cooking*. Translated by Timothy J. Tomasik. Minneapolis: University of Minnesota Press.

Chaplowe, Scott G. 1996. "Havana's Popular Gardens: Sustainable Urban Agriculture." *World Sustainable Agriculture Association Newsletter (WSAA) Newsletter* (A Publication of the World Sustainable Agriculture Association) 5 (22): 266.

Cole, Johnnetta B., and Gail Reed. 1986. "Women in Cuba: Old Problems and New Ideas." *Urban Anthropology and Studies of Cultural Systems and World Economies* 15 (3/4): 321–353.

Cole, Steven M., and Gelson Tembo. 2011. "The Effect of Food Insecurity on Mental Health: Panel Evidence from Rural Zambia." *Social Science & Medicine* 73 (7) :1071–1079.

Collier, Stephen J. 2011. *Post-Soviet Social: Neoliberalism, Social Modernity, Biopolitics*. Princeton, NJ: Princeton University Press.

Coté, Charlotte. 2017. *Spirits of Our Whaling Ancestors: Revitalizing Makah and Nuu-chah-nulth Traditions*. Seattle: University of Washington Press.

Counihan, Carole. 1999. *The Anthropology of Food and Body: Gender, Meaning and Power.* New York: Routledge.

———. 2004. *Around the Tuscan Table: Food, Family, and Gender in Twentieth-Century Florence.* New York: Routledge.

Csordas, Thomas J. 2013. "Morality as a Cultural System?" *Current Anthropology* 54 (5): 523–546.

———. 2014. "Afterword: Moral Experience in Anthropology." *Ethos* 42 (1): 139–152.

Das, Veena. 2003. "Trauma and Testimony: Implications for Political Community." *Anthropological Theory* 3, 293–307.

———. 2007. *Life and Words: Violence and the Descent into the Ordinary.* Berkeley: University of California Press.

Davis, Angela Y. 1998. *Blues Legacies and Black Feminism: Gertrude "Ma" Rainey, Bessie Smith and Billie Holiday.* New York: Vintage.

Dawdy, Shannon Lee. 2002. "La Comida Mambisa: Food, Farming, and Cuban Identity, 1839–1999." *New West Indian Guide* 76: 47–80.

de la Fuente, Alejandro. 2001. *A Nation for All: Race, Inequality, and Politics in Twentieth-Century Cuba.* Chapel Hill: The University of North Carolina Press.

———. 2011. "Race and Income Inequality in Contemporary Cuba." *NACLA Report on the Americas* 44 (4): 30–33.

Deere, Carmen Diana. 1995. "The New Agrarian Reforms." *NACLA Report on the Americas* Special Issue on Cuba: Adapting to a Post-Soviet World 29 (2): 13–17.

del Real, Patricio, and Anna Cristina Pertierra. 2008. "Inventar: Recent Struggles and Inventions in Housing in Two Cuban Cities." *Buildings and Landscapes* 15 (1): 78–92

Desjarlais, Robert. 1994. "Struggling Along: The Possibility for Experience among the Homeless Mentally Ill." *American Anthropologist* 96 (4): 886–901.

DeVault, Marjorie L. 1994. *Feeding the Family: The Social Organization of Caring as Gendered Work.* Chicago: University of Chicago Press.

Dewing, Sarah, Mark Tomlinson, Ingrid M. le Roux, Mickey Chopra, and Alexander C. Tsai. 2013. "Food Insecurity and Its Association with Co-occurring Postnatal Depression, Hazardous Drinking, and Suicidality among Women in Peri-urban South Africa." *Journal of Affective Disorders* 150 (2): 460–465.

Domínguez, Jorge I. 2005. "Cuba's Economic Transition: Successes, Deficiencies, and Challenges." In *Transforming Socialist Economies: Lessons for Cuba and Beyond,* edited by Shahid Javed Burki and Daniel P. Erikson, 10–34. New York: Palgrave.

Dossa, Parin. 2014. *Afghanistan Remembers: Gendered Narrations of Violence and Culinary Practices.* Toronto: University of Toronto Press.

Douglas, Mary. 1966. *Purity and Danger: An Analysis of Concepts of Pollution and Taboo.* New York and London: Routledge.

———. 1972. "Deciphering a Meal." *Daedalus* 101: 61–81.

Dunn, Elizabeth C. 2004. *Privatizing Poland: Baby Food, Big Business, and the Remaking of Labor.* Ithaca, NY: Cornell University Press.

———. 2005. "Standards and Person-making in East Central Europe." In *Global Assem-*

blages: Technology, Politics and Ethics as Anthropological Problems, edited by Aihwa Ong and Stephen J. Collier, 173–193. Oxford, UK: Blackwell.

Eckstein, Susan, and Timothy Wickham-Crowley. 2003. *What Justice? Whose Justice? Fighting for Fairness in Latin America.* Berkeley: University of California Press.

Espín, Vilma.1975. *Memories, 2nd Congress: FMC.* Havana: Orbe.

Esquivel, Miguel, and Karl Hammer. 1988. "The 'Conuco'–An Important Refuge of Cuban Plant Genetic Resources." *Kulturpflanz* 3: 451–463.

Fagan, Richard. 1969. *The Transformation of Political Culture in Cuba.* Stanford, CA: Stanford University Press.

Fanon, Franz.1967. *Black Skin, White Masks.* New York: Grove Press.

Farber, Samuel. 2006. *The Origins of the Cuban Revolution Reconsidered.* Chapel Hill: University of North Carolina Press.

Farquhar, Judith. 2002. *Appetites: Food and Sex in Post-socialist China.* Durham, NC: Duke University Press.

Farquhar, Judith, and Qicheng Zhang. 2005. "Biopolitical Beijing: Pleasure, Sovereignty, and Self-Cultivation in China's Capital." *Cultural Anthropology* 20 (3): 303–327.

Fassin, Didier. 2008. "Beyond Good and Evil? Questioning the Anthropological Discomfort with Morals." *Anthropological Theory* 8 (4): 333–344.

Faubion, James D. 2001. *The Ethics of Kinship: Ethnographic Inquiries.* New York: Rowman & Littlefield.

———. 2011. *An Anthropology of Ethics.* Cambridge: Cambridge University Press.

Federation of Cuban Women (FMC). 1975. *Memories, Second Congress Cuban Women's Federation.* Havana: Editorial Orbe.

Ferguson, James. 1999. *Expectations of Modernity: Myths and Meanings of Urban Life on the Zambian Copperbelt.* Berkeley and Los Angeles: University of California Press.

———. 2015. *Give a Man a Fish: Reflections on the New Politics of Distribution.* Durham, NC: Duke University Press.

Ferguson, James, and Akhil Gupta. 2002. "Spatializing States: Toward an Ethnography of Neoliberal Governmentality." *American Ethnologist* 29: 981–1002.

Fernandes, Sujatha. 2006. *Cuba Represent!: Cuban Arts, Power, and the Making of Revolutionary Cultures.* Durham, NC: Duke University Press.

Fernández, Damián J. 2000. *Cuba and the Politics of Passion.* Austin: University of Texas Press.

Fernandez, Nadine. 2010. *Revolutionizing Romance: Interracial Couples in Contemporary Cuba.* New Brunswick, NJ: Rutgers University Press.

Fernández Robaina, Tomás. 1990. *El negro en Cuba, 1902–1958 : apuntes para la historia de la lucha contra la discriminación racial.* La Habana : Editorial de Ciencias Sociales.

Ferrer, Ada. 1999. *Insurgent Cuba: Race, Nation, and Revolution, 1868–1898.* Chapel Hill: University of North Carolina Press.

Finch, Aisha. 2015. *Rethinking Slave Rebellion in Cuba: La Escalera and the Insurgencies of 1841–1844.* Chapel Hill: University of North Carolina Press.

Fischer, Edward F. 2014. *The Good Life: Aspiration, Dignity, and the Anthropology of Wellbeing.* Stanford, CA: Stanford University Press.

Fischer, Edward F., and Peter Benson. 2006. *Broccoli and Desire: Global Connections and Maya Struggles in Postwar Guatemala.* Stanford, CA: Stanford University Press.

Fischer, Michael M. J. 2003. *Emergent Forms of Life and the Anthropological Voice.* Durham, NC: Duke University Press.

Fosado, Gisela. 2004. "The Exchange of Sex for Money in Contemporary Cuba: Masculinity, Ambiguity, and Love." Unpublished PhD diss., University of Michigan.

Foucault, Michel. 1985. *The Use of Pleasure.* Vol. 2, *The History of Sexuality.* Translated by Robert Hurley. New York: Random House.

———. 1988a. *The History of Sexuality.* Vol. 3, *The Care of the Self.* Translated by Robert Hurley. New York: Vintage Books.

———. 1988b. "Technologies of the Self." In *Technologies of the Self: A Seminar with Michel Foucault,* edited by Luther H. Martin, Huck Gutman, and Patrick H. Hutton, 16–49. Amherst, MA: University of Massachusetts Press.

———. 1990. *The Use of Pleasure.* Vol. 2, *History of Sexuality.* Translated by Robert Hurley. New York: Vintage Books.

———. 1991. "Governmentality." In *The Foucault Effect: Studies in Governmentality,* edited by G. Burchell, C. Gordon, and P. Miller, 87–104. London: Harvester/Wheatsheaf.

———. 1998. *The Essential Works of Michel Foucault.* Vol. 2, *Aesthetics, Method, and Epistemology,* edited by James D. Faubion. New York: The New Press.

Franco, M., Orduñez, P., Caballero, B., Tapia Granados, J. A., Lazo, M., Bernal, J. L., et al. 2007. "Impact of Energy Intake, Physical Activity, and Population-Wide Weight Loss on Cardiovascular Disease and Diabetes Mortality in Cuba, 1980–2005." *American Journal of Epidemiology* 166 (12): 1374–1380. DOI: 10.1093/aje/kwm226.

Frederik, Laurie A. 2012. *Trumpets in the Mountains: Theater and the Politics of National Culture in Cuba.* Durham, NC: Duke University Press.

Freeman, Carla. 1997. "Reinventing Higglering across Transnational Zones: Barbadian Women Juggle the Triple Shift." In *Daughters of Caliban: Caribbean Women in the Twentieth Century,* edited by Consuelo Lopez Springfield, 68–95. Bloomington: Indiana University Press.

Friedmann, Harriet. 1993. "International Political Economy of Food: A Global Crisis." *New Left Review* 197: 29–57.

Funes, Fernando, Luis Garcia, Martin Bourque, Nilda Perez, and Peter Rosset, eds. 2001. *Transformando el Campo Cubano: Avances de la Agricultura Sostenible.* Asociación Cubana de Técnicos Agrícolas y Forestales.

Funes, Fernando, Luis García, Martin Bourque, Nilda Pérez, and Peter Rosset. 2002. *Sustainable Agriculture and Resistance: Transforming Food Production in Cuba.* Oakland, CA: Food First Books.

Funes Monzote, Reinaldo. 2008. *From Rainforest to Cane Field in Cuba: An Environmental History since 1492.* Durham, NC: University of North Carolina Press.

Fusco, Coco. 1998. "Hustling for Dollars: Jineterismo in Cuba." In *Global Sex Workers: Rights, Resistance, and Redefinition,* edited by Kamala Kempadoo and Jo Doezema, 155–66. New York: Routledge.

Gaceta Oficial de Cuba Articulo 42–44. Accessed June 22, 2013. http://www.gacetaoficial. cu/html/constitucion_de_la_republica.html.

Garcia, Alyssa. 2008. "(Re) covering Women: The State, Morality, and Cultural Discourses of Sex-Work in Cuba." PhD diss., University of Illinois Urbana-Champaign.

Garcia, Angela. 2010. *The Pastoral Clinic: Addiction and Dispossession along the Rio Grande.* Berkeley: University of California Press.

———. 2014. "The Promise: On the Morality of the Marginal and the Illicit." *Ethos* 42 (1): 51–64

Garth, Hanna. 2009. "'Things Became Scarce': Food Availability and Accessibility in Santiago de Cuba Then and Now." *NAPA Bulletin* 32: 178–192.

———. 2010. "Toward Being a Complete Woman:" Reflections on Mothering in Santiago de Cuba. *UCLA Center for Study of Women Newsletter,* December.

———. 2012. "'Things Became Scarce': Food Availability and Accessibility in Santiago de Cuba Then and Now." In *Taking Food Public: Redefining Foodways in a Changing World,* edited by Carole Counihan and Psyche Williams-Forson. New York: Routledge/Taylor & Francis.

———. 2013. "Cooking Cubanidad: Food Importation and Cuban Identity in Santiago de Cuba." In *Food and Identity in the Caribbean,* edited by Hanna Garth, 95–106. London and New York: Bloomsbury Academic.

———. 2014a. "Cuba to Eliminate Dual Currency System." Association for Cultural Anthropology Section, *Anthropology News* 55 (7).

———. 2014b. "'They Started to Make Variants'": The Impact of Nitza Villapol's Cookbooks and Television Shows on Contemporary Cuban Cooking." *Food, Culture & Society* 17 (3): 359–376.

———. 2017. "'There is No Food': Coping with Food Scarcity in Cuba Today." Hot Spots, *Fieldsights.* March 23, 2017. https://culanth.org/fieldsights/there-is-no-food-coping-with-food-scarcity-in-cuba-today.

———. 2019. "Alimentary Dignity: Defining a Decent Meal in Post-Soviet Cuban Household Cooking." *Journal of Latin American and Caribbean Anthropology.* 24(2): 424–42.

Gerassi, John, ed. 1968. *!Venceremos!: The Speeches and Writings of Ernesto Che Guevara.* New York: Simon and Schuster.

Gilbert, Sandra M. 2014. *The Culinary Imagination: From Myth to Modernity.* New York: W.W. Norton & Company.

Gonçalves, João Felipe. 2014, "The Ajiaco in Cuba and Beyond: Preface to 'The Human Factors of Cubanidad' by Fernando Ortiz." *HAU: Journal of Ethnographic Theory* 4 (3): 445–480.

González, Pablo Alonso. 2016. Transforming Ideology into Heritage: A Return of Nation and Identity in Late Socialist Cuba? *International Journal of Cultural Studies* 19 (2): 139–159.

Good, Byron. 2012. "Theorizing the 'Subject' of Medical and Psychiatric Anthropology." *The Journal of the Royal Anthropological Institute* 18: 515–535.

Good, Byron J., Mary-Jo DelVecchio Good, Sandra Teresa Hyde, and Sarah Pinto. 2008. "Postcolonial Disorders: Reflections on Subjectivity in the Contemporary World." In

Postcolonial Disorders, edited by Mary-Jo DelVecchio Good, Sandra Teresa Hyde, Sarah Pinto, and Byron Good, 1–40. Berkeley: University of California Press.

Goodman, David, and Michael Watts, eds. 1997. *Globalising Food: Agrarian Questions and Global Restructuring*. London: Routledge.

Gordy, Katherine. 2015. *Living Ideology in Cuba: Socialism in Principle and Practice*. Ann Arbor: University of Michigan Press.

Grewal, Inderpal and Caren Kaplan. 1994. *Scattered Hegemonies. Postmodernity and Transnational Feminist Practices*. Minneapolis: University of Minnesota Press.

Guerra, Lillian. 2005. *The Myth of Jose Marti Conflicting Nationalisms in Early Twentieth-Century Cuba*. Chapel Hill: University of North Carolina Press.

Guevara, Ernesto. 1965. *El socialismo y el hombre en Cuba*. Semanario Marcha. Montevideo, Uruguay.

Gupta, Akhil. 1995. "Blurred Boundaries: The Discourse of Corruption, the Culture of Politics, and the Imagined State." *American Ethnologist* 22: 375–402.

———. 2012a. "A Different History of the Present: The Movement of Crops, Cuisines, and Globalization.". In *Curried Cultures: Globalization, Food, and South Asia*, edited by Krishnendu Ray and Tulasi Srinivas, 29–46. Berkeley: University of California Press.

———. 2012b. *Red Tape: Bureaucracy, Structural Violence and Poverty in India*. Durham, NC: Duke University Press.

Gupta, Akhil, and Aradhana Sharma. 2006. "Globalization and Postcolonial States." *Current Anthropology* 47 (2): 277–307.

Guthman, Julie. 2008. "'If They Only Knew': Color Blindness and Universalism in California Alternative Food Institutions." *The Professional Geographer* 60: 387–397.

Hadley, Craig, and Deborah L. Crooks. 2012. "Coping and the Biosocial Consequences of Food Insecurity in the 21st Century." *American Journal of Physical Anthropology* 149 (S55): 72–94.

Hadley, Craig, Edward Geoffrey, Jedediah Stevenson, Yemesrach Tadesse, and Tefera Belachew. 2012. "Rapidly Rising Food Prices and the Experience of Food Insecurity in Urban Ethiopia: Impacts on Health and Well-Being." *Social Science & Medicine* 75 (12): 2412–2419.

Hamilton, Carrie. 2012. *Sexual Revolutions in Cuba: Passion, Politics, and Memory*. Chapel Hill: University of North Carolina Press.

Harrison, Faye. 1995. "The Persistent Power of 'Race' in the Cultural and Political Economy of Racism." *Annual Review of Anthropology* 24: 47–74.

Hatheway, William H. 1957. *Races of Maize in Cuba*. National Academy of Sciences-National Research Council: Washington D.C. Publication 453.

Hearn, Adrian H. 2008. *Cuba: Religion, Social Capital and Development*. Durham, NC: Duke University Press.

Hearn, Adrian H. 2016. *Diaspora and Trust: Cuba, Mexico and the Rise of China*. Durham, NC: Duke University Press.

Henken, Ted A. 2006. "From Son to Salsa: The Roots and Fruits of Cuban Music." *Latin American Research Review* 41 (3): 185–200.

Helg, Aline. 1995. *Our Rightful Share: The Afro-Cuban Struggle for Equality, 1886–1912.* Chapel Hill: University of North Carolina Press.

Hernández, Rafael. 2003. *Looking at Cuba: Essays on Culture and Civil Society.* Gainesville: University of Florida Press.

Hernandez-Reguant, Ariana. 2004. "Copywriting Che: Art and Authorship under Cuban Late Socialism." *Public Culture* 16 (1): 1–29.

———. 2005. "Cuba's Alternative Geographies." *Journal of Latin American Anthropology* 10 (2): 275–313.

———, ed. 2009. *Cuba in the Special Period: Culture and Ideology in the 1990s.* New York: Palgrave MacMillan.

Hodge, G. Derrick. 2001. "Colonization of the Cuban Body: The Growth of Male Sex Work in Havana." *NACLA Report on the Americas* 34 (5): 20–28

Holbraad, Martin. 2014. Revolución o muerte: Self-Sacrifice and the Ontology of Cuban Revolution. *Ethnos: Journal of Anthropology* 79 (3): 365–387.

Holmes, Seth. 2013. *Fresh Fruit, Broken Bodies: Migrant Farmworkers in the United States.* Berkeley: University of California Press.

Holtzman, Jon D. 2006. "Food and Memory." *Annual Review of Anthropology* 35: 361–378.

Humphreys, Laura-Zoë. 2012. "Symptomologies of the State: Cuba's 'Email War' and the Paranoid Public Sphere." In *Digital Cultures and the Politics of Emotion: Feelings, Affect and Technological Change,* edited by A. Kuntsman and A. Karatzogianni. Basingstoke and New York: Palgrave Macmillan

James, Joel, Jose Millet, and Alexis Alarcon. 1992. *El Vodú en Cuba.* Santo Domingo: Ediciones. CEDEE.

James Figarola, Joel. 1974. *Cuba 1900–1928: La republica dividida contra si misma [Cuba 1900–1928: The republic divided against itself].* La Habana: Editorial Arte y Literatura.

Jiménez Acosta, S., C. Porrata, M. Pérez. 1998. Evolución de algunos indicadores alimentario-nutricionales en Cuba a partir de 1993. Rev Cubana Med Trop;50 (suppl):270–2.

Jenkins, Janis H. 2015. *Extraordinary Conditions: Culture and Experience in Mental Illness.* Berkeley: University of California Press.

Johnson, Sara. 2012. *The Fear of the French Negroes: Transcolonial Collaboration in the Revolutionary Americas.* Berkeley: University of California Press.

Kapcia, Antoni. 2000. *Cuba: Island of Dreams.* Oxford, UK: Berg.

Khan, Aisha. 2001. "Journey to the Center of the Earth: The Caribbean as Master Symbol." *Cultural Anthropology* 16 (3): 271–302.

Kleinman, Arthur. 2006. *What Really Matters.* Oxford: Oxford University Press.

Kligman, Gail. 1998. *The Politics of Duplicity: Controlling Reproduction in Ceausescu's Romania.* Berkeley: University of California Press.

Knight, Franklin W. 1970. *Slave Society in Cuba During the Nineteenth Century.* Madison: University of Wisconsin Press.

Lambek, Michael. 2008. "Value and Virtue." *Anthropological Theory* 8 (2): 133–157.

———, ed. 2010. *Ordinary Ethics: Anthropology, Language, and Action.* New York: Fordham University Press.

Latour, Bruno. 2005. *Reassembling the Social: An Introduction to Actor-Network Theory*. New York and Oxford: Oxford University Press.

Lauria, Anthony, Jr. 1964. "'Respeto,' 'Relajo' and Inter-Personal Relations in Puerto Rico." *Anthropological Quarterly* 37 (2): 53–67.

Ledeneva, Alena V. 1990. *How Russia Really Works: The Informal Practices That Shaped Post-Soviet Politics and Business*. New York: Cornell University Press.

Levy, Robert I., and Douglas W. Hollan. 1998. "Person-Centered Interviewing and Observation." In *Handbook of Methods in Cultural Anthropology*, edited by H. Russell Bernard, 333–364. Walnut Creek, CA: Altamira Press.

Lin, K. 2004. "Sectors, Agents, and Rationale: A Study of the Scandinavian States with Special Reference to the Society Model." *Acta Sociologica* 47 (2): 141–157.

Louis, Bertin M., Jr. 2014. *My Soul Is in Haiti: Protestantism in the Haitian Diaspora of the Bahamas*. New York: New York University Press.

Lyon, Sarah, Tad Mutersbaugh, and Holly Worthen. 2017. "The Triple Burden: The Impact of Time Poverty on Women's Participation in Coffee Producer Organizational Governance in Mexico." *Agriculture Human Values* 34: 317–331. https://doi.org/10.1007/s10460-016-9716-1

Maes, Kenneth C., Craig Hadley, Fikru Tesfaye, and Selamawit Shifferaw. 2010. "Food Insecurity and Mental Health: Surprising Trends among Community Health Volunteers in Addis Ababa, Ethiopia during the 2008 Food Crisis." *Social Science & Medicine* 70 (9): 1450–1457.

Mankekar, Purnima. 2015. *Unsettling India: Affect, Temporality, Transnationality*. Durham, NC: Duke University Press.

Mannur, Anita. 2007. "Culinary Nostalgia: Authenticity, Nationalism, and Diaspora." *Melus* 32 (4): 11–31.

Mares, Teresa M. 2017. "Navigating Gendered Labor and Local Food: A Tale of Working Mothers in Vermont." *Food and Foodways* 25 (3): 177–192.

Martínez-Alier, Verena. 1989. *Marriage, Class and Colour in Nineteenth-Century Cuba: A Study of Racial Attitudes and Sexual Values in a Slave Society*. Ann Arbor: University of Michigan Press.

Mattingly, Cheryl. 2010. *The Paradox of Hope: Journeys through a Clinical Borderland*. Berkeley: University of California Press.

———. 2013. "Moral Selves and Moral Scenes: Narrative Experiments in Everyday Life." *Ethnos* 78 (3): 301–327.

Maurer, Bill. 2004. "Understanding Knowledges Offshore: Caribbean Studies, Disciplinarity, and Critique." *Comparative American Studies* 2 (3): 324–341.

McFarlane, Colin. 2011. "The City as Assemblage: Dwelling and Urban Space." *Environment and Planning D: Society and Space* (29) 4: 649–671.

McGranahan, Carole. 2016. "Theorizing Refusal: An Introduction." *Cultural Anthropology* 31 (3): 319–325.

Menjivar, Cecilia. 2011. *Enduring Violence: Ladina Women's Lives in Guatemala*. Berkeley: University of California Press.

Mesa-Lago, Carmelo. 1978. *Cuba in the 1970s: Pragmatism and Institutionalization*. Albuquerque: University of New Mexico Press.

———. 2013a. "Los cambios en la propiedad en las reformas económicas estructurales de Cuba," *Espacio Laical*, No. 223, February.

———. 2013b. *Social Protection Systems in Latin America and the Caribbean: Cuba*. Santiago de Chile: ECLAC

Millet, Jose, and Rafael Brea. 1989. *Grupos folkloricos de Santiago de Cuba*. Santiago de Cuba: Editorial Oriente.

Mintz, Sidney. 1985. *Sweetness and Power*. New York: Viking Penguin.

———. 1998. "The Localization of Anthropological Practice: From Area Studies to Transnationalism." *Critique of Anthropology* 18 (2): 117–133.

———. 2006. "Food at Moderate Pace." In *Fast Food/Slow Food: The Cultural Economy of the Global Food System*, edited by Richard Wilk. Lanham, MD: Altamira.

Molé, Noelle J. 2012. "Hauntings of Solidarity in Post-Fordist Italy." *Anthropological Quarterly* 85 (2): 371–396.

Moore, Carlos. 1988. *Castro, the Blacks, and Africa*. Los Angeles: University of California, Center for African American Studies.

Muehlebach, Andrea. 2012. *The Moral Neoliberal: Welfare and Citizenship in Italy*. Chicago: University of Chicago Press.

———. 2013. "On Precariousness and the Ethical Imagination: The Year 2012 in Sociocultural Anthropology." *American Anthropologist* (115) 2: 297–311.

Mullings, Leith. 1997. *On Our Own Terms: Race, Class, and Gender in the Lives of African American Women*. New York: Routledge.

Mullings, Leith, and Alaka Wali. 2001. *Stress and Resilience: The Social Context of Reproduction in Central Harlem*. New York: Kluwer Academic.

Murphy, Keith. 2015. *Swedish Design: An Ethnography*. Ithaca, NY: Cornell University Press.

Nanama, Siméon, and Edward A. Frongillo. 2011. "Altered Social Cohesion and Adverse Psychological Experiences with Chronic Food Insecurity in the Non-market Economy and Complex Households of Burkina Faso." *Social Science & Medicine* 74 (3): 444–51

Nettles-Barcelon, Kimberly D. 2007. "'Saving'" Soul Food." *Gastronomica* 7 (3): 106–113.

Nova González, Armando. 2000. El Mercado Interno y el Aceso a los Alimentos en Cuba. Centro de Estudios de la Economía Cubana, Universidad de la Habana, Ciudad de la Habana. Mimeographed.

Núñez Sarmiento, Marta. 2001. "Cuban Strategies for Women's Employment in the 1990s: A Case Study of Professional Women." *Socialism and Democracy* 15 (1): 41–64.

Nunley, John W., and Judith Bettelheim. 1988. *Caribbean Festival Arts*. Seattle: University of Washington Press.

Ong, Aihwa. 1999. *Flexible Citizenship: The Cultural Logics of Transnationality*. Durham, NC: Duke University Press

Orr, David M. R. 2013. "'Now He Walks and Walks, as if He Didn't Have a Home Where He Could Eat'": Food, Healing, and Hunger in Quechua Narratives of Madness." *Culture, Medicine, and Psychiatry* 37 (4): 694–710.

Ortiz, Fernando.1940. *Contrapunteo cubano del tabaco y el azúcar.* Havana: Jesús Montero.

Ortiz, Fernando. 1947 [1995]. *Cuban Counterpoint: Tobacco and Sugar.* Translated by H. De Onis. Durham, NC: Duke University Press.

———. 1985. *Nuevo cautauro de cubanismos.* [New basket of Cubanisms]. Ediciones de Ciencias Sociales: La Habana.

Oxfeld, Ellen. 2017. *Bitter and Sweet: Food, Meaning, and Modernity in Rural China.* Berkeley: University of California Press.

Page-Reeves, Janet. 2014. *Women Redefining the Experience of Food Insecurity: Life off the Edge of the Table.* Lanham, MD: Lexington Books.

Palmié, Stephan. 2004. "Fascinans or Tremendum? Permutations of the State, the Body, and the Divine in Late-Twentieth-Century Havana." *New West Indian Guide* 78: 229–268.

———. 2005. "Ackee and Saltfish vs. Amalá con Quimbombó?: Sidney Mintz' Contribution to the Historical Anthropology of African American Cultures." *Journal de la Société des Américanistes* 91 (2): 89–122.

———. 2013. *The Cooking of History: How Not to Study Afro-Cuban Religion.* Chicago: University of Chicago Press.

Parish, Steven M. 1996. *Hierarchy and Its Discontents: Culture and the Politics of Consciousness in Caste Society.* Philadelphia: University of Pennsylvania Press.

Patterson, Tiffany Ruby, and Robin D. G. Kelley. 2000. "Unfinished Migrations: Reflections on the Africa Diaspora and the Making of the Modern World." *African Studies Review* 43 (1): 11–45.

Paxson, Heather. 2013. *The Life of Cheese: Crafting Food and Value in America.* Berkeley: University of California Press.

Pérez, Elizabeth. 2016. *Religion in the Kitchen: Cooking, Talking, and the Making of Black Atlantic Traditions.* New York: New York University Press.

Pérez, Humberto. 1979. "Humberto Perez en el Congreso de la ANEC Che: El mas destacado economista de nuestro pais duespues del trinunfo de la revolución." *Bohemia* 71, no. 25 (June 22, 1979): 51–60.

Pérez, Louis A., Jr. 1992. "History, Historiography, and Cuban Studies: Thirty Years Later." In *Cuban Studies since the Revolution*, edited by Damien Fernández, 53–78. Gainesville: University Press of Florida.

———. 1995 [1988]. *Cuba between Reform and Revolution.* New York: Oxford University Press.

———. 1999. *On Becoming Cuban: Identity, Nationality, and Culture.* Chapel Hill: University of North Carolina Press.

———. 2009. "Thinking Back on Cuba's Future: The Logic of Patria." *NACLA Report on the Americas* 42 (2): 12–17.

Pérez Firmat, Gustavo. 1987. "From Ajiaco to Tropical Soup: Fernando Ortiz and the Definition of Cuban Culture (Dialogue #93) LACC Occasional papers series." *Dialogues* (1980–1994). Paper 16. http://digitalcommons.fiu.edu/laccopsd/16

———. 1997. "A Willingness of the Heart: Cubanidad, Cubaneo, Cubanía." *Cuban Studies Association Occasional Papers.* Paper 8.

Pérez-Stable, Marifeli. 2011 [1993]. *The Cuban Revolution: Origins, Course, and Legacy.* Oxford, UK: Oxford University Press.

Perry, Marc D. 2016. *Negro Soy Yo: Hip Hop and Raced Citizenship in Neoliberal Cuba.* Durham, NC: Duke University Press.

Pertierra, Anna Cristina. 2011. *Cuba: The Struggle for Consumption.* Coconut Creek, FL: Caribbean Studies Press.

Porter, Amy L. 2008. "Fleeting Dreams and Flowing Goods: Citizenship and Consumption in Havana, Cuba." *PoLAR: Political and Legal Anthropology Review* 31 (1): 134–149.

Pottier, Johan. 1999. *Anthropology of Food: The Social Dynamics of Food Security.* Malden, MA: Polity.

Postero, Nancy. 2017. *The Indigenous State: Race, Politics, and Performance in the Plurinational Bolivia.* Berkeley: University of California Press.

Preeg, E. II, and Levine, J. D. 1993. *Cuba and the New Caribbean Economic Order.* Washington DC: The Center for Strategic and International Studies.

Premat, Adriana. 2012. *Sowing Change: The Making of Havana's Urban Agriculture.* Nashville, TN: Vanderbilt University Press.

Queeley, Andrea J. 2015. *Rescuing Our Roots: The African Anglo-Caribbean Diaspora in Contemporary Cuba.* Gainesville: University Press of Florida.

Rabinow, Paul, ed. 1994. *Michel Foucault Ethics: Subjectivity and Truth, Volume 1.* Translated by Robert Hurley and Others. New York: The New Press.

Reese, Ashanté. 2018. "'We will not perish; we're going to keep flourishing': Race, Food Access, and Geographies of Self-Reliance." *Antipode* 50 (2):407–424.

Ries, Nancy. 2009. "Potato Ontology: Surviving Postsocialism in Russia." *Cultural Anthropology* 24 (2): 181–212.

Robertson, A. 1988. "Welfare State and Welfare Society." *Social Policy and Administration* 22 (3): 222–234.

Roitman, Janet. 2006. "The Ethics of Illegality in the Chad Basin." In *Law and Disorder in the Postcolony,* edited by Jean Comaroff and John Comaroff, 240–263. Chicago: University of Chicago Press.

Roland, L. Kaifa. 2011. *Cuban Color in Tourism and La Lucha: An Ethnography of Racial Meanings.* New York: Oxford University Press.

Rolando, Gloria. 2014. *Reembarque/Reshipment.* Film (59 minutes). Available at http://www.afrocubaweb.com/gloriarolando/gloriarolando.htm.

Rosaldo, Michelle Zimbalist, and Louise Lamphere, eds. 1974. *Woman, Culture, and Society.* Stanford, CA: Stanford University Press.

Rose, Nikolas. 1999. *Powers of Freedom: Reframing Political Thought.* New York: Cambridge University Press.

Rosendahl, Mona. 1997. *Inside the Revolution: Everyday Life in Socialist Cuba.* Ithaca, NY: Cornell University Press.

Ryer, Paul. 2008. "Cubanidad, La Yuma and África: Racial and National Consciousness in Contemporary Cuba." PhD diss., Department of Anthropology, University of Chicago.

———. 2015. "The *Maine*, the *Romney*, and the Threads of Conspiracy in Cuba." *International Journal of Cuban Studies* 7 (2): 200–211.

Safa, Helen. 1995. *The Myth of the Male Breadwinner: Women and Industrialization in the Caribbean*. Boulder, CO: Westview Press

———. 2005. "The Matrifocal Family and Patriarchal Ideology in Cuba and the Caribbean." *Journal of Latin American Anthropology* 10 (2): 314–338.

Salmi, Anna-María. 2003. "Health in Exchange: Teachers, Doctors, and the Strength of Informal Practices in Russia." *Culture, Medicine, and Psychiatry* 27 (2): 109–130.

Santí, Enrico Mario. 2002. Introduction to *Contrapunteo Cubano del tabaco y el azúcar* [Cuban counterpoint of tobacco and sugar], by Fernando Ortiz, 23–103. Madrid: Ediciones Catédra.

Sassen, Saskia. 1998. *Globalization and Its Discontents: Essays on the New Mobility of People and Money*. New York: New Press.

Saunders, Tanya L. 2009. "La Lucha Mujerista: Krudas cubensi and Black Feminist Sexual Politics in Cuba." *Caribbean Review of Gender Studies* 3: 1–20.

———. 2010. "Black Lesbians and Racial Identity in Contemporary Cuba." *Black Women, Gender and Families* 4 (1): 9–36.

Schild, Verónica. 2007. "Empowering Consumer Citizens or Governing Poor Female Subjects? The Institutionalization of 'Self-Development' in the Chilean Social Policy Field." *Journal of Consumer Culture* 7 (2): 179–203.

———. 2013. "Care and Punishment in Latin America: The Gendered Neoliberalisation of the Chilean State." In *Neoliberalism, Interrupted: Social Change and Contested Governance in Contemporary Latin America* edited by Mark Goodale and Nancy Postero, 195–224. Stanford, CA: Stanford University Press.

Schmidt, Jalane. 2015. *Cachita's Streets: The Virgin of Charity, Race, and Revolution in Cuba*. Durham, NC: Duke University Press.

Schwenkel, Christina. 2015. "Reclaiming Rights to the Socialist City: Bureaucratic Artefacts and the Affective Appeal of Petitions." *South East Asia Research* 23 (2): 205–225.

Scott, James C. 1985. *Weapons of the Weak: Everyday Forms of Peasant Resistance*. New Haven, CT: Yale University Press.

Scott, Rebecca J. 1985. *Slave Emancipation in Cuba: The Transition to Free Labor, 1860–1899*. Pittsburgh, PA: University of Pittsburgh Press.

Sen, Amartya. 1987. "Food and Freedom." Sir John Crawford Memorial Lecture, Washington DC. http://wphna.org/wp-content/uploads/2015/02/1985-Sen-Food-and-freedom.pdf.

———. 1998. "Mortality as an Indicator of Economic Success and Failure." *The Economic Journal* 108 (446): 1–25.

Sharma, Aradhana, and Akhil Gupta, eds. 2006. *The Anthropology of the State: A Reader*. Malden, MA: Blackwell.

Sharpe, Christina. 2016. *In the Wake: On Blackness and Being*. Durham, NC: Duke University Press.

Simmons, Kimberly E. 2009. *Reconstructing Racial Identity and the African Past in the Dominican Republic*. Gainesville: University Press of Florida.

Simoni, Valerio. 2015. "Intimacy and Belonging in Cuban Tourism and Migration." *The Cambridge Journal of Anthropology* 33 (2): 26–41.

Simpson, Audra. 2007. "Ethnographic Refusal: Indigeneity, 'Voice' and Colonial Citizenship." *Junctures: The Journal for Thematic Dialogue*, 9: 67–80. http://junctures.org/index.php/junctures/issue/view/11/showToc.

———. 2014. *Mohawk Interruptus: Political Life across the Borders of Settler States*. Durham, NC: Duke University Press.

Slocum, Karla, and Deborah A. Thomas. 2003. "Rethinking Global and Area Studies: Insights from a Caribbeanist Anthropology." *American Anthropologist* 105 (3): 553–565.

———. 2007. "Introduction: Locality in Today's Global Caribbean: Shifting Economies of Nation, Race, and Development." *Identities: Global Studies in Culture and Power* 14: 1–18.

Smith, Lois M., and Alfred Padula. 1996. *Sex and Revolution: Women in Socialist Cuba*. New York: Oxford University Press.

Smith, M. G. 1962. *West Indian Family Structure*. Seattle: University of Washington Press

Smith, Raymond T. 1996. *The Matrifocal Family: Power, Pluralism and Politics*. New York: Routledge.

Sojoyner, Damien. 2016. *First Strike: Educational Enclosures in Black Los Angeles*. Minneapolis: University of Minnesota Press.

Speed, Shannon, R. Aída Hernández Castillo, and Lynn M. Stephen, eds. 2006. *Dissident Women: Gender and Cultural Politics in Chiapas*. Austin: University of Texas Press.

Spivak, Gayatri Chakravorty. 1988. "Can the Subaltern Speak?" In *Marxism and the Interpretation of Cultures*, edited by Cary Nelson and Lawrence Grossberg, 271–313. Urbana: University of Illinois Press.

Spence Benson, Devyn. 2016. *Anti-Racism in Cuba: The Unfinished Revolution*. Chapel Hill: University of North Carolina Press.

Stewart, Kathleen. 2007. *Ordinary Affects*. Durham, NC: Duke University Press.

———. 2012. "Precarity's Forms." *Cultural Anthropology* 27 (3): 518–525.

Stolcke, Verena. 1995. "Talking Culture: New Boundaries, New Rhetorics of Exclusion in Europe." *Current Anthropology* 36 (1): 1–23.

Stoler, Ann Laura. 2002. *Carnal Knowledge and Imperial Power: Race and the Intimate in Colonial Rule*. Berkeley: University of California Press.

Storper, Michael. 1995. "The Resurgence of Regional Economies, Ten Years Later: The Region as a Nexus of Untraded Interdependencies." *European Urban and Regional Studies* 2 (3): 191–221.

Stout, Noelle M. 2008. "Feminist, Queers, and Critics: Debating the Cuban Sex Trade." *Journal of Latin American Studies* 40 (4): 721–742.

———. 2014. *After Love: Queer Intimacy and Erotic Economies in Post-Soviet Cuba*. Durham, NC: Duke University Press.

Stowers, Sharon. 2014. "Salvadoran Immigrant Women and the Culinary Making of Gendered Identities: 'Food Grooming' as a Class and Meaning-Making Process." In *Women Redefining the Experience of Food Insecurity: Life off the edge of the Table*, edited by Janet Page-Reeves, 193–226. Lanham, MD: Lexington Books.

Sutton, David. 2001. *Remembrance of Repasts: The Anthropology of Food and Memory*. New York: Berg.

Tanaka, Maki. 2011. "Heritage Modern: Cityscape of the Late Socialist Political Economy in Trinidad, Cuba." Unpublished diss. Department of Anthropology, University of California, Berkeley.

Tankha, Mrinalini. 2016. "The Heads and Tails of Monetary Duality." *Cuba Counterpoints: Public Scholarship about a Changing Cuba.* https://cubacounterpoints.com/archives/3261.

———. 2018. "Chiastic Currency Spheres: Postsocialist 'Conversions' in Cuba's Dual Economy." In *Money at the Margins: Global Perspectives on Technology, Inclusion and Design,* edited by Bill Maurer, Smoki Musaraj, and Ivan Small. New York and Oxford: Berghahn.

Texler Segal, Marcia, and Vasilikie Demos, eds. 2016. *Gender and Food: From Production to Consumption and After.* Bingley, UK: Emerald Group Publishing Limited.

Thomas, Deborah A. 2004. *Modern Blackness: Nationalism, Globalization, and the Politics of Culture in Jamaica.* Durham, NC: Duke University Press.

———. 2011. *Exceptional Violence: Embodied Citizenship in Transnational Jamaica.* Durham, NC: Duke University Press

Thornton, Brendan Jamal. 2016. *Negotiating Respect: Pentecostalism, Masculinity, and the Politics of Spiritual Authority in the Dominican Republic.* Gainesville: University Press of Florida.

Throop, C. Jason. 2009. "Intermediary Varieties of Experience." *Ethnos* 74 (4): 535–558.

Trouillot, Michel-Rolph. 1988. *Peasants and Capital: Dominica in the World Economy.* Baltimore: Johns Hopkins University Press.

———. 1995. *Silencing the Past: Power and the Production of History.* Boston: Beacon Press.

———. 2003. *Global Transformations: Anthropology and the Modern World.* New York: Palgrave MacMillan.

Trudelle Schwarz, Maureen. 2013. *Fighting Colonialism with Hegemonic Culture: Native American Appropriation of Indian Stereotypes.* Albany: State University of New York Press.

Tsing, Anna L. 1993. *In the Realm of the Diamond Queen: Marginality in an Out-of-the-Way Place.* Princeton, NJ: Princeton University Press.

Ulysse, Gina Athena. 2015. *Why Haiti Needs New Narratives: A Post-Quake Chronicle.* Middletown, CT: Wesleyan University Press.

Unamuno, Miguel de. 1927. "Hispanidad." *Síntesis* 6 (1): 305–310.

United Nations Committee on World Food Security (UN CFS). 2018. http://www.fao.org/cfs/en/.

United States Department of Agriculture (USDA). 2008. "Cuba's Food and Agriculture Situation Report." Accessed April 10, 2019. https://thecubaneconomy.com/wp-content/uploads/2012/02/Cuba's-Food-Agriculture-Situation-Report-USDA-2008.pdf.

Van Esterik, Penny. 1999. "The Right to Food; Right to Feed; Right to Be Fed: The Intersection of Women's Rights and the Right to Food." *Agriculture and Human Values* 16 (2): 225–232.

Vann, Elizabeth F. 2005. "Domesticating Consumer Goods in the Global Economy: Examples from Vietnam and Russia." *Ethnos* 70 (4): 465–488.

Varma, Saiba. 2016. "Love in the Time of Occupation: Reveries, Longing, and Intoxication in Kashmir." *American Ethnologist* 43 (1): 50–62.

Verdery, Katherine. 1996. *What Was Socialism, and What Comes Next?* Princeton, NJ: Princeton University Press.

Vester, Katharina. 2015. *A Taste of Power: Food and American Identities.* Berkeley: University of California Press.

Viddal, Grete. 2006. "'Sueno de Haiti': Danced Identity in Eastern Cuba." *Journal of Haitian Studies* 12 (1): 50–64.

———. 2013. "Vodú Chic: Cuba's Haitian Heritage, the Folkloric Imaginary, and the State." PhD diss., Department of African and African American Studies, Harvard University.

Wade, Peter. 1993. *Blackness and Race Mixture: The Dynamics of Racial Inequality in Columbia.* Baltimore, MD: Johns Hopkins University Press.

———. 2001. "Racial Identity and Nationalism: A Theoretical View from Latin America." *Ethnic and Racial Studies* 24 (5): 845–865.

Waterson, Roxana. 2007. *Southeast Asian Lives: Personal Narratives and Historical Experience.* Singapore: NUS Press.

Weinreb, Amalia. 2009. *Cuba in the Shadow of Change: Daily Life in the Twilight of the Revolution.* Gainesville: University of Florida Press.

Weismantel, Mary J. 1989. *Food, Gender and Poverty in the Ecuadorian Andes.* Philadelphia: University of Pennsylvania Press.

Weiss, Brad. 2011. "Making Pigs Local: Discerning the Sensory Character of Place." *Cultural Anthropology* 26, (3): 438–461.

———. 2012. "Configuring the Authentic Value of Real Food: Farm-to-Fork, Snout-to-Tail, and Local Food Movements." *American Ethnologist* 39 (3): 614–626.

———. 2016. *Real Pigs: Shifting Values in the Field of Local Pork.* Durham, NC: Duke University Press.

White, Daniel. 2017. "Affect: An Introduction." *Cultural Anthropology* 32 (2): 175–180.

Wilk, Richard. 2006. *Fast Food/Slow Food: The Cultural Economy of the Global Food System.* Lanham, MD: Altamira Press.

Willen, Sarah S. 2014. "Plotting a Moral Trajectory, Sans Papiers: Outlaw Motherhood as Inhabitable Space of Welcome." *Ethos* 42 (1): 84–100.

Williams-Forson, Psyche. 2006. *Building Houses Out of Chicken Legs.* Chapel Hill: University of North Carolina Press.

Willoughby-Herard, Tiffany. 2008. "The Rape of an Obstinate Woman: Frantz Fanon's Wretched of the Earth." In *Shout Out: Women of Color Respond to Violence,* edited by María Ochoa and Barbara K. Ige, 264–280. Emeryville, CA: Seal Press.

———. 2010. "'I'll give you something to cry about': Intraracial Violence of Uplift Feminism in the Carnegie Poor White Study Volume, *The Mother and Daughter of the Poor Family.*" *South African Review of Sociology* 41 (1): 78–104.

Wilson, Ara. 2004. *The Intimate Economies of Bangkok: Tomboys, Tycoons, and Avon Ladies in the Global City.* Berkeley: University of California Press.

Wirtz, Kristina. 2004. "Santeria in Cuban National Consciousness: A Religious Case of the Double Moral." *Journal of Latin American and Caribbean Anthropology* 9 (2): 409–438.

———. 2014. *Performing Afro-Cuba: Image, Voice, Spectacle in the Making of Race and History.* Chicago: University of Chicago Press.

———. 2017. "Mobilizations of Race, Place, and History in Santiago de Cuba's Carnivalesque." *American Anthropologist* 119 (1): 58–72.

Wright, Julia. 2009. *Sustainable Agriculture and Food Security in the Era of Oil Scarcity: Lessons from Cuba.* London: Earthscan.

Yan, Yunxiang. 2000. "Of Hamburger and Social Space: Consuming McDonald's in Beijing." In *The Consumer Revolution in Urban China*, edited by Deborah Davis, 201–225. Berkeley: University of California Press.

Yates-Doerr, Emily. 2014. *The Weight of Obesity: Hunger and Global Health in Postwar Guatemala.* Berkeley: University of California Press.

———. 2015. "Does Meat Come from Animals? A Multispecies Approach to Classification and Belonging in Highland Guatemala." *American Ethnologist* 42: 309–23.

Yelvington, Kevin A. 2001. "The Anthropology of Afro-Latin America and the Caribbean: Diasporic Dimensions." *Annual Review of Anthropology* 30: 227–260.

Yurchak, Alexei. 2003. "Soviet Hegemony of Form: Everything Was Forever, Until it Was No More." *Comparative Studies of Society and History* 45 (3): 480–510.

———. 2005. *Everything Was Forever, Until It Was No More: The Last Soviet Generation.* Princeton and Oxford: Princeton University Press.

Zigon, Jarrett. 2007. "Moral Breakdown and the Ethical Demand: A Theoretical Framework for an Anthropology of Moralities." *Anthropological Theory* 7 (2): 131–150.

———. 2008. *Morality: An Anthropological Perspective.* Oxford, UK: Berg.

Zigon, Jarrett, and C. Jason Throop. 2014. "Moral Experience: Introduction." *Ethos* 42 (1): 1–15.

Index

Made in the USA
Monee, IL
19 March 2023

30204860R00135